Decorative PAINTING *techniques for*
WALLS, FLOORS, CEILINGS & FURNITURE

Elise C. Kinkead & Gail E. McCauley

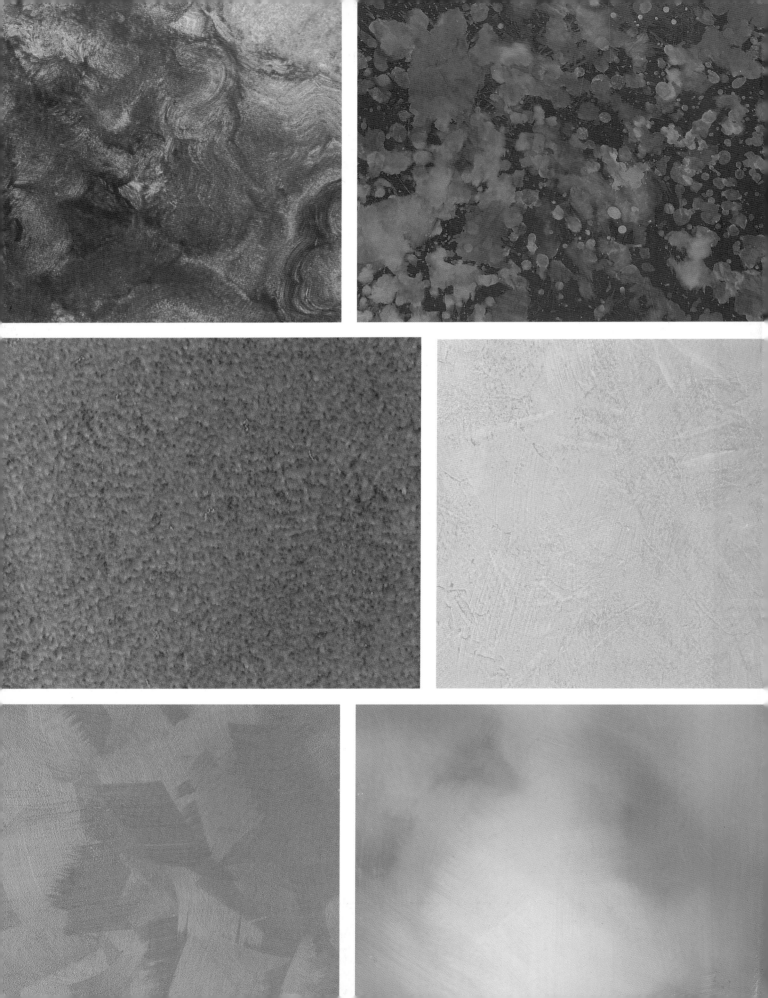

Decorative PAINTING _techniques for_
WALLS, FLOORS, CEILINGS _&_ FURNITURE

Elise C. Kinkead & Gail E. McCauley

Creative Publishing
international

Contents

Copyright © 2009
Creative Publishing international, Inc.
400 First Avenue North, Suite 300
Minneapolis, Minnesota 55401
1-800-328-3895
www.creativepub.com
All rights reserved

Printed in China

10 9 8 7 6 5 4 3 2 1

Library of Congress Cataloging-in-Publication Data

Kinkead, Elise.
 Decorative painting techniques for walls, floors, ceilings & furniture/
[authors, Elise C. Kinkead and Gail E. McCauley].
  p. cm.
  Includes index.
  Summary: "Features concise, illustrated instructions for 150 of the most
popular interior decorative painting techniques"--Provided by publisher.
  ISBN-13: 978-1-58923-453-6 (soft cover)
  ISBN-10: 1-58923-453-7 (soft cover)
 1. House painting--Amateurs' manuals. 2. Finishes and finishing--Amateurs'
manuals. 3. Interior decoration--Amateurs' manuals. I. McCauley, Gail E.
II. Creative Publishing International. III. Title.

TT323.K383 2009
747'.3--dc22

2008048744

President/CEO: Ken Fund
VP for Sales & Marketing: Kevin Hamric

Home Improvement Group
Publisher: Bryan Trandem
Acquisition Editor: Barbara Harold
Managing Editor: Tracy Stanley
Senior Editor: Mark Johanson
Editor: Jennifer Gehlhar

Creative Director: Michele Lanci-Altomare
Senior Design Managers: Brad Springer, Jon Simpson
Design Manager: James Kegley
Page Layout Artist: Nicole Hepokoski

Lead Photographer: Steve Galvin
Photographer: Andrea Rugg
Photo Coordinator: Joanne Wawra

Shop Manager: Bryan McLain
Shop Assistant: Cesar Fernandez Rodriguez
Shop Help: David Hartley, Scott Boyd

Authors: Elise C. Kinkead & Gail E. McCauley

Production Managers: Linda Halls, Laura Hokkanen

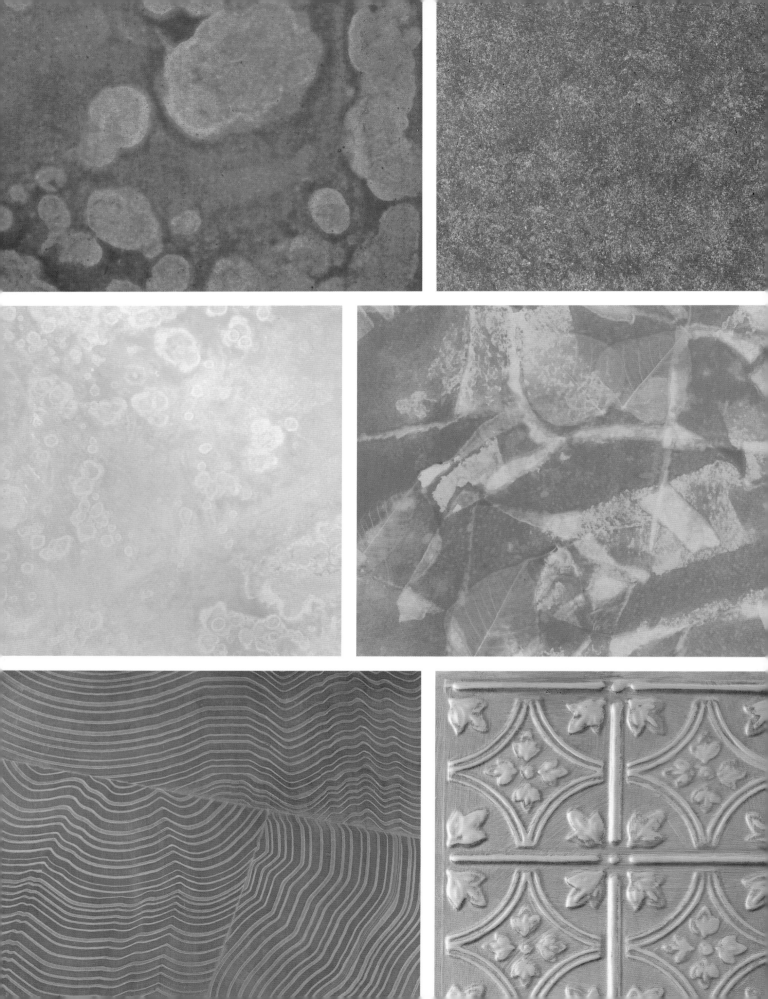

Introduction

You now hold in your hands the guide to over 150 of the most employed decorative painting techniques for walls, ceilings, floors, and furniture. The secrete to how these textures are created are revealed in the pages that follow. This book offers creative ways to revamp furniture, walls, ceilings, and floors; it stirs the imagination and inspires you to give new life to your home décor. It supplies you with techniques to complete a wide variety of finishes—with sensational results. These foundational techniques form the basis on which you can lay your imagination.

As you delve into this wonderful world of decoration, keep in mind this very important point: *Decorative Painting Techniques for Walls, Floors, Ceilings & Furniture* contains technical information. You, the craftsperson, provide the creativity. Give yourself the aesthetic permission to explore, imagine, and realize that you can render beautiful work. Your inspiration will then be true and accurate. The desire to produce an intriguing piece of art (for that is what your finished work becomes) is an ancient yearning. This book will help you satisfy that urge.

When you select your finish, open your paints, and roll up your sleeves, you start a creative process. You are the artist. So allow your self-expression to come forward. Allow yourself to create what you find desirable.

There are no rules, only compatibilities. Does this finish work with this piece? Does this paint work with that paint? What if I did this? What if I try that? And what if I purposely put two incompatibles together?

While striving for beauty and elegance, accept that you are not a machine. Your personality, in combination with that of the furniture piece, will work together to create a harmonious and graceful result. You are the one to satisfy. Use the techniques outlined in the following pages to please yourself. How do you know when a piece of furniture or a finish is done? When you like it!

Go forth—bravely and boldly—but relaxed. Enjoy the process as your hands produce. Satisfy your desire to bring a bit of beauty into your home for the enjoyment of all. Use the techniques outlined in this book as a springboard—a suggestion—to create finished work that you will be proud of, amused by, intrigued with, and that will enhance your home.

It's a wonderful journey. Have fun along the way and your enjoyment will be reflected in your final result.

Walls

Decorative **WALLS**

1   Color Washing

2   Overlaying Color

3   Sponging

4   Ragging

5   Double Rolling

6   Dragging/Strié

7   Color Weaving

8   Combing

DECORATIVE PAINTING TECHNIQUES

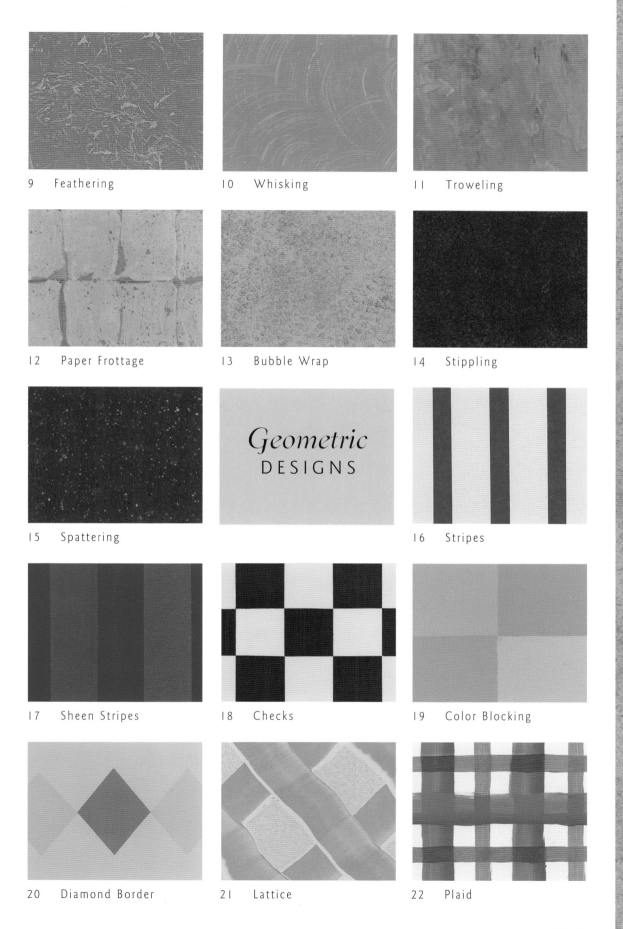

9   Feathering

10   Whisking

11   Troweling

12   Paper Frottage

13   Bubble Wrap

14   Stippling

15   Spattering

Geometric DESIGNS

16   Stripes

17   Sheen Stripes

18   Checks

19   Color Blocking

20   Diamond Border

21   Lattice

22   Plaid

Faux FINISHES

23 Polka Dots

24 Basket Weave

25 Textured Metallic

26 Pearl

27 Fresco

28 Venetian Plaster

29 Denim

30 Linen

31 Parchment

32 Grass Cloth

33 Bamboo

34 Suede

35 Leather

36 Wood Graining

37   Granite

38   Stone Blocks

39   Fossil Rock

40   Clouds

41   Crackle

Wall EMBELLISHMENTS

42   Stamping

43   Reverse Stamping

44   Stenciling

45   Dimensional Stenciling

46   Caulking

47   Decoupage

48   Collage

49   Painted Tiles

50   Words

Choosing a Paint Style

Today's decorative paint techniques will transform any room with their intriguing patterns, tantalizing colors, and rich textures. The following pages show you how to work this magic yourself. There are fifty techniques that follow, including faux finishes that mimic everything from stone to cloth, bold geometric designs, and a variety of wall embellishments. You can achieve a range of looks with each method simply by varying the paint colors or applicators.

Although some techniques require special paint tools, many require only an ordinary paintbrush and roller or common items (for example, bubble wrap!). Follow the instructions and photos and you will be successful even if you have no experience with painting. The next few pages cover types of paint, wall preparation (which is important), and basic brushwork and rollering to help you get a good start.

Consider the Décor

A room's architectural features, the amount of natural light, and floor covering and furnishings should all be considered when choosing paint. Less tangible but equally important is the mood you want to create.

While the techniques shown in this book complement a variety of room décors, many seem particularly well suited to specific styles. For example, an iridescent finish, such as textured metallic or pearl, teamed with sleek furnishings offers a sophisticated, contemporary look. Techniques that look like natural surfaces — such as stone blocks, granite, fossil rock, and bamboo — create an earthy ambience well suited to rustic country or Southwestern interiors. Classic paint techniques that emphasize patterns like diamonds and stripes are particularly at home with traditionally styled architecture and furnishings. Burgundy sheen stripes can lend grandeur to the walls of a formal dining room. Walls painted to look like rich leather bring classic sophistication to a home office or study.

More subtle techniques produce a background for small spaces and rooms where you want the walls to blend with existing décor. Geometric designs and wall embellishments produce obvious patterns more suitable for large spaces, where they complement (rather than overwhelm) the area.

Paint techniques can draw attention to architectural elements, such as pillars, niches, alcoves, or built-in shelving, or create a focal point in an otherwise ordinary room. Using the same or coordinating paint treatments on walls unifies open concept living spaces.

Select Colors

Besides picking a technique, you have to pick the color. Colors are extremely powerful. They affect our emotions and energy levels and even influence our perceptions of space and temperature. Reds, yellows, and oranges are warm colors. They are cheerful and uplifting; they energize and stimulate. Warm colors advance walls, making a large space cozier. Blues, greens, and violets are cool colors. They are calming and relaxing, making them popular choices for bedrooms and bathrooms. Cool colors tend to recede visually, making a small area appear more spacious.

Pure, saturated colors are clear and bright. Muted colors calm and impart an air of sophistication. These include neutrals, such as grays, beiges, and tans.

The lightness or darkness of a color (its "value") makes a big difference, too.

- Light or pastel colors are soothing and gentle. Dark and bold colors are dramatic.
- A mixture of light, medium, and dark values in a room creates interest by keeping the eye moving from one area to another.

- Combining light and dark colors intensifies the effect of both colors and creates drama. Painting the short end walls of a long, narrow room darker than the long side walls creates the illusion that the room is more square.
- Any color appears more intense next to white. If you want to boost a soft pastel pink in a girl's bedroom, for example, paint the woodwork white.

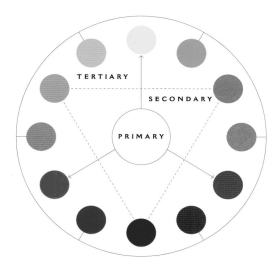

A color wheel is a great tool for developing color combinations. Here are some basic color schemes to consider for your home:

- Monochromatic schemes include various values of the same color. These combinations are subtle, sophisticated, and calming.
- Complementary colors (those that are opposite on the color wheel) increase intensity. For the best effect use more of one color than the other, allowing one color to dominate and the other to accent.
- Analogous color combinations are hues that appear side by side on the color wheel. They harmonize naturally.
- Triadic schemes include colors located equal distances apart, such as the three primary colors (red, blue, and yellow) or the three secondary colors (green, orange, and purple).

Always try color samples on the wall first, in both natural and artificial light. Rooms that receive indirect light benefit from brighter, bolder colors. Direct sunlight that enters the room from the south can intensify colors and add a subtle yellow tone. Incandescent light brings out the warm colors in a room, and fluorescent lights emphasize cool colors.

Some techniques commonly require specific colors, which the introductions will note. For example, denim (pg. 86) and skies (pg. 108) are traditionally blue.

Practical Considerations

How much time do you want to spend on your project? Some paint techniques are quick to finish, while others have several steps that require drying time. Also, a few decorative paint techniques, including fresco, Venetian plaster, collage, and fossil rock, result in raised surfaces that cannot be changed with a simple coat of paint — you will have to replace the plasterboard. Think of them for small, isolated areas. Most techniques can easily be painted over, though, which is a reason to be bold and try something new.

Have Fun

If this is your first experience with decorative painting, it's fine to start small. Expand your paint horizons by introducing surprising color, design, or texture to one wall. If you are satisfied with the results, consider taking on a larger decorative paint project next. Why not add dimensional color and pattern to a narrow hallway, small front entry space, or dark kitchen? When you see the results, you'll be looking for more walls to paint. Experiment with paint and add your own touches. The possibilities are endless!

Wall Painting Basics

The success of your painting project depends greatly on the care that goes into selecting the paints and tools and preparing the walls. These are a crucial parts of the process that will reward you with professional results.

All About Paint

Paint is available in a wide variety of types and finishes, with color choices limited only by your imagination. Whether you want a tough, childproof finish or a soft, sophisticated wash of color, you'll find just the right paint on the shelf of your paint store.

These simple guidelines for choosing paint will help steer you toward the paint products necessary for the look you want.

Types of Paint

Paint falls into two basic categories: water-based and oil-based paint. Both water-based and oil-based paints are available in various sheens, each recommended for different areas of your house.

Virtually all interior painting jobs today—including walls, ceilings, and woodwork—are done using water-based paint, which is commonly called latex paint. Water-based paint is safer for the environment and easier to use than oil-based paint. You can clean up brushes and rollers quickly with soap and water, and just as easily remove spatters from your skin. Latex paint dries quickly on the surface, so you can apply second coats in a few hours. Most latex paints have comparatively mild odors, so room ventilation is less of a concern.

Oil-based paints, also called alkyd paints, give a durable, smooth finish. They do, however, require longer drying times; and because you must use harsh solvents like mineral spirits or turpentine, cleanup is more complicated.

Glazes

A glaze is a translucent film applied over a painted surface to create depth and visual texture. By manipulating a glaze with various tools or materials, you can create interesting effects. Glazes are usually a mixture of glazing liquid (which is basically paint binder without the pigment), water, and pigmented paint in proportions suggested by the manufacturer. The resulting glaze has a prolonged drying time, beneficial for creating decorative and faux finishes.

Primers & Sealers

Unseen beneath the top paint coat, primers and sealers are nonetheless key ingredients in a quality paint job. Although they usually have very little pigment, these products help cover flaws and ensure that the paint adheres well to the surface. It is usually not necessary to prime a nonporous surface in good condition, like painted wood, painted plaster, or painted drywall.

Primers are available in both water-based and oil-based varieties. Different types are recommended for different jobs.

PAINT	CHARACTERISTICS & APPLICATIONS
Flat latex	No sheen; for walls and ceilings
Satin latex	Low sheen; for walls, ceilings, trim
Semigloss latex	Slightly glossy sheen; for walls and trim; durable
High-gloss latex	Reflective sheen; for doors, cabinets, trim; washable; durable
Satin-enamel latex	Low sheen; smooth, hard finish; for trim and furniture
Gloss-enamel latex	Very glossy; smooth, hard finish; for trim and furniture
Oil-based enamels	Very glossy sheen; smooth, hard finish; for trim and furniture

Flat Latex Primer

Used for sealing unfinished drywall or previously painted surfaces, this primer dries quickly so your top coat can be applied on the same day.

Deep Color Primer

When you plan to apply a very deep, dark color to your walls, prime first with this type of latex primer. It is designed to be tinted with a color similar to your top coat and will provide better top-coat coverage and appearance.

Latex Enamel Primer

Used primarily for sealing raw wood, enamel undercoat closes wood pores and provides a smooth top finish. Do not use the primer on cedar, redwood, or plywood that contains water-soluble dyes, because the dyes will bleed through the primer.

Stain-Killing Primer

Available in both alkyd and latex forms, these primers are designed to seal stains like crayon, ink, and grease so they will not bleed through your top coat of paint. Use them to seal knotholes in wood and for cedar, redwood, and plywood that contain water-soluble dyes.

Metal & Masonry Primer

Designed specifically for use with metal, brick, or cement block surfaces, these latex primers can be used on the interior or exterior of your home.

You may find metal primers for both clean, rust-free metal surfaces and for surfaces where rusting has already occurred. Both types inhibit rusting and allow the top coat to adhere evenly to the metal.

How Much to Buy?

To calculate how much paint you will need to finish your project, use this standard formula. Work in square feet (or square meters).

1. Measure each wall to figure the area:
  • Height × width = area.
  • Add the wall totals together for the sum total of wall area.

2. Measure each window and door to figure the area:
  • Height × width = area.
  • Add the window and door areas together for the sum total of window and door area.

3. Now subtract the total window and door area from the total wall area:
  • Wall area – window/door area = total area of the wall space you will need to paint.

4. Measure ceilings and floors to figure total area you need to paint:
  • Length × width = area.

Most interior paint products are designed to cover approximately 400 square feet per gallon (36 square meters per 3.56 liters). To figure how many gallons of wall paint you will need, simply divide your total wall area by 400. (Check the paint can label for the manufacturer's coverage recommendation.) Don't forget to double your final amount if you plan to apply two coats.

Drying Times

It is a good idea to estimate how long your painting project will take to complete. While every painter works at a different pace, remember that as a rule, preparation time takes longer than most people anticipate. If you are planning to work on weekends, for instance, complete your wall preparation on one weekend; then on the next weekend move furniture, drape and mask surfaces, and apply paint.

TYPICAL DRYING TIMES		
	WATER-BASED	OIL-BASED
PRIMERS	1–4 hours	4–10 hours; do not recoat for 24 hours
PAINTS	1–4 hours	6–10 hours; do not recoat for 24 hours
STAINS	1–4 hours	6–10 hours; do not recoat for 24 hours

The Right Tools

For most home improvement projects, choosing the right tools for the job is half the battle. Painting is no different. So before you grab the first brush or roller cover you spot on the store shelf, bone up on some basics. Because of the abundance of quality, specialized painting products on the market today, you'll have no trouble finding the right tools for your job. With this information, you'll know how to make the best choices.

Rollers

A good roller can be invaluable to your painting project. Inexpensive and efficient, this simple tool can save you time and energy. Rollers are commonly used for painting large wall areas, ceilings, and floors. Two simple components make up the roller: the frame and the cover. Covers are easily changeable, according to the job at hand.

SELECTING A ROLLER FRAME
Choose a standard 9" (23 cm) roller with wire frame and nylon bearings. Check the handle to make sure the molded grip is comfortable in your hand. The handle should also have a threaded end so you can attach an extension handle for painting ceilings and high walls.

SELECTING A ROLLER COVER
Roller covers, or *pads*, come in either synthetic or natural lamb's wool and are available in a variety of nap thicknesses. In general, synthetic covers are used for water-based paint; while lamb's-wool covers are used for oil-based paint. Select roller covers with longer-lasting plastic interiors, as opposed to the cheaper versions.

- Short-nap roller covers have $1/4$" to $3/8$" (6 mm to 1 cm) nap. Choose short nap covers for applying glossy paints to smooth surfaces like wallboard, wood, and smooth plaster.

- Medium-nap roller covers have $1/2$" to $3/4$" (1.3 to 2 cm) nap. These are commonly called all-purpose covers. They give flat surfaces a slight texture and are a good choice for walls and ceilings with small imperfections.
- Long-nap roller covers have a 1" to $11/4$" (2.5 to 3.2 cm) nap. Choose long-nap covers for painting textured surfaces including stucco and concrete block.

Brushes

Paintbrushes fall into two basic categories: natural bristle and synthetic bristle. Do not assume that natural is better, which was once the common wisdom about paintbrushes. In fact, natural-bristle brushes should only be used with alkyd, or oil-based, paint. If natural-bristle brushes are used with water-based paints, the bristles will bunch together. Choose synthetic-bristle brushes for water-based latex paints.

Look for quality. A bargain brush will save you a few dollars but may well cost you more in the long run. Invest in a few quality brushes; with proper care, they should last through many paint projects. As a starting point, choose a straight-edged 3" (7.5 cm) wall brush, a 2" (5 cm) straight-edged trim brush, and a tapered sash brush.

A good brush has a strong, hardwood handle. Dense bristles should be flagged, or split, at the ends. Always check to make sure the bristles are attached securely to the handle. If some pull out when you tug, you can expect the bristles to fall out into your paint job. The metal band, or ferrule, should be firmly attached. Inside the bristles, check that the spacer plugs are made of wood, not cardboard, which may soften when wet.

- A $11/2$" (3.8 cm) trim brush works well for painting narrow woodwork.
- A 2" (5 cm) trim brush works well for painting woodwork and windows.
- Choose a 2" (5 cm) tapered sash brush for painting windows.
- Choose a 4" (10 cm) brush for painting walls and ceilings.

Paint Pads

Paint pads come in a wide variety of shapes and sizes to accommodate many different tasks. Use these foam pads with water-based paints. Small pads with tapered edges are helpful for painting narrow areas like window trim or louvers, while the larger sizes can be used on wall surfaces. Specialty pads are available for painting corners and hard-to-reach areas. Paint pads generally apply paint in a thinner coat than a brush or roller, so additional coats may be necessary.

Preparing the Surface

Preparation is the key to a good paint job. Taking the time to repair, clean, and prime your walls will guarantee a longer-lasting paint finish. Because dirt and grease will interfere with a good, smooth paint finish, every surface should be thoroughly cleaned before painting.

Don't rush the preparation process and you'll be rewarded with a beautiful, durable finish once the project is completed.

SURFACE PREPARATION AT A GLANCE		
SURFACE TO BE PAINTED	PREPARATION	PRIMER
Unfinished wood	1. Sand surface smooth. 2. Wipe with tack cloth to remove grit. 3. Apply primer.	Latex enamel undercoat
Painted wood	1. Clean surface to remove grease and dirt. 2. Rinse with clear water; let dry. 3. Sand surface lightly to degloss, smooth, and remove loose paint. 4. Wipe with tack cloth to remove grit. 5. Apply primer to bare wood spots.	Latex enamel undercoat only on areas of bare wood
Unfinished wallboard	1. Dust with hand broom, or vacuum with soft brush. 2. Apply primer.	Flat latex primer
Painted wallboard	1. Clean surface to remove dirt and grease. 2. Rinse with clear water; allow to dry. 3. Apply primer only if making a dramatic color change.	Not necessary, except when painting over spot repairs or dark or strong color; then use flat latex primer
Unpainted plaster	1. Sand surfaces as necessary. 2. Dust with hand broom, or vacuum with soft brush.	Polyvinyl acrylic primer
Painted plaster	1. Clean surface to remove dirt and grease. 2. Rinse with clear water; allow to dry. 3. Repair any cracks or holes. 4. Sand surface to smooth and degloss.	Not necessary, except on spot repairs or when painting over strong or dark colors; then use polyvinyl acrylic primer

Clean the Surface First

To avoid messy streaking, begin washing your walls from the bottom up. While you can use common household cleansers for the job, many professional painters use a TSP (trisodium phosphate) solution.

Wearing rubber gloves, wash with a damp, not dripping, sponge. Rinse thoroughly with clean water. After the surface is dry, sand lightly where need; then wipe the surface with a clean cloth.

As you clean, you will discover any small problems, like cracks or stains, on the surface. Make those repairs before beginning to paint.

Fixing Common Problems

WATER STAINS

Problem: Unsightly water or rust stains require immediate attention because they may indicate a leak somewhere.

Solution: Check for leaking pipes or damaged flashing on the roof. Before you paint, repair the leak. If the wall surface is soft or crumbling, repair the area. To seal and cover a water-stained area that is not otherwise damaged, use a stain-sealing primer that contains shellac. If left unsealed, the stain will eventually show through your new paint job.

COLORED STAINS

Problem: Black marks and other wall stains like crayon or marker are not always easily removed.

Solution: Apply a stain remover to a clean, dry cloth and rub lightly on the stain. Cover any stain that is not completely removed with a stain-sealing primer that contains shellac.

MILDEW AND MOLD

Problem: Because mold and mildew grow in damp areas, check kitchen and bathroom surfaces carefully.

Solution: Test the stain by washing it with water and detergent. If it is mildew, it will not wash away. Wash the area with a solution of one part chlorine bleach to four parts water, which will kill the mildew spores. Scrub with a soft-bristle brush. Then wash the mildew away with a TSP solution, rinse with clear water, and allow the area to dry thoroughly before painting.

PEELING PAINT

Problem: Peeling paint occurs for a number of reasons, and it must be removed before you repaint.

Solution: Scrape away the loose paint with a putty knife or paint scraper. Apply a thin coat of spackle to the edges of the chipped paint, using a putty knife. Allow it to dry. Sand the area with 150-grit sandpaper, creating a smooth transition between bare wall and surrounding painted surfaces. Wipe clean with a damp sponge. Spot-prime the area with polyvinyl acrylic (PVA) primer.

FILLING SMALL NAIL HOLES

1. Using a putty knife or your finger, force a small amount of drywall compound or spackle into the hole, filling it completely. Scrape the area smooth with the putty knife and let dry (see photo left).

2. Sand the area lightly with 150-grit sandpaper. Wipe clean with a damp sponge, let dry, and dab on PVA primer.

Fixing Popped Drywall Nails

Drywall nails can work themselves loose, either popping through the drywall or creating a small bulge on the surface.

1. Drive a new wallboard screw into place 2" (5 cm) below the popped nail, sinking the head slightly below the wall surface. Be sure the screw hits the stud and pulls the drywall tight against the framing (see top photo), taking care not to damage the wall surface.

2. Scrape away loose paint or drywall material around the popped nail. Drive the popped nail back into the framing, sinking the head slightly below the drywall surface.

3. Using a drywall knife, cover both the nail hole and the new screw hole with spackle. Sand and prime the patched areas.

Filling Dents and Gouges in Drywall

1. Scrape away any drywall paper using a drywall knife, if necessary. Sand the dented or gouged area lightly. Using a drywall knife, fill the dent or hole with spackle (see top, middle photo). For deep holes or dents, build up the spackle in layers, allowing each layer to dry before adding another.

2. Sand the patched area with fine-grit sandpaper; seal the area with PVA primer.

Patching Holes in Drywall

1. Cut a rectangle around the hole using a drywall saw. Cut backer strips from drywall or wood; hot-glue them to the back of the opening (see lower, middle photo).

2. Cut a rectangular drywall patch slightly smaller than the opening; secure it in place to the backing strips, using hot glue.

3. Apply self-adhesive drywall tape over the cracks; then spackle. After drying, sand the area smooth and apply PVA primer.

Option: Self-adhering fiberglass and metal repair patches are available. Apply the patch over the hole. Then coat the area with spackle, blending into the surrounding wall (see lower, right photo). After drying, sand it smooth and apply primer.

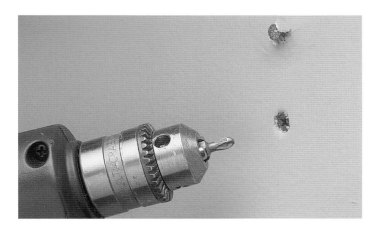

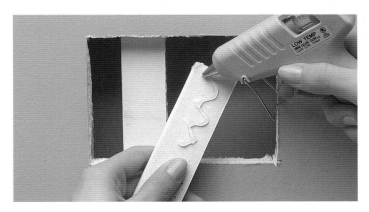
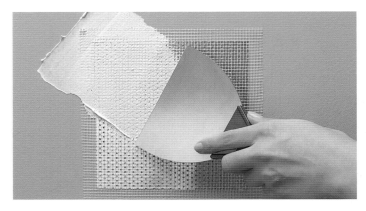

Repairing Cracks in Plaster

1. Scrape away any loose plaster or textured surface along the crack. Reinforce the crack with self-adhesive fiberglass drywall tape.

2. Apply a thin layer of joint compound over the taped crack, using a taping knife or trowel (see top right photo). Allow it to dry. Apply a second thin coat, if necessary, to hide the tape edges.

3. Sand the area lightly using 150-grit sandpaper. Apply PVA primer. Retexture the surface, if necessary, using texturized paint.

Repairing Holes in Plaster

1. Gently scrape away any loose material and clean the damaged area. Undercut the edges of the hole where possible.

2. Cut a piece of wire lath to fit the damaged area and staple it to the wood lath. Mix a small amount of patching plaster, following the manufacturer's directions.

3. Using a drywall knife or trowel, apply a thin coat of plaster to the wire lath, working the material under the hole edges (see photo right).

4. Score a grid pattern into the surface of the patching plaster with the tip of your knife; allow to dry.

5. To apply a second coat, first dampen the area with a sponge; then apply another layer of patching plaster, even with the surrounding wall (see lower right photo). Allow it to dry thoroughly.

6. Sand the area lightly using 150-grit sandpaper. Apply PVA primer. Retexture the surface, if necessary, using texturized paint.

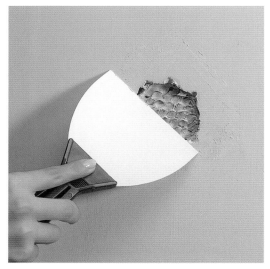

Preparing the Room

Once your repairs have been made, you're almost ready to paint. Take the time now to remove or cover anything in the room that could be spattered by paint as you work. Furniture should be moved into the center of the room and draped with plastic (readily available in large sheets at hardware stores and home improvement centers). Cover floors with canvas drop cloths (paint will not pool

up on canvas like it will on plastic), and remove things like switch plates, window and door hardware, duct covers, and wall lights. Use tape to mask off wood moldings. Taking the time to mask and drape thoroughly will save both cleanup time and unnecessary damage to furnishings and fixtures.

TAPING

It is always wise to protect areas like woodwork and window glass that butt up against the surfaces you'll be painting. Taping these areas may save you cleanup time and ensure a clean, straight finish. To mask woodwork, use painter's tape, which is a wide strip of brown paper with adhesive along one edge. Cut off short lengths of the tape, and, working one section at a time, smooth the adhesive edge onto the woodwork with a putty knife (see top photo). Keep your edges as straight as possible. The paper edge will stick out past the molding, protecting it from paint spatters.

Painter's masking tape (not to be confused with the masking tape used for packages) is specially designed to be applied and removed without damaging painted surfaces. Still, it's best not to leave the tape in place longer than necessary. Carefully removing the tape before the paint dries usually produces a smoother line. Look for these masking tapes in the paint section of your home improvement store. They are available in a wide range of widths and are often colored red or blue.

COVER LIGHT FIXTURES

To protect hanging fixtures, unscrew the collar from the ceiling and lower it to expose the rough opening in the ceiling. Then wrap the fixture with a plastic bag.

DRAPING

When painting the ceiling only, drape your walls (see lower photo) with sheet plastic to prevent damage from paint spatters. Use 2" (5 cm) masking tape to hold the plastic sheets to the wall along the ceiling line.

How to Paint

Using Your Paintbrush

- Transfer some paint from the can into a small paint bucket with a handle. It will be easier to carry with you as you move around the room.
- Double-check your paintbrush. If you are using water-based (latex) paint, you should have a synthetic-bristle brush.
- Don't overload your paintbrush! Dip the bristles only about 2" (5 cm) into the paint. Tap, don't drag, the bristles on the side of the can.

1. Begin painting with horizontal strokes in a back-and-forth manner using first one side of the brush then the other (see top photo). Press the brush against the surface just hard enough to flex the bristles slightly. Always paint from dry areas back into wet areas to avoid lap marks.

2. Smooth the paint evenly across the surface using vertical strokes. Feather, or blend, the edges of your painted area by brushing lightly with just the tip of your brush.

3. Along edges where a wall meets the ceiling or woodwork, use a technique called "cutting in." Hold the brush at a slight angle. Stroking slowly, move the brush slightly away from your edge as you go (see lower photo). This will allow paint to bead up along the straight line of the edge.

Using Your Paint Roller

- Paint surfaces in small sections, working from dry surfaces back into wet paint to avoid roller marks.
- If you notice roller marks or lines of beaded paint beginning to form on your paint job, feather the edges immediately. Also, try easing up on the pressure you're applying to the roller.
- If your paint job will take more than one day, cover the roller tightly with plastic wrap overnight to prevent the paint from drying out. Be sure to run the roller over a piece of scrap material before you begin painting again the next day.

1. Load your roller by dipping it into the paint tray, then rolling it back and forth on the textured ramp (see top photo). The cover should be soaked but not dripping.

2. With the loaded roller settled comfortably in your hand, roll paint onto the surface in smooth, crisscrossing strokes. When working on walls, roll upward on your first stroke to avoid spilling paint (see middle photo).

3. Distribute the paint across the surface using horizontal back-and-forth strokes.

4. Smooth the painted area by lightly drawing the roller down the surface, from top to bottom. Lift the roller at the bottom of each stroke, and then return to the top.

Painting Walls

1. Using a narrow brush, cut in a 2" (5 cm) strip of paint where the walls meet woodwork and ceiling. Begin in the upper right-hand corner if you are right-handed, upper left if you are left-handed.

2. Using your roller, paint one small wall section at a time. Work on the wall sections while your edges are still wet. When painting near the cut-in edge, slide the roller cover slightly off the roller. This helps to cover the cut-in edge as much as possible (brushed paint dries differently than rolled-on paint). Continue painting adjacent wall sections, cutting in with a brush and then rolling wall areas (see lower photo). Work from top to bottom. All finish strokes should be rolled toward the door.

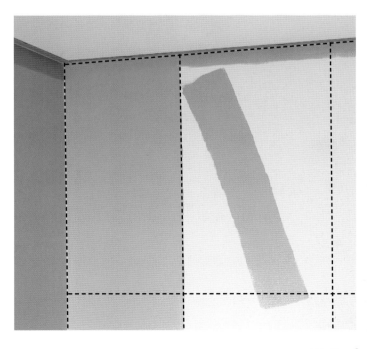

Decorative WALLS

1 | Color Washing

COLOR WASHING gives walls a subtle, watercolored appearance. Using a wide paintbrush, a translucent paint glaze is applied over a base coat in simple, crosshatch strokes, leaving a finish that has soft texture and color depth. Flat, smooth walls can be color washed to add visual dimension. The rough texture of a plaster or stucco wall is amplified by color washing.

This versatile finish is commonly used for rustic and country styled interiors and for casual spaces, such as family rooms, dens, and kitchens. Color washing provides a more interesting background for stenciled or stamped designs than a plain painted wall. It is also an effective way to "age" the walls of new homes or to mellow a painted wall that turned out brighter or bolder than expected.

The color-washing glaze can be either lighter or darker than the base coat color. The farther apart the base coat and glaze are in value, the more pronounced the effect. Often white or off-white is used for either the base coat or glaze. You can also use two tones or shades of the same color. Two different colors will blend together—yellow over blue will turn green. The glaze coat color will be the strongest.

MATERIALS & TOOLS

- ❖ Painter's masking tape
- ❖ Drop cloths
- ❖ Paint roller and tray
- ❖ Satin or semigloss latex paint for base coat
- ❖ Rubber gloves

- ❖ Water-based glazing liquid
- ❖ Flat latex paint for top coat
- ❖ Paint bucket and mixing tool
- ❖ Paintbrush, 4" to 6" (10 to 15 cm) wide

1 Prepare the walls for painting (page 17). Protect the area around the walls with painter's masking tape and drop cloths (page 21). Apply the base coat and let it dry completely.

2 Put on rubber gloves. In the bucket, prepare the glaze, mixing four parts glazing liquid with one part top-coat paint. If you want a more translucent glaze, add some water.

3 Beginning in a top corner, brush the mixture over a 3-ft. (1 m) square section with a crosshatch or "X" motion. Go over the area several times, lightly blending the strokes. There will be light lines in the finish (they will be less visible if the wall is textured).

4 Immediately move to an adjacent section and repeat step 3. While the glaze from the previous section is still wet, blend the areas together. Work from corner to corner, moving down toward the floor in small sections until you have color-washed the entire wall. Allow the wall to dry completely.

5 If desired, repeat steps 2 to 4 with a lighter or darker shade of glaze to give the wall more depth.

2 | Overlaying Color

THIS IS AN EASY technique for even the first-time decorative painter because it doesn't require skillful handling of a paintbrush or other tools. Paints are dabbed onto the wall with a wad of cotton knit fabric called "jersey." Every pounce of the cloth produces a soft, textured imprint. As more color layers are applied, the imprints blend together, building texture and depth. Because of its complex, dappled appearance, overlaying color disguises any surface flaws and an errant stroke can simply be dabbed over.

The size and "landscape" of the scrunched cotton jersey determine the finished look. Large, loosely scrunched pieces of fabric produce a coarsely textured appearance, suitable for bedrooms, family rooms, and casual areas of the home. Smaller, tightly wadded fabric produces a finer-grained, more controlled texture, appropriate for the dining room, living room, home library, and other formal living areas.

For best results, select a light, neutral hue for the base-coat color. Select the overlay colors to coordinate with the room furnishings. Choose a light and dark value of the same color or colors that are close to each other on the color wheel.

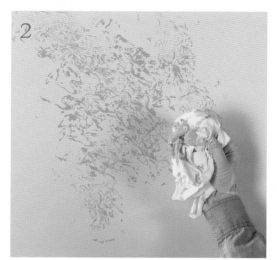

- ❖ Painter's masking tape
- ❖ Drop cloths
- ❖ Paint roller and tray
- ❖ Flat latex paint for base coat
- ❖ Rubber gloves

- ❖ Lint-free, loosely knit, cotton cloth, such as jersey, cut into 18" (46 cm) squares
- ❖ Dark flat latex paint for top coat
- ❖ Light flat latex paint for top coat

1 Prepare the walls for painting (page 17). Protect the area around the walls with painter's masking tape and drop cloths (page 21). Apply the base coat and let it dry completely.

2 Put on rubber gloves. Scrunch up a piece of cloth and dip it into the dark paint. Squeeze out the excess paint. Beginning in an upper corner, dab the cloth over the wall surface in a 2-ft. (0.6 m) square area. Continue dabbing over the area, lifting any excess paint and reapplying it until the cloth is nearly dry. Allow some of the base coat to show through.

3 Use a clean piece of scrunched cloth to apply the light paint in the same manner. Allow some of the base coat and first over-lay color to show through.

4 Repeat steps 2 and 3 in adjacent wall sections, blending areas together, until the entire wall is finished. Switch to clean cloths when they become saturated. Allow the wall to dry completely.

5 Dab more base-coat color onto any areas that appear too dense. Build depth and texture by dabbing on more dark paint. Add highlights by dabbing on more light paint.

3 | Sponging

POUNCING PAINT onto the wall with a natural sea sponge produces a pebbly, mottled finish with color depth that invites a closer look. Sponge painting has changed through the years, yet continues to be popular because it is so easy to master and works well with so many décor styles. Today sponging is subtle and blended, unlike the high contrast in color that was once popular.

Different sponged effects can be produced, depending on the color choices, the number of color layers, and the density of the sponging. Colors that are similar in tone to the base-coat color produce the most harmonious results. Understated monochromatic looks can be achieved by sponging various shades of the same color over a neutral base coat. Rich depth and color interest develop when two or three analogous hues are used. In general, the more open the sponged design, the more casual the appearance.

Sponging is often combined with other paint techniques and design elements. It can be teamed with solid-color painted walls in a guest room or whitewashed wainscoting in a formal dining area. Sponged stripes on a guest bath wall or a sponged border in a nursery can be very effective.

MATERIALS & TOOLS

- ❖ Painter's masking tape
- ❖ Drop cloths
- ❖ Paint roller and tray
- ❖ Flat or semigloss latex paint for base coat
- ❖ Flat latex paint for top coat
- ❖ Water & bucket
- ❖ Paint bucket and mixing tool
- ❖ Rubber gloves
- ❖ Large natural sea sponge
- ❖ Small natural sea sponge
- ❖ Small paintbrush

1 Prepare the walls for painting (page 17). Protect the area around the walls with painter's masking tape and drop cloths (page 21). Apply the base coat and let it dry completely.

2 Put on rubber gloves. In the bucket, prepare the glaze, mixing equal amounts of top-coat paint and water. Pour some of the paint mixture into the paint tray.

3 Soak the large sponge in water and squeeze tightly so the sponge is damp. Dip the sponge into the paint mixture and blot the excess onto the flat part of the tray.

4 Beginning at an upper corner, lightly pounce the sponge onto the wall in a 2-ft. (0.6 m) square area, getting as close as possible to the ceiling, corners, and moldings. Turn the sponge often to avoid repeating the pattern, and leave an irregular edge. Allow some of the base-coat color to show through.

5 Repeat step 4, moving down the wall to the bottom in a checkerboard pattern. Then go back to the top and fill in the open areas, blending into the irregular edges. Rinse the sponge often in warm water to keep it from clogging with paint. Squeeze out the sponge until it is only damp and start again.

6 Repeat steps 4 and 5 until each wall is covered. Use a small sea sponge or paintbrush to fill in corners and around moldings.

4

5

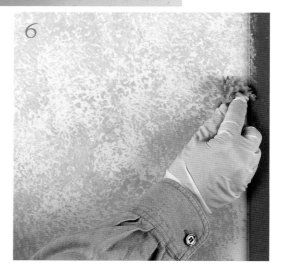

6

4 | Ragging

RAGGING ENHANCES A WALL with a softly mottled layer of translucent color. In this technique, a crumpled rag saturated with glaze is pounced onto the wall. Although easy to master, ragging tends to be messy, so careful room preparation is important. Ragging is a good choice for hiding minor wall imperfections. It can be subtle enough for every wall in a room or applied to only one wall to create a focal point. Ragging can also be combined with a geometric technique, such as checks, stripes, or a harlequin design.

The colors selected for the base coat and glaze will influence the look and the style of décor for which it will be most suitable. Ragging is particularly attractive in cottage or country styled spaces with soft colors that clearly reveal the rag imprints. Two or three closely related colors can be ragged in layers. Values of the same color will have a quieter effect; contrasting colors will be more dramatic.

Any clean, lint-free rags can be used, including gauze, burlap, chamois cloth, or jersey. Woven cotton rags (used for the sample above) produce a blended look. Ragging can be applied sparsely, leaving much of the base color showing, or densely, creating a more solid appearance.

❖ Painter's masking tape
❖ Drop cloths
❖ Paint roller and tray
❖ Flat latex paint for base coat

❖ Paint bucket and mixing tool
❖ Latex paint for glaze mixture
❖ Water-based glazing liquid
❖ Rubber gloves

❖ Lint-free cotton rags, approximately 2 ft. (0.6 m) square
❖ Bucket and water
❖ Cardboard

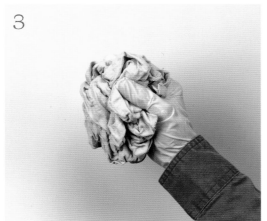

3

4

5

1 Prepare the walls for painting (page 17). Protect the area around the walls with painter's masking tape and drop cloths (page 21). Apply the base coat and let it dry completely.

2 In the bucket, prepare the glaze, mixing equal amounts of paint, water, and glazing liquid to achieve a thin, creamy consistency.

3 Put on rubber gloves. Soak a rag in water and wring it out well. Dip the damp rag into the paint mixture and wring it out well. Draw the edges to the center and bunch the rag into random folds and creases.

4 Beginning in a top corner, pounce the rag randomly onto the wall, moving your entire arm in order to cover an area approximately 2 ft. (0.6 m) square. Work as close as possible to the ceiling, corners, and moldings. Leave irregular edges around the section. Reposition the rag in your hand to avoid repetitious patterns.

5 Repeat step 4 in another section, moving down the wall to the bottom in a checkerboard pattern. Then go back to the top and fill in the open areas, blending into the irregular edges. Reload the rag with paint as needed. When the cloth becomes slimy, rinse it in warm water, wring it out, and reload with paint, or begin with a clean rag.

6 Repeat steps 4 and 5 until each wall is covered.

7 To finish the room, hold a piece of cardboard against wall corners, ceiling, and moldings. Fill in gaps by dabbing lightly with a small piece of paint-filled cloth.

8 If additional colors are desired, allow the wall to dry completely before applying a second or third color.

5 | Double Rolling

DOUBLE ROLLING allows even a beginner to apply an impressive decorative paint finish with minimal effort. Two paint colors are rolled onto the wall at once using a special roller that is split down the middle. As the roller moves back and forth through the paint, the colors mingle together, leaving a dramatic marbled effect that looks more complicated than it really is.

Colors that blend rather than contrast produce the most pleasing double-roller effects. For a monochromatic scheme, select two colors from one paint color card at least two or three value steps apart. Rolling colors that are close to each other on the color wheel (like the orange and yellow-orange shown here) produces a more complex appearance with mottled patches of each paint color plus intermediate shades.

Double rollers fit onto standard 9" (23 cm) roller cages. Paint trays and tray liners with divided wells are also available. The double roller used in the photographs has a deep pile, which blends the colors with a soft, blurry texture. Double-roller covers with close-cropped sculpted shapes are also available. They blend colors in more distinct patterns.

MATERIALS & TOOLS

- ❖ Painter's masking tape
- ❖ Drop cloths
- ❖ Paint roller and tray
- ❖ Latex paint for base coat
- ❖ Rubber gloves
- ❖ Latex paint for top coat in two colors
- ❖ Double roller with divided paint tray
- ❖ Small foam edging tool or paintbrush

1 Prepare the walls for painting (page 17). Protect the area around the walls with painter's masking tape and drop cloths (page 21). Apply the base coat and let it dry completely.

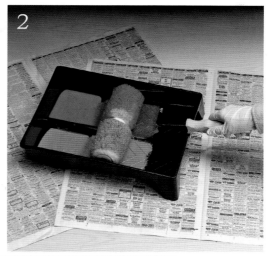

2 Put on rubber gloves. Pour the two paint colors into the divided paint tray. Dip the double roller into the paint. Each side of the roller will be loaded with a different paint color.

3 Beginning in a top corner, roll the paint over a 3-ft. (1 m) square section, moving the roller up and down and back and forth, covering the base coat and slightly blending the colors. Leave irregular edges. Reload the roller as necessary.

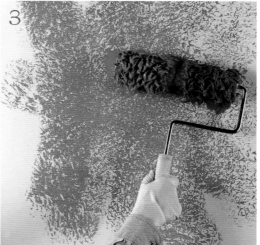

4 Repeat step 3 in adjacent areas from top to bottom and continuing around the room, blending along the irregular edges.

5 Load a small foam edging tool or paintbrush with both colors. Dab it onto the wall to blend both paint colors into corners and around woodwork.

6 | Dragging/Strié

DRAGGING CREATES a patterned wall with fine, irregular streaks. It is also called strié, the French word for streak or groove. Dragging can be used to create a dignified, tailored background for paintings, antiques, and collections in a formal setting. With its sleek appearance, dragging also works well for contemporary spaces. For dining rooms with chair rails, dragging can be combined with plain painted or papered walls above or below the rail.

Dragging involves pulling a brush or similar tool vertically through wet paint glaze. You can use a wide paintbrush, wallpaper brush, steel wool, or a specialty strié brush; different tools create different patterns. The technique may take practice because it is important to keep the dragging strokes straight. The process tends to be messy, so prepare the room carefully. It is a good idea to work with someone—one person applies the glaze and the other drags.

Similar colors or different shades of one color will have a subtle effect. High-contrast colors create more apparent streaks. Pastels dragged over various shades of white or deeper colors dragged over a pastel base are popular choices for dragging. Deep jewel tones, such as emerald green or royal blue, are favorites for dragging in traditionally styled spaces.

❖ Painter's masking tape

❖ Drop cloths

❖ Paint roller and tray

❖ Satin latex paint for base coat

❖ Rubber gloves

❖ Paint bucket and mixing tool

❖ Latex paint for glaze mixture

❖ Water-based glazing liquid

❖ Wide, stiff, natural-bristle brush or other dragging tool

❖ Clean rags

1 Prepare the walls for painting (page 17). Protect the area around the walls with painter's masking tape and drop cloths (page 21). Apply the base coat and let it dry completely.

2 Put on rubber gloves. In the bucket, prepare the glaze, mixing one part latex paint with one part glazing liquid.

3 Apply the glaze from ceiling to floor in an 18" (46 cm) wide strip using a roller. Make sure the wall surface is evenly covered.

4 While the glaze is still wet, lay the bristles flat against the surface and apply slight, even pressure on the back of the bristles as you pull the dragging tool downward through the glaze. Work from the ceiling to the baseboard in long, overlapping strokes.

5 Wipe off excess glaze from the brush onto rags after each downward stroke.

6 Repeat steps 3 to 5, moving around the room until all the walls are finished.

7 | Color Weaving

COLOR WEAVING IS THREE layers of dragging (page 36) applied in alternating directions. Because each layer is a different color, the result is a rich, dimensional effect that resembles woven fabric. This technique is a budget-wise alternative to wallpapers or fabric wall treatments.

The dragging tools and colors selected will vary the look. Specialty dragging brushes are usually 2" to 3" (5 to 7.5 cm) wide, though regular paintbrushes are available in a wide variety of sizes and work just as well. Coarse weave brushes leave wider streaks, revealing more color and making the space appear more casual. Bright colors combined in a coarse weave

work well for casual living spaces such as a family room. For the example above, a standard 4" (10 cm) paintbrush and warm colors with high value contrast were used, resulting in a casual, imperfect look. Fine weave brushes and a subtle color scheme produce a more sophisticated look. Monochromatic tones and a fine weave would be elegant in a formal dining room.

Although different color combinations may be used, three distinct values (light, medium, and dark) are recommended. It is always best to apply the dark value in the bottom layer, the light value in the middle, and the medium value on top.

MATERIALS & TOOLS

- ❖ Painter's masking tape
- ❖ Drop cloths
- ❖ Three paint rollers and tray with liners
- ❖ Light color latex paint for base coat
- ❖ Rubber gloves
- ❖ Paint bucket and mixing tool
- ❖ Water-based glazing liquid
- ❖ Latex paint in three colors for glaze mixtures
- ❖ Paintbrush, 4" (10 cm) wide
- ❖ Clean rags

1 Prepare the walls for painting (page 17). Protect the area around the walls with painter's masking tape and drop cloths (page 21). Apply the base coat and let it dry completely.

2 Put on rubber gloves. Mix the first glaze, following manufacturer's instructions. Apply the glaze to the wall and drag through it *vertically*, following the steps for dragging on page 37. Let the wall dry completely.

3 Mix the second glaze. Apply the glaze to the wall and drag through it *horizontally*, following the steps for dragging. Let the wall dry completely.

4 Mix the third glaze slightly thinner than the first two. Apply the glaze to the wall and drag through it *vertically*, following the steps for dragging. Let the wall dry completely. The thinner glaze will allow more of the first two colors to show through.

8 | Combing

COMBING COVERS A WALL with narrow, distinct lines by drawing a comb through wet glaze to reveal the base coat. The technique is fairly simple but requires a steady hand to produce an even, straight pattern. Working with a partner creates more consistent results; one person applies the glaze, and the other combs through it. The technique works best on smooth walls where the combing tool won't skip.

Depending upon the comb, colors, and pattern used, combing can appear delicate or bold. Painting combs and rubber squeegees with notches cut into them are the most common combing tools. Walls can be combed horizontally or vertically. Combed pinstripes in upscale earthy browns are attractive in formal spaces. Soft pastels with low contrast can be used to comb an entire wall or room, creating a soothing, relaxed atmosphere. Vertical combing under a chair rail mimics wainscoting. Combing can also be done in patterns, such as zigzags, swirls, or wavy lines. This effect, however, can be distracting, so it's best to use such designs in small spaces. Molding-framed wall areas can be attractively emphasized with subtle-colored combed swirls. Vibrant combed hues in a contemporary design above a fireplace or wet bar serve as a dramatic focal point that enlivens the entire space.

MATERIALS & TOOLS

- ❖ Painter's masking tape
- ❖ Drop cloths
- ❖ Paint roller and tray
- ❖ Latex paint for base coat
- ❖ Rubber gloves
- ❖ Paint bucket and mixing tool

- ❖ Latex paint for glaze mixture
- ❖ Water-based glazing liquid
- ❖ Combing tool of choice
- ❖ Clean rags

1 Prepare the walls for painting (page 17). Protect the area around the walls with painter's masking tape and drop cloths (page 21). Apply the base coat and let it dry completely.

2 Put on rubber gloves. In the bucket, prepare the glaze, mixing one part latex paint with two parts glazing liquid.

3 Apply the glaze from ceiling to floor in a 2-ft. (0.6 m) wide strip using a roller. Make sure the wall surface is evenly covered.

4 While the glaze is still wet, pull the combing tool downward through the glaze from the ceiling to the baseboard, applying even, relaxed pressure. The teeth of the combing tool remove lines of glaze, allowing the base coat to show through.

5 Wipe off excess glaze from the combing tool onto rags after each downward stroke.

6 Repeat steps 3 to 5, moving around the room until all the walls are finished.

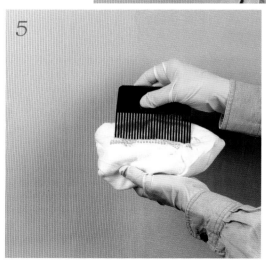

9 | Feathering

A SIMPLE WAY to produce a custom look, feathering is a technique that even the beginning painter can master. Contrasting paint is lightly pounced onto the wall, using an ordinary feather duster. Feathering doesn't require patience or a steady hand, and the tools are inexpensive. As easy as the technique may be, however, it is always a good idea to practice on a large piece of tagboard before applying the paint to the wall.

Purchase several feather dusters made from long wing feathers, rather than short, fluffy breast and back feathers. They cost less because they don't dust as well, but they produce better results for this technique.

Feathering with white or off-white paint can be used to tone down an intense base coat. Colorful, rich, and creamy shades feathered over walls of the same color in a lighter or darker value create a dreamy appearance for walls in a nursery or a young child's bedroom and bathroom. Feathering can also be applied in wide vertical stripes or as a high border.

1 Prepare the walls for painting (page 17). Protect the area around the walls with painter's masking tape and drop cloths (page 21). Apply the base coat and let it dry completely.

2 Put on rubber gloves. Gently dab the end of a feather duster into the top-coat paint and lightly tap off the excess paint onto newspaper.

3 Beginning at a top corner and working out and down, gently pounce the feather duster onto the wall. Turn the duster often to vary the pattern. Reload the duster with paint as necessary. Leave irregular edges.

4 Continue around the room, always working back into the irregular edges. Stand back from the wall often to check for a consistently dense feathering pattern. If the feathers become clogged with paint and the design becomes too heavy, simply switch to a new duster.

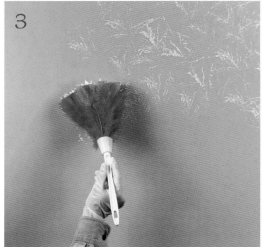

10 | Whisking

WHISKING DRESSES A WALL with curved streaks. It is similar to dragging (page 36), though the tool used to pattern the wall is a whisk broom, drawn through top-coat paint in short swirls. The technique is easy and inexpensive. Buy a new whisk broom and count on throwing it away when you finish painting the wall.

In addition to the swirled pattern shown here, other whisking options include pulling the whisk broom vertically through the paint, free-form crisscrossing curves, and wavy lines. When whisking, it is important to apply enough pressure to leave string-like stripes. Whenever possible, complete an entire wall without stopping to achieve a uniform look.

For the most effective results, select colors with high contrast for the base coat and top coat. The top coat will be the most apparent color. Use satin or semigloss paint for the base coat so the broom bristles can easily sweep off some of the top coat. Whisked walls can be quite "busy," so it is best to use this technique for small wall spaces, such as below a chair rail or as a border. Apply enough pressure to leave string-like stripes.

- ❖ Painter's masking tape
- ❖ Drop cloths
- ❖ Paint roller and tray
- ❖ Satin or semigloss latex paint for base coat
- ❖ Rubber gloves
- ❖ Satin latex paint for top coat
- ❖ Whisk broom
- ❖ Paper towels or clean rags

1 Prepare the walls for painting (page 17). Protect the area around the walls with painter's masking tape and drop cloths (page 21). Apply the base coat and let it dry completely.

2 Put on rubber gloves. Starting at the upper corner, roll on a single, 2-ft. (0.6 m) wide, vertical stripe of paint with the paint roller.

3 Sweep the whisk broom through the wet paint in overlapping swirling motions. Keep a narrow wet edge unwhisked.

4 Repeat steps 2 and 3 immediately alongside the first whisked stripe, working back into the wet edge. Use paper towels or clean rags to clean the bristles, as needed. Continue across the wall without stopping in order to whisk the entire surface while the paint is wet.

11|Troweling

TROWELING LAYERS PAINT on the wall with a hand trowel. Dark, medium, and light color values applied to the wall this way produce a dramatically textured, weathered appearance. This method provides only the illusion of texture, leaving the wall very smooth, so the wall can be easily repainted at a future date. Troweling works best on flat, uninterrupted walls where it is easy to manipulate the trowel. No base coat is necessary and the technique is extremely forgiving, making this an easy finish.

The randomness of the application and the wide range of color choices will make the results unique. Although troweling requires at least three color values, more colors can be added if desired. To achieve powerful color effects, use deep earth tones or striking jewel tones. Paler hues, such as soft pastels or various tinted whites combined with neutral tones, produce more muted effects.

Concentrating darker colors in the corners and along the baseboard lends an overall timeworn look to the wall, perfect for aging a vintage-styled kitchen in a new home. A combination of deep mustard, golden honey, rich sand, and slate tones would tone down a sun-drenched breakfast room to create a more soothing dining area.

MATERIALS & TOOLS

- ❖ Painter's masking tape
- ❖ Drop cloths
- ❖ Rubber gloves
- ❖ Semigloss latex paint in three color values
- ❖ Large aluminum foil roasting pan
- ❖ Small plastic trowel
- ❖ Clean rags

1 Prepare the walls for painting (page 17). Protect the area around the walls with painter's masking tape and drop cloths (page 21).

2 Put on rubber gloves. Pour the three paints into the foil pan, with the dark value on one side, the medium value in the center, and the light value on the other side. Add more of each color until the paint is at least 2" (5 cm) deep.

3 Dip the trowel about 1" (2.5 cm) deep into the dark paint. Beginning in an upper corner of the wall, apply the paint by wiping it from the trowel in short strokes in random directions. Repeat to cover an area about 3 ft. (1 m) square. Much of the bare wall will show through.

4 Repeat step 3 with the medium paint, applying it in areas not covered by the dark paint. It is not necessary to clean the trowel, as it is desirable to have the colors mix together slightly.

5 Repeat step 3 with the light paint, building depth and texture.

6 Apply more of each paint value as desired, blending them slightly and creating a rough plaster look. Clean the trowel, as necessary, with clean rags.

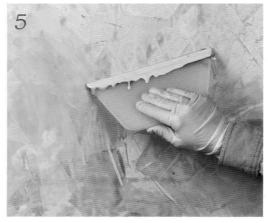

7 Repeat steps 3 to 6 in adjacent areas, moving down and across the entire wall. Stand back and look at the wall occasionally. Go back and add more paint to areas that need highlights or shadows.

12 | Paper Frottage

PAPER APPLIED OVER WET GLAZE and then removed will absorb some of the glaze and leave a distinctive imprint on the wall. This technique, called paper frottage, gives unique depth and color variation to the wall. It can be used alone or as a stylish background for other applications, such as stencils, freehand designs, or even murals.

In the example above, ordinary copy-machine paper was applied to the glaze and removed in rows, producing a finish that resembles stone blocks. Variations of the paper frottage theme can be achieved by using different kinds of paper. Lining paper, tissue paper, corrugated paper, craft paper, newspaper, or paper shopping bags can be used; each produces a distinctive look. You can also overlap papers at random angles or lightly crumple and manipulate the paper before applying it to the glaze.

Using two different intensities of one color for the base coat and glaze results in a subtle appearance. Bolder effects happen with two highly contrasting colors. The paper will absorb a lot of the glaze and leave a sheer veil of glaze color over the base coat with patches of concentrated color.

MATERIALS & TOOLS

- Painter's masking tape
- Drop cloths
- Paint roller and tray
- Latex paint for base coat
- Rubber gloves
- Paint bucket and mixing tool
- Latex paint for top coat
- Flat water-based glazing liquid
- Paper (8½" × 11" or larger)

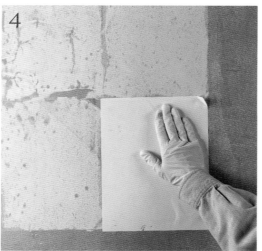

1 Prepare the walls for painting (page 17). Protect the area around the walls with painter's masking tape and drop cloths (page 21). Apply the base coat and let it dry completely.

2 Put on rubber gloves. In the bucket, prepare the glaze, mixing one part paint with one part glazing liquid.

3 Beginning at the top of the wall and working downward, apply glaze to the wall in a 4-ft. (1.2 m) square section using the paint roller.

4 Fold up one corner of the paper so it will be easier to remove. Press the paper directly into the wet glaze.

5 Peel the paper from the wall by carefully pulling the folded corner.

6 Repeat steps 4 and 5 throughout the glazed area, leaving a narrow wet edge of glaze. Align sheets of paper in rows as shown or overlap papers at various angles for a less distinct pattern.

7 Repeat steps 3 to 6 until the entire wall is complete.

13 | Bubble Wrap

THIS DECORATIVE PAINT technique produces a pebbled imprint of little "bubbles" all over the wall. Glaze is applied to the wall and manipulated with common plastic bubble wrap that has been secured to a rubber grout float for easy handling. This process is fun, but it can get a bit messy, so prepare the room well and have lots of clean rags handy.

Any compact area that could use a healthy dose of pattern and color is a good candidate for the bubble wrap technique. Cool pastel colors, such as muted blue, pale green, soft aqua, and gentle turquoise, result in soothing, lighthearted effects. Applying bubbles onto a half-wall in a nursery using soft pastel tones creates a subtle pattern for the space. Bubbles are a festive way to add a border of bright, primary colors in a children's bathroom. Stripes of bubbles in a bright, sunny color scheme could liven up a laundry room. Using a deep-toned metallic paint color, the pebbled pattern would be a dramatic effect for a backsplash wall behind a wet bar in a family room.

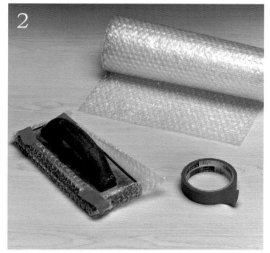

1 Prepare the walls for painting (page 17). Protect the area around the walls with painter's masking tape and drop cloths (page 21). Apply the base coat and let it dry completely.

2 Cover the bottom and sides of the rubber float with bubble wrap. Secure the edges with masking tape.

3 Put on rubber gloves. In the bucket, prepare the glaze, mixing one part latex paint with one part glazing liquid.

4 Apply the glaze from ceiling to floor in a 18" (46 cm) wide strip using a roller. Make sure the wall surface is evenly covered.

5 Beginning in an upper corner, press the bubble wrap into the glaze and lift it straight back. Repeat several times, turning the float at different angles, creating bubble impressions. Wipe excess glaze from the bubble wrap onto clean rags, as necessary. Continue until the entire strip is bubbled. Leave a wet edge.

6 Apply another strip of glaze next to the first one and repeat step 5, blending the bubble impressions back into the first area. Continue until the entire wall is bubbled. Rewrap the float with fresh bubble wrap as necessary.

14 | Stippling

STIPPLING COVERS THE WALL with fine, pinpoint dots that produce a delicate texture. The finish is most effective on walls that are in good condition, as the glaze can accentuate surface imperfections.

Unless you are stippling only a small area, use a two-person team to speed up the process. The first partner applies the vertical strips of glaze and the other stipples the glaze. It is a good idea to wipe the stippling brush frequently to be sure the glaze is manipulated, not removed. Work continuously and quickly for even results.

The stippling technique works with many colors. Though translucent, the glaze color will be dominant, as most of it will remain on the wall. Light tones and pastel-colored base coats will soften and lighten a dark or bold glaze color. Stippling a light glaze over a bright jewel tone mellows the base-coat color considerably, but allows bright color to peek through.

MATERIALS & TOOLS

- ❖ Painter's masking tape
- ❖ Drop cloths
- ❖ Paint roller and tray
- ❖ Rubber gloves
- ❖ Latex paint for base coat
- ❖ Paint bucket and mixing tool
- ❖ Latex paint for top coat
- ❖ Water-based glazing liquid
- ❖ Paintbrush, 2" (5 cm) wide
- ❖ Foam applicator, 2" (5 cm) wide
- ❖ Block stippler
- ❖ Edge stippler or stencil brush

1 Prepare the walls for painting (page 17). Protect the area around the walls with painter's masking tape and drop cloths (page 21). Apply the base coat and let it dry completely.

2 Put on rubber gloves. In the bucket, prepare the glaze, mixing equal amounts of top-coat paint and glazing liquid. Pour some of the mixture into the well of the paint tray.

3 Beginning in an upper corner, apply the glaze mixture to the wall in a 2-ft. (0.6 m) vertical strip. Use a 2" (5 cm) paintbrush to cut in along the ceiling and wall corner; use the paint roller to fill in the wall.

4 Apply a small amount of the glaze mixture to the block stippler, using a foam applicator, to ensure that the first pounce will not remove an excessive amount of glaze. This is called "buttering" the stippler.

5 Stipple the wall with a pouncing action. Move your arm in a circular motion, overlapping the imprints as you work from the top of the wall to the bottom. Leave an unstippled wet edge where the adjacent strip will be applied.

6 Repeat steps 3 to 5 until the entire wall is complete. Use a small edge stippler or stencil brush to stipple the corners and around woodwork.

15 | Spattering

FLICKING SMALL DOTS of different colored paint haphazardly onto a wall results in a speckled, casual wall. The colors selected for spattering and the density that each color is spattered determine the look. Spattering is often used effectively in country-styled interiors. Picture a vintage farmhouse kitchen with spattered walls that serve as a backdrop to black, white, and red collections and antiques.

Although easy to master, the process can be messy. Use a stiff, short-bristled brush to load the paint and a paint stirring stick or wooden craft stick to cause the spatters. Test the technique against a sheet of tagboard before you begin. If some of the dots drip, add more paint to the glaze mixture.

Apply the spatters sparsely at first, as an area can always be spattered again. If more than one color of dots is being applied, spatter the first round sparsely and then go back and add colors.

The base coat will remain the dominant color. When colors are spattered on a light-colored base coat, the effect is much lighter and airier than when the same colors are spattered on a darker base-coat color.

1 Prepare the walls for painting (page 17). Protect the area around the walls with painter's masking tape and drop cloths (page 21). Apply the base coat and let it dry completely.

2 Put on rubber gloves. In the bucket, prepare the glaze, mixing two parts paint, two parts glazing liquid, and one part water. It should be the consistency of heavy cream.

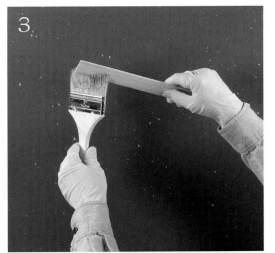

3 Dip the brush about ½" (1.3 cm) into the glaze mixture. Remove excess paint. Hold the brush upright with the bristles perpendicular to the wall. Holding the spatter stick parallel to the wall, pull it toward you across the tips of the bristles, releasing a spray of paint flecks onto the wall. Begin in an upper corner and work outward and down, directing the spatters by turning the brush slightly. Reload the brush when the spatters get too fine.

4 Repeat step 3 until the walls are complete. Repeat with a second color of glaze mix, if desired.

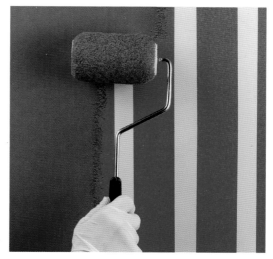

Geometric DESIGNS

16 | Stripes

VERSATILE AND APPEALING, stripes can be part of many décors. Stripes provide an eye-catching backdrop for a gallery of artwork. They can visually expand a small foyer or perk up a boring hallway or landing. In a kitchen, stripes can be an innovative treatment above upper cabinets. Wide stripes can relax formal furnishings in a living room.

There are lots of color choices for stripes. Colors with high contrast produce a dramatic effect that can be used for showcasing contemporary spaces. Pinstripes in rich colors look formal. Stimulating, vivid stripes are often found in children's play areas. Exciting inspiration for striped designs

can be found in clothing and home décor fabrics. Stripes are also combined with other paint techniques such as sponging, ragging, or combing.

The success of a striped design depends on accurate measuring and taping. Though shown with a carpenter's level, a laser level will make the technique easier. When choosing the width of the stripes, consider the size of the wall as well as the time you want to dedicate to the project. Traditional stripes are 3" to 5" (7.5 to 12.7 cm) wide. The spaces between the stripes can be wider, narrower, or equal to the stripes. Spaces the same width as painter's tape can be taped off quickly.

- ❖ Painter's masking tape
- ❖ Drop cloths
- ❖ Paint roller and tray
- ❖ Latex paint for base coat
- ❖ Pencil
- ❖ Carpenter's or laser level
- ❖ Ruler
- ❖ Small plastic smoothing tool
- ❖ Rubber gloves
- ❖ Latex paint for top coat
- ❖ Small roller or paintbrush
- ❖ Artist's paintbrush

1 Prepare the walls for painting (page 17). Protect the area around the walls with painter's masking tape and drop cloths (page 21). Apply the base coat and let it dry completely.

2 For even stripes, use the carpenter's level to mark a series of tick marks from floor to ceiling at the center of the wall. Mark a line of tick marks on each side of the first line a distance away equal to half the desired width of the stripes. These lines indicate your center stripe. For uneven stripes, measure the width of the first stripe from one corner of the wall; mark a series of tick marks from floor to ceiling.

3 Continue marking the measurements to indicate subsequent stripes. When you reach a corner, either adjust the stripe widths to end exactly in the corner or keep constant widths and wrap a stripe around the corner.

4 Apply painter's masking tape to mask the areas between stripes. Smooth down the edge of the tape along the marked lines, using a small plastic smoothing tool. This prevents the paint from seeping under the tape, producing an imperfect edge.

5 Put on rubber gloves. Apply a top-coat paint to the exposed areas using a small roller or paintbrush.

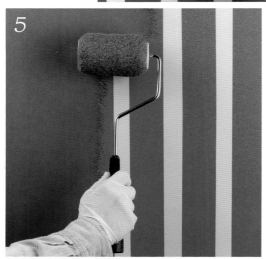

6 Carefully remove the masking tape before the paint dries. If there has been any seepage under the tape, touch it up with a small artist's paintbrush.

17 | Sheen Stripes

SHEEN STRIPING is a simple and subtle way to add interest to the wall without expanding the existing color palette. Glossy stripes are painted over a flat background of the same color, creating an elegant contrast that is particularly suitable for formal spaces. Consider using sheen striping in a room that holds treasured antiques or traditionally styled furnishings.

Variations in the width of the stripes add visual interest and distinctiveness to the striped design. You can alternate extra-wide stripes with very narrow stripes or gradually increase the width of the stripes at regular intervals from narrow to wide. Apply the glossy stripes to one focus wall or to all the walls in the room.

Color options for sheen stripes are directly related to the existing color scheme in the room. The effect is more pronounced, however, with deep colors, such as the brilliant blue shown above, rich burgundy, or emerald green. Light, muted sheen stripes work well in smaller spaces, rooms that contain low ceilings, and areas that lack natural lighting. Deeper, richer sheen stripes add warmth and coziness to oversized rooms and open-concept homes with high ceilings.

MATERIALS & TOOLS

- ❖ Painter's masking tape
- ❖ Drop cloths
- ❖ Paint roller and tray
- ❖ Flat latex paint for base coat
- ❖ Pencil
- ❖ Carpenter's or laser level
- ❖ Small plastic smoothing tool
- ❖ Water-based glazing liquid
- ❖ Rubber gloves
- ❖ Small paintbrush
- ❖ Semigloss latex paint for top coat in same color as base coat

1 Prepare the walls for painting (page 17). Protect the area around the walls with painter's masking tape and drop cloths (page 21). Apply the flat base coat and let it dry completely.

2 Mark and mask off stripes, as in steps 2 to 4 on page 59.

3 Put on rubber gloves. Apply glazing liquid along the inside edges of the tape using the small paintbrush. Allow to dry completely. This will ensure crisp, straight edges by preventing the paint from seeping under the tape.

4 Paint the stripes, using the semigloss paint. Remove the tape. Allow to dry completely.

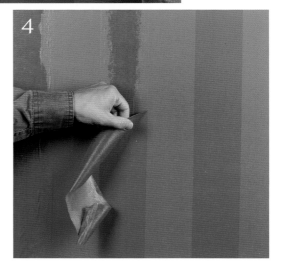

18 | Checks

CLASSIC CHECKS consist of squares painted in a repeating, alternating pattern over a background color. They can be a stylish accent in a casual-styled kitchen, either under a chair rail or as a border around the room. Bright colored checks are playful and charming in a child's bedroom. So the strong pattern does not overwhelm the area, take color and scale into consideration. You can apply surprisingly oversized checks to one wall in a room.

For the most effective checked design, choose a light background color and paint the checks in a medium or dark value color. This is especially important if complementary colors are used, so the colors will not fight for dominance. Colors that are close to each other on the color wheel, such as blue and green, produce handsome combinations. Along with solid colors, decorative paint techniques, such as sponging (page 30), can be used.

Though it may take a lot of time, careful masking of the checks is crucial to the success of this application. A laser level will make the job faster and easier.

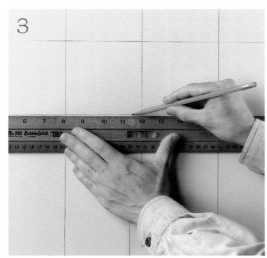

3

- ❖ Painter's masking tape
- ❖ Drop cloths
- ❖ Paint roller and tray
- ❖ Latex paint for base coat
- ❖ Tape measure

- ❖ Pencil
- ❖ Carpenter's or laser level
- ❖ Putty knife
- ❖ Latex paint for top coat
- ❖ Paintbrush or small roller

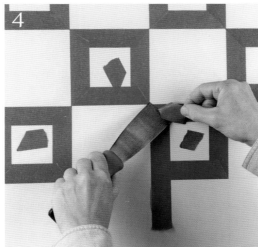

4

5

1 Prepare the walls for painting (page 17). Protect the area around the walls with painter's masking tape and drop cloths (page 21). Apply the base coat and let it dry completely.

2 Measure the height and width of the wall to be painted. Decide on the scale of your check. If the wall cannot be divided evenly, begin the design at the ceiling, allowing it to run out at the floor, where smaller squares will be less obvious.

3 Mark a series of tick marks from floor to ceiling for the sides of the first row of squares. Use a carpenter's level to ensure the line is plumb. Join the marks using a pencil. Repeat to mark all the vertical lines. Then mark the horizontal lines, measuring evenly from the baseboard.

4 Apply painter's masking tape to mask off the squares that will remain the base-coat color; use a putty knife to trim masking tape diagonally at the corners, as shown. Smooth down the tape edges to prevent seepage. Mark the inside of each square not being painted at this time with a piece of tape.

5 Paint the remaining squares using a paintbrush or small roller. Carefully remove the tape. Allow the paint to dry. Touch up any areas where paint may have seeped under the tape.

19 | Color Blocking

SQUARES AND RECTANGLES painted in various sizes and colors are a fresh, dramatic look, especially suitable for contemporary spaces. Large, oversized blocks make the most effective design statement. Due to the large scale of the blocks, quantity of blocks, and number of colors used, the technique is most effective when painted on only one wall in a room.

It is not uncommon for blocks of color to take the place of artwork on the wall. Consider using the technique above a whirlpool in a master bathroom, behind a sofa in a family room, or above a sideboard in a dining room.

Choose a family of colors in tasteful, muted shades and paint them in one-yard blocks or larger to create a striking wall treatment. For a small focus area, slightly brighter hues in 12" to 18" (30.5 to 46 cm) blocks will produce a bolder overall look. Soothing monochromatic effects can be achieved by using varying intensities of the same color.

1 Prepare the walls for painting (page 17). Protect the area around the walls with painter's masking tape and drop cloths (page 21). Apply the base coat in the lightest color and let it dry completely.

2 Map out the block design on the wall using a carpenter's level or laser level and the colored pencils that coordinate with each paint color.

3 Apply painter's masking tape around the blocks that will be painted with the first color, aligning the tape to the outer edges of the colored pencil lines.

4 Apply glazing liquid along the inside edge of the tape, using a foam applicator. Let the glaze dry completely. This will ensure crisp, straight edges by preventing the paint from seeping under the tape.

5 Paint the first set of blocks in the desired color, using the small roller. Carefully remove the tape while the paint is still wet. Let the paint dry completely.

6 Repeat steps 3 to 5 for the blocks in each paint color.

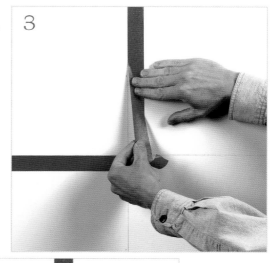

20 | Diamond Border

THE DIAMOND BORDER is a simple pattern with timeless appeal. Tailored, formal settings can be accented with traditional black and white diamonds. Bright-colored diamond borders are a cheerful motif in children's rooms. Subtle looks can be achieved by painting the diamonds in two shades from the same paint color card or by choosing the same color and alternating the paint sheens.

Scale the size of the diamond border to suit the size of the wall and the room. Consider the colors of the fabrics and furnishings in the room when choosing the diamond colors. Popular large-scale diamonds have a greater impact when the furnishings are sleek and simple. Blend the décor of adjoining rooms by extending the diamond border from one room onto one wall of the next room. Unify an open-concept living space by painting sections of the diamond border in several areas.

There are many creative ways to personalize a diamond border. The diamonds can be color washed (page 26), sponge painted (page 30), ragged (page 32), or combed (page 40). Applying upholstery tacks or beads at the points where the diamonds intersect gives a distinctive touch to the border.

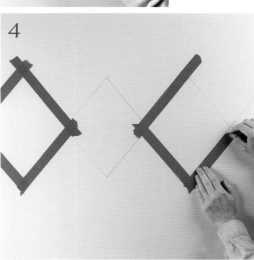

3

4

5

1 Prepare the walls for painting (page 17). Protect the area around the walls with painter's masking tape and drop cloths (page 21). Apply the base coat and let it dry completely. Using a carpenter's level or laser level and tape measure, mark a faint horizontal pencil line on the wall at the desired center line of the border.

2 Measure the width of the wall space to be covered. Divide by the approximate desired diamond width, and round up to the nearest whole number to determine the number of diamonds. Then divide the space measurement by the number of diamonds to determine the exact diamond width. Make a cardboard diamond template with this width and the desired height. Draw a line across the center.

3 Match up the line on the template to the line on the wall, and trace the diamonds along the border with a pencil.

4 Apply masking tape to the outside of every other diamond, overlapping the tape at each corner of the diamond.

5 Apply the first top-coat color inside the taped-off diamonds, using the small roller.

6 Remove the tape while paint is still wet. Allow the paint to dry completely.

7 Repeat steps 4 to 6 with the second color to paint the remaining diamonds.

21 | Lattice

THIS LATTICE FINISH is a freehand glaze manipulation technique that results in a sheer diagonal grid. The Color Shaper tool used to create the lattice is shaped like a paintbrush but has a solid, flat, rubber end instead of bristles. It is available from specialty paint stores or art supply centers. A small putty knife could also be used.

White or off-white glaze applied over a medium or dark base-coat color will give the most realistic appearance. Bright, vivid base-coat colors can liven up an art studio or craft area. Soft pastel colors may enhance a child's bedroom. Washed, earthy tones look natural in a sunroom or behind a potting bench.

Lattice works well as a companion to other techniques. Painted on the bottom half of the wall in dining area, the lattice technique resembles wainscoting. A stenciled or freehand painted climbing vine can be applied over the lattice design as part of a botanical themed bathroom. Alongside stairs, the lattice design forms an interesting backdrop where family portraits can be hung.

1 Prepare the walls for painting (page 17). Protect the area around the walls with painter's masking tape and drop cloths (page 21). Apply the base coat and let it dry completely.

2 Put on rubber gloves. In the bucket, prepare the glaze, mixing three parts glazing liquid with one part paint. Using the paintbrush, apply the glaze mixture evenly over the wall surface.

3 While the wall is wet, draw the Color Shaper through the glaze in freehand diagonal stripes. After each stripe, wipe excess paint from the tool onto clean rags.

4 Repeat step 3 in the opposite direction, creating a lattice effect.

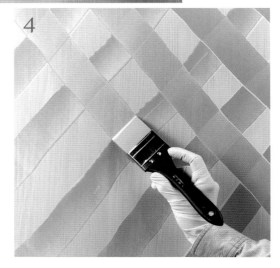

22 | Plaid

IN THIS PLAID design, horizontal and vertical stripes of alternating colors and widths are applied freehand, resulting in a casual, wonderfully imperfect appearance. The multicolor plaid design is most effective and easiest to paint where there are no windows, doors, or other interruptions in the wall surface.

Two-color blended lines are achieved by "double loading" the paintbrush. It is critical to always load and hold the brush in the same position to avoid reversing the paint colors. Pouring only a small amount of paint at a time into shallow containers helps prevent the paint colors from mixing together. If an entire stripe

cannot be completed with one stroke, it is better to begin the next stroke from the opposite direction, painting it back into the first stroke. This results in a more continuous joining of colors and a more harmonious look. Chalk guidelines help space the strokes evenly.

Size and scale are important. Small rooms are prime candidates for smaller scale plaids in light or neutral colors. If there are other strong design elements in the room, consider painting the plaid on only one wall or half-wall. A bold hue that is part of the existing color scheme can be accentuated by bringing that color into the plaid design.

❖ Painter's masking tape
❖ Drop cloths
❖ Paint roller and tray
❖ Satin latex paint for base coat
❖ Pencil
❖ Chalk
❖ Foam applicators in desired widths
❖ Latex paint for top coat in two to four colors
❖ Shallow container for each top-coat color

1 Prepare the walls for painting (page 17). Protect the area around the walls with painter's masking tape and drop cloths (page 21). Apply the base coat and let it dry completely.

2 Mark the plaid pattern on the wall with tick marks, using a pencil. Use chalk to sketch out the plaid pattern on the wall.

3 Pour small amounts of the first two colors into shallow containers. Dip the foam applicator into one color; gently tap the back of the applicator against the container rim to remove excess paint. Next, dip one edge of the applicator into the second color of paint. This method of adding paint to the applicator is called "double loading."

4 Paint the first vertical stripe of the plaid, beginning at the top of the wall and pulling the applicator downward until the paint gets too thin.

5 Double load the applicator again and complete the stripe, painting back into the first stroke to blend the strokes together.

6 Repeat steps 4 and 5 until all the vertical stripes have been painted. Allow the vertical stripes to dry for two hours.

7 Repeat steps 3 to 6 for the horizontal stripes.

23 | Polka Dots

A LIVELY, LIGHTHEARTED paint technique, polka dots are often inspired by a fun dotted fabric. This playful effect is perfect for children's rooms, craft rooms, laundry rooms, bathrooms, and more. Part of the success of this technique depends on adjusting the spacing of the polka dots to suit the size of the room. Do not worry if the polka dots are imperfect, as randomness is part of what makes this technique special.

Choice of color depends mostly on where the polka dots are used. Consider brighter colors for lively spaces like children's playrooms, bedrooms, and bathrooms. If you select complementary colors, as shown above, use a lighter value for the background so the dots pop. Use subdued colors, perhaps two shades of the same color, for a guest bedroom or guest bathroom where the goal is to create a one-of-a-kind look. Color washing (page 26) the walls before applying polka dots will soften the look. For a reversible scheme, choose colors for the background and dots on one wall and reverse the colors on an adjacent wall.

MATERIALS & TOOLS

- ❖ Painter's masking tape
- ❖ Drop cloths
- ❖ Paint roller and tray
- ❖ Latex paint for base coat
- ❖ Latex paint in desired colors for dots

- ❖ Paper plates
- ❖ Styrofoam cups
- ❖ Paper towels
- ❖ Small foam applicator

1 Prepare the walls for painting (page 17). Protect the area around the walls with painter's masking tape and drop cloths (page 21). Apply the base coat and let it dry completely.

2 Plan the spacing of the polka dots. Place small pieces of masking tape wherever you would like the dots placed.

3 Pour a puddle of paint onto a paper plate. Dip the open end of a Styrofoam cup into the puddle and dab lightly onto several paper towels to remove excess paint.

4 Press the cup firmly over the tape mark on the wall. Repeat to outline each polka dot.

5 Using a small foam applicator, fill in each polka dot with its paint color.

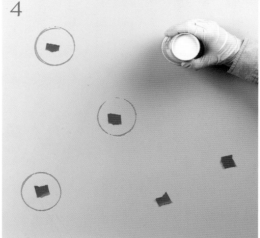

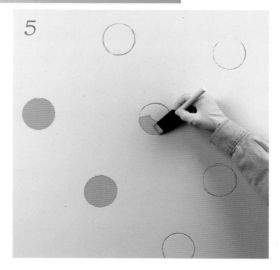

24 | Basket Weave

THE BASKET WEAVE technique is a variation of combing (page 40), worked with a triangular graining tool. The sides of the graining tool are rubber combs with teeth of different widths and spacing. The repeated dragging, lifting, and repositioning of the tool in the wet glaze results in a fluid, imperfect design resembling woven wicker.

A somewhat time-consuming process with effective but busy results, the basket weave technique is best used in small, casual areas such as a laundry room or mudroom or on the wall space between kitchen cabinets and the countertop. The basket weave can be attractively applied to part of a wall when the rest of the wall is a solid base color. A basket weave border near the ceiling in a guest bedroom would complement wicker furniture. Set at chair-rail height, a basket weave border adds interest in a casual dining room or breakfast nook. Soft, muted colors in a monochromatic scheme can add subtle texture to an otherwise dull space.

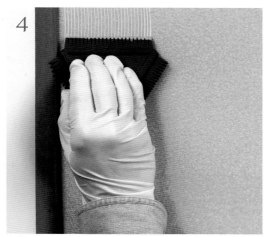

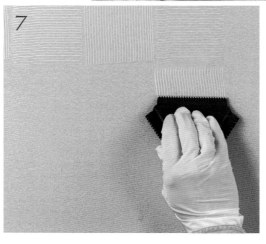

1 Prepare the walls for painting (page 123). Protect the area around the walls with painter's tape and drop cloths (page 126). Apply the base coat and let it dry.

2 In the bucket, prepare the glaze mixture, mixing one part latex paint with two parts glazing liquid.

3 Apply the glaze in a 2-ft. (0.6 m) wide area from ceiling to floor using the roller. Make sure the wall surface is evenly covered.

4 Using the fine-toothed side of the triangular graining tool, vertically comb a section from the top corner of the wall downward. The section should only be as deep as the comb is wide, resulting in a square. Lift the tool from the surface.

5 Turn the tool perpendicular to the lines of the first square. Beginning alongside the first square, horizontally comb a square of the same size. Wipe excess glaze from the comb onto clean rags, as necessary.

6 Continue combing the top row of squares in the 2-ft. (0.6 m) wide area, alternating vertical and horizontal squares. Leave a 2" (5 cm) wet edge of glaze and move down to the next row, beginning with a horizontal square and continuing to alternate directions. A checkerboard pattern will develop.

7 Apply another strip of glaze alongside the wet edge. Comb a basket-weave column vertically before the wet edge dries. Then continue combing each row horizontally, again leaving a 2" (5 cm) wet edge of glaze.

8 Repeat step 7, moving around the room until all the walls are finished.

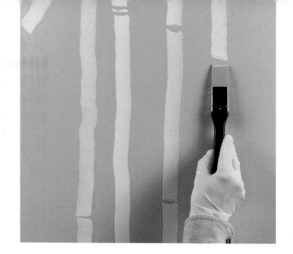

Faux
FINISHES

25 | Textured Metallic

RICH METALLIC COLORS applied with dramatic texture produce a finish that has a unique aged appearance. It is best to apply the textured metallic paint finish to a distinct, compact wall area, such as a built-in niche or a slender divider wall between two rooms. A modest alcove wall or the minimal wall space above upper cabinets will come alive when the textured metallic finish is applied.

For the best results, select a brown and green of the same intensity. The "washing" of the light green latex paint over the bronze, copper, and brown creates the hint of metal. Or partner pewter, brushed silver, matte gold, or any other popular metallic hue with a light green latex paint. Because of the textured plaster in this technique, the only way to remove it is to replace the wall board, so practice before you begin.

MATERIALS & TOOLS

- ❖ Painter's masking tape
- ❖ Drop cloths
- ❖ Vinyl spackle
- ❖ Wide plastic spackling knife
- ❖ Rubber gloves
- ❖ Water
- ❖ Sea sponges
- ❖ Brown satin latex paint for base coat
- ❖ Paintbrush
- ❖ Bronze metallic paint
- ❖ Copper metallic paint
- ❖ Light green latex paint
- ❖ Cotton rags

1 Prepare the walls for painting (page 17). Protect the area around the walls with painter's masking tape and drop cloths page 21). Using the spackling knife, apply a very thin layer of vinyl spackle to the wall.

2 Put on rubber gloves. Slightly dampen a sea sponge with water. Beginning at the top of the wall, pull the sponge down over the vinyl spackle to create small ridges. Let the surface dry completely.

3 Apply the brown base coat to the wall, using the paintbrush. Let it dry completely.

4 Dip a clean, damp sea sponge into the bronze metallic paint; dab off excess. Beginning at the top of the wall, apply the bronze paint over the brown base coat, pulling the sponge in vertical strokes. Reload the sponge with paint as needed. Let the surface dry completely.

5 Repeat step 4 using the copper metallic paint. Let the surface dry completely.

6 For a verdigris effect, apply the light green paint as in step 4, but wipe off as much of the excess paint as you desire, using a damp rag.

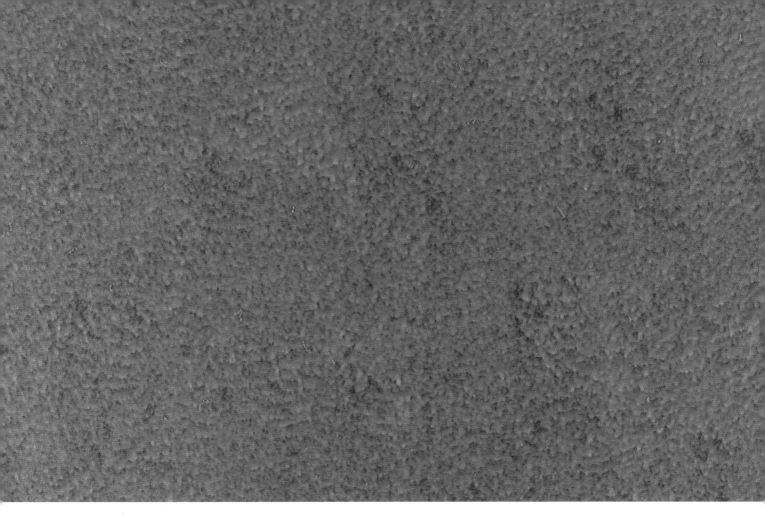

26 | Pearl

THE PEARL FINISH casts a soft, white shimmer over the wall surface. The walls appear to subtly change color as you walk by or as the lighting in the room changes.

Pearlescent or opalescent paint is a translucent finishing product, much like a glaze, that is applied over a base coat. It is available in a few white or off-white colors. An additive creates the luster. Because the additive tends to settle to the bottom, the product should be stirred often during application.

Strong colors can be used for the base coat because the sheer pearl finish will soften the color a lot. If a pastel is used for the base coat, the wall will have a soft white shimmer with only a hint of color.

Pearlescent walls can be a stunning focal point around a tub in a master bathroom or as a fireplace wall in a master bedroom. When painted as vertical stripes (page 58), the pearl technique will lend height and drama to a formal living room. The technique is especially striking when used in a contemporary interior that features furnishings with sleek lines and glass or metal surfaces.

❖ Painter's masking tape
❖ Drop cloths
❖ Paint roller and tray
❖ Semigloss latex paint for base coat
❖ Rubber gloves

❖ Pearlescent or opalescent paint
❖ Paintbrush, 2" (5 cm) wide
❖ Block stippler
❖ Small edge stippler
❖ Clean rags

1 Prepare the walls for painting (page 17). Protect the area around the walls with painter's masking tape and drop cloths (page 21). Apply the base coat and let it dry completely.

2 Put on rubber gloves. Beginning in an upper corner, apply a 2-ft. (0.6 m) square area of pearlescent paint. Use the paintbrush to cut in along the ceiling and wall corner; use the paint roller to fill in the area.

3 Butter the block stippler, as in step 4 on page 53. While the paint is wet, stipple the area with a pouncing action. Move your arm in a circular motion, overlapping the imprints. Leave an unstippled wet edge where the adjacent square will be applied.

4 Repeat steps 2 and 3 in adjacent areas until the entire wall is complete. Wipe excess paint from the stippler onto clean rags, as necessary. Use the edge stippler to stipple the corners and around woodwork.

27 | Fresco

FRESCO IS AN advanced paint technique that creates a stucco-like textured surface. It is well suited for walls that already have irregularities or imperfections. It is important to work quickly, as the drywall joint compound used to texture the wall dries rapidly. Working with a partner helps to speed transitions from one area of the wall to another.

After drying, the textured surface is painted and color washed (page 26). Light or medium shades of the same color used for the base coat and glaze most dramatically show the fresco's texture. Pale, earth-tone colors are attractive choices for fresco color schemes. Although fresco is found in many rustic and country-styled homes, it also provides a warm backdrop for even the most contemporary interior that lacks pattern, color, or texture.

You can change the color of your fresco wall, but the only way to successfully remove the texture is to replace the plasterboard. Therefore, it is essential that you test the application on a small piece of plasterboard to be sure you will like the results.

MATERIALS & TOOLS

- ❖ Painter's masking tape
- ❖ Drop cloths
- ❖ Rubber gloves
- ❖ Drywall joint compound
- ❖ Wide spackling knife
- ❖ Dust mask
- ❖ Sandpaper
- ❖ Vacuum
- ❖ Drywall primer

- ❖ Paint roller with ¾" (2 cm) nap; tray
- ❖ Latex paint for base coat
- ❖ Paint bucket and mixing tool
- ❖ Water-based glazing liquid
- ❖ Latex paint for glaze mixture
- ❖ Paintbrush, 4" to 6" (10 to 15 cm) wide

1 Prepare the walls for application of the drywall joint compound (page 17). Protect the area around the walls with painter's masking tape and drop cloths (page 21).

2 Put on rubber gloves. Beginning at the upper corner and working downward, apply an ⅛" (3 mm) layer of compound to the wall with a spackling knife. Use random sweeping motions to produce a rough wall surface. Allow the compound to dry completely.

3 Put on a dust mask and sand down any areas of compound that contain high ridges and bumps, for a smoother look. Vacuum the entire wall.

4 Apply drywall primer to the wall surface using the roller. Let it dry completely.

5 Apply the base coat to the wall surface using the roller. Let it dry completely.

6 In the bucket, prepare the glaze mixture, mixing one part latex paint with four parts glazing liquid.

7 Beginning in an upper corner, apply the glaze mixture using the color washing technique on page 26. Allow the base coat to be subtly exposed.

28 | Venetian Plaster

VENETIAN PLASTER has the mellow, weathered appearance of old plaster walls that can be found in Italy. This elegant finish is often applied by craftspeople to the walls of upscale retail stores and restaurants because of its architectural interest and durability. Home owners can buy the tinted plasters at paint stores, along with the proper trowels for applying the finish. The three-part process of layering the plaster is easy to learn.

Venetian plaster is available in a limited number of colors, usually in earthy, faded, sun-drenched hues.

Trust the color card when choosing a shade of Venetian plaster. Unlike wet paint, which can be a couple of shades lighter than the color represented on the sample card, wet Venetian plaster is about 40 percent darker than the color indicated on the sample card. The true color will develop as the plaster dries.

Venetian plaster is a permanent finish. The wet plaster can be scraped off the wall if you are not satisfied with your results, but after it dries, the only way to successfully remove it is to replace the plasterboard.

MATERIALS & TOOLS

- ❖ Painter's masking tape
- ❖ Drop cloths
- ❖ Rubber gloves
- ❖ Primer tinted the same color as the plaster
- ❖ Venetian plaster

- ❖ Small trowel
- ❖ Large trowel
- ❖ Handsanding block with 220-grit and 400-grit sandpapers
- ❖ Clean rags

1 Prepare the walls for the plaster treatment (page 17). Protect the area around the walls with painter's masking tape and drop cloths (page 21). Apply the primer and let it dry completely.

2 Put on rubber gloves. Apply the first thin coat of plaster to a section of the wall using a small trowel. Using the large trowel, smooth out the plaster. Let the plaster dry completely.

3 Apply a second thin coat of plaster, using the small trowel and working in broad crisscross motions. The walls should appear textured. Allow the second coat of plaster to dry completely.

4 Apply a third and final thin coat of plaster to the wall surface using the large trowel, smoothing it over the second layer. Allow the third coat of plaster to dry completely.

5 Sand the wall very lightly in an up and down motion using a hand sanding block and 220-grit sandpaper. Then sand with 400-grit sandpaper to subtly polish the top coat of the plaster.

6 Wipe off the plaster dust using a slightly damp rag.

29 | Denim

PAINT GLAZE MANIPULATED with a special brush can produce the distinct appearance of worn denim fabric. Fine vertical and horizontal lines created in the glaze mimic the weave of this casual cotton fabric.

The denim technique is a favorite for the family room, game room, and other relaxed family spaces. It is often used in children's and teens' bedrooms and bathrooms. The denim finish can be attractively customized by hand painting "stitches," "seams," or "pockets" as they appear on denim clothing. Team the denim wall finish with plaids and floral upholstered furnishings and fabrics.

Although it is most recognizable when it appears in classic blue shades, the denim technique can be applied in a variety of colors. Consider pastel colors such as soft pinks, pale yellows, or gentle peaches.

MATERIALS & TOOLS

- ❖ Painter's masking tape
- ❖ Drop cloths
- ❖ Paint roller and tray
- ❖ Neutral color latex paint for base coat

- ❖ Rubber gloves
- ❖ Paint buckets and mixing tools
- ❖ Latex paint for glaze in two differing shades of one color

- ❖ Water-based glazing liquid
- ❖ Water
- ❖ Wide denim weaver brush or wallpaper brush
- ❖ Clean rags

1 Prepare the walls for painting (page 17). Protect the area around the walls with painter's masking tape and drop cloths (page 21). Apply the base coat and let it dry completely.

2 Put on rubber gloves. In a bucket, prepare the first glaze, mixing two parts of the first paint color with two parts glazing liquid and one part water.

3 Beginning at the top of the wall, apply the glaze horizontally in an 18" (46 cm) wide strip, using the roller.

4 While the glaze is wet, drag the denim weaver brush or wallpaper brush horizontally through the glaze in continuous strokes from corner to corner. Wipe excess glaze from the brush onto rags after each stroke.

5 Repeat steps 3 and 4, working from top to bottom on each wall. Much of the neutral base coat should show through the glaze. Allow the glaze to dry completely.

6 In another bucket, prepare the second glaze, mixing equal amounts of the darker color, glazing liquid, and water. Note that the increase in the amount of water will produce a thinner mixture.

7 Beginning in the top corner, apply the glaze and drag through it as in steps 3 and 4, but working vertically. Some of the background color and much of the first glaze color should show through.

30 | Linen

DRAGGING A BRUSH through wet glaze in horizontal and vertical strokes creates the woven look of linen. This finish is soft and subtle and will not compete with heavily patterned fabrics, ornate furnishings, or artwork and collections found in the room.

The most effective colors for this technique resemble actual linen fabric. Consider using light, natural tones, such as soft sand and wheat, or pale pastels, such as muted yellows and washed blues.

The linen paint finish is versatile enough to be used throughout the home and teamed with several styles of décor. Though commonly used in cottage-style or country settings, the linen finish also works in contemporary spaces. This technique can be an attractive partner to wide vertical stripes (page 58) in adjacent rooms with similar color schemes.

In preparation for applying the linen paint finish, the walls are taped off in vertical sections that mimic the width of actual linen fabric. Thin lines of deeper color where the sections overlap will appear as seams in the fabric, adding to the illusion that the walls are covered with linen.

3

4

1 Prepare the walls for painting (page 17). Protect the area around the walls with painter's masking tape and drop cloths (page 21). Apply the base coat and let it dry completely.

2 Divide the room into a series of vertical sections that you can work with easily and quickly from top to bottom. Using painter's tape, mask off every other section.

3 Put on rubber gloves. In the bucket, prepare the glaze, mixing five parts glazing liquid with one part paint. Apply the glaze mixture onto the first wall section using the roller. While the glaze is still wet, drag the linen weaver brush in long horizontal strokes, back and forth, through the entire section. Wipe off excess glaze from the brush with a lint-free cloth after each stroke.

4 Turn the brush and drag it through the glaze in long vertical strokes, from top to bottom.

5 Repeat steps 3 and 4 for each alternating wall section. Remove the tape and allow each section to dry completely.

6 Mask off the painted sections, positioning the tape ⅛" (3 mm) inside the painted edges. As the glaze overlaps in these thin lines, it will create the look of seams. Repeat steps 3 and 4 in the remaining sections. Remove the tape and let the glaze dry completely.

31 | Parchment

RICH COLORS and sophisticated dimensional texture are combined in a parchment finish. Crumpled tissue paper is sealed into the paint, leaving a network of wrinkled ridges. The wall becomes a delight to the eye and invites admiring touches. Since the paper is sealed into the paint, the wall can be touched often, and even wiped with a damp cloth when necessary, without fear of damaging the finish.

Parchment, a popular wall treatment in many designer showcase homes, can be incorporated tastefully into any style of décor. Deep, strong colors highlight the dimension of the wrinkled ridges. Consider burgundy, dark brown, maroon, plum, black, or forest green. Light, natural tans and creams will create a subdued appearance. A slightly darker color-wash finish can be added to emphasize the texture.

Decide carefully where to use the parchment finish, as removing it from walls requires replacing the plasterboard.

MATERIALS & TOOLS

- ❖ Painter's masking tape
- ❖ Drop cloths
- ❖ Tissue paper, enough to cover the wall in a single layer
- ❖ Paint roller and tray
- ❖ Latex paint for base coat
- ❖ Rubber gloves
- ❖ Paint bucket and mixing tool, optional
- ❖ Satin latex paint for color washing glaze, optional
- ❖ Water-based glazing liquid, optional
- ❖ Paintbrush, 4" to 6" (10 to 15 cm) wide, optional

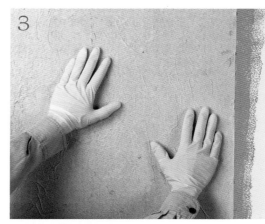

1 Prepare the walls for painting (page 17). Protect the area around the walls with painter's masking tape and drop cloths (page 21).

2 Scrunch up whole pieces of tissue paper and set them aside.

3 Put on rubber gloves. Beginning in an upper corner, apply the base-coat paint to an area slightly larger than a sheet of tissue paper using the roller. While the paint is wet, open up a sheet of crumpled tissue paper and apply it to the wall using your hands to smooth the paper into the wet paint. Leave small crinkles in a random pattern.

4 Roll over the surface carefully with a second coat of the base-coat paint.

5 Repeat steps 3 and 4, slightly overlapping the tissue papers until the entire surface has been covered evenly and completely. Let the wall dry completely.

6 If an aged look is desired, apply a colorwash finish, following steps 2 to 5 on page 26.

32 | Grass Cloth

WOVEN GRASS WALL COVERINGS are an expensive investment, but you can create the same look with paint and a squeegee. The grass cloth paint technique is a variation of combing (page 40). Sawtooth points cut into the edge of a rubber squeegee manipulate the top coat of paint, removing fine lines of color to expose the base coat. The walls are taped off in sections similar in width to wallpaper. When the painting is complete, narrow lines of color where the sections overlap resemble butted wallpaper seams.

For a realistic appearance, select paint colors, such as sand and wheat, that closely resemble natural grasses. Because of the earthy nature of the technique, grass cloth walls work well in a casual sunroom where plants and natural textures are key design elements. The grass cloth look when married to rich reds and classic black exudes luxurious elegance in an Asian or other ethnically inspired décor.

The walls will have to be sanded and primed before repainting at a later date.

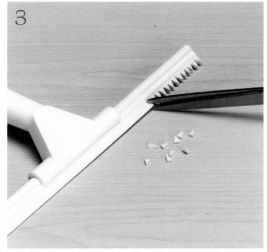

MATERIALS & TOOLS

- Painter's masking tape
- Drop cloths
- Paint roller and tray
- Latex paint for base coat
- Pencil
- Long carpenter's level
- Scissors

- Window squeegee
- Rubber gloves
- Latex paint for top coat
- Sash brush
- Small paint comb
- Clean rags

1 Prepare the walls for painting (page 17). Protect the area around the walls with painter's masking tape and drop cloths (page 21). Apply the base coat and let it dry completely.

2 Using the pencil, mark off 3-ft. (1 m) vertical panels around the room. Pencil in the edge lines with the level. Tape off every other panel.

3 Using the scissors, cut the squeegee into a sawtooth pattern, with pointed teeth about ¼" (6 mm) apart.

4 Put on rubber gloves. Cut in the top and bottom of the panel with the top-coat paint using the sash brush. Immediately fill in the rest of the panel, using the paint roller.

5 Draw the squeegee across the painted panel horizontally, beginning at the top and moving downward. Overlap the passes to create a grass cloth look. After each pass, wipe excess paint from the squeegee onto clean rags. Use a small paint comb for hard-to-reach areas like corners, and around switches and outlets. Remove the tape before the paint dries.

6 Repeat steps 4 and 5 for each alternating wall section. Allow each section to dry completely.

7 Mask off the painted sections, positioning the tape ⅛" (3 mm) inside the painted edges. As the paint overlaps in these thin lines, it will create the look of seams in wallpaper. Repeat steps 4 and 5 in the remaining sections. Remove the tape and let the paint dry completely.

33 | Bamboo

THIS TECHNIQUE REPLICATES the look of slender, graceful bamboo stalks. A special paint tool, called a Color Shaper, is drawn through the wet top coat to remove slim lines of paint. The realistic look is enhanced by leaving short breaks in the lines, like the divisions in real bamboo, and by creatively overlapping and angling some of the stalks.

This look works well with Asian and tropical themes. It also works well with contemporary interiors.

For an authentic appearance, use a base-coat color in a natural, woody tone that closely resembles actual bamboo. A realistic effect will be created if the top-coat color is a slightly darker shade than the base coat. An entire room of bamboo stalks would be overwhelming, so limit the effect to a focal corner or wall, or leave wide, irregularly spaced gaps of plain painted wall between clusters of stalks.

1 Prepare the walls for painting (page 17). Protect the area around the walls with painter's masking tape and drop cloths (page 21). Apply the base coat and let it dry completely.

2 Put on rubber gloves. Using the top-coat paint, roll approximately two widths of the roller onto the wall, creating a vertical strip. Beginning at the top of the wall, pull the Color Shaper downward through the wet paint in a straight, slightly angled line, removing some of the paint. Break the line every 12" to 18" (30.5 to 46 cm), leave a short space, and begin again, to mimic the divisions in a real bamboo stalk. After completing the stalk, wipe excess paint from the tool onto clean rags.

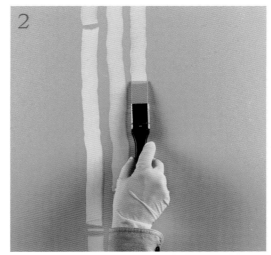

3 Repeat step 2 several times in the same strip of wet paint, pulling the tool at slightly different angles and crisscrossing some of the stalks.

4 Paint a small section of the top-coat color and leave it plain. Then repeat steps 2 and 3 alongside the plain section. Continue until all of the walls are complete.

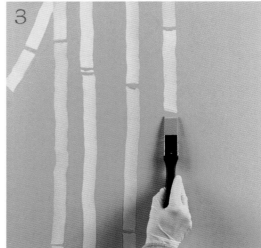

34 | Suede

THE SUEDE PAINT FINISH provides the soft, grainy visual texture of real suede and brings a cozy feeling to a room. Suede-finish latex paint contains a special additive that produces the characteristic grainy appearance. Suede-finish latex paint base is available from several paint manufacturers and can be tinted to any color. Because the additive tends to settle to the bottom, the product should be stirred often during application.

For a traditional suede appearance, select from any of the classic earthy colors that resemble real suede: shades of brown, cream, sand, and tan, or variations of red such as cinnamon, clay, or terra cotta.

The suede finish is a technique that easily adapts to many styles of décor, ranging from traditional to rustic to contemporary to Southwestern. Topped with an elegant wallpaper border, the suede finish offers high style in a formal dining area. Dark and dramatic suede colors add distinction to a home library. The appearance of suede walls lends instant texture to a compact space.

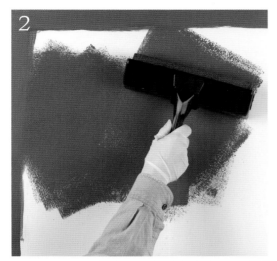

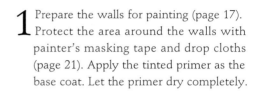
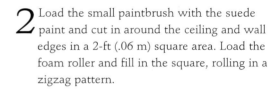

❖ Painter's masking tape

❖ Drop cloths

❖ Primer, tinted to the top-coat color

❖ Paint roller with spatter guard and tray

❖ Suede-finish latex paint

❖ Small paintbrush for cutting in

❖ Foam roller

❖ Paintbrush, 4" (10 cm) wide

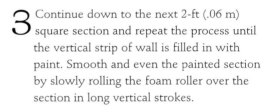

1 Prepare the walls for painting (page 17). Protect the area around the walls with painter's masking tape and drop cloths (page 21). Apply the tinted primer as the base coat. Let the primer dry completely.

2 Load the small paintbrush with the suede paint and cut in around the ceiling and wall edges in a 2-ft (.06 m) square area. Load the foam roller and fill in the square, rolling in a zigzag pattern.

3 Continue down to the next 2-ft (.06 m) square section and repeat the process until the vertical strip of wall is filled in with paint. Smooth and even the painted section by slowly rolling the foam roller over the section in long vertical strokes.

4 Repeat steps 2 and 3 until the entire wall is painted with the first coat. Allow to dry completely.

5 Using the 4" (10 cm) paintbrush, apply a second coat of suede paint, in crosshatch strokes over the entire wall. Begin in the upper corner and work from top to bottom, then left to right. This will produce the soft shading characteristic of suede.

35 | Leather

IN THIS LEATHER painting technique, plastic sheeting, in the form of garbage bags, is used to manipulate the glaze and leave an imprint in the paint that imitates the fine cracks and wrinkled texture apparent in aged leather. To obtain a true leather appearance, choose deep, rich colors. Deep slate grays and rich chocolate browns offer realistic interpretations of actual leather. The most effective results are produced with two distinctly different shades of the same color, using the lighter shade for the base coat and the darker shade for the glaze.

Walls painted with the leather technique are traditional favorites for studies or home offices. However, do not overlook the possibility of using the leather finish in an unexpected area of the home, such as a bathroom or foyer. It's also hip in a teenager's bedroom!

MATERIALS & TOOLS

- ❖ Painter's masking tape
- ❖ Drop cloths
- ❖ Paint roller and tray
- ❖ Latex paint for base coat
- ❖ Scissors
- ❖ Large plastic garbage bags
- ❖ Rubber gloves
- ❖ Paint bucket and mixing tool
- ❖ Latex paint for top coat
- ❖ Water-based glazing liquid
- ❖ Paintbrush

1 Prepare the walls for painting (page 17). Protect the area around the walls with painter's masking tape and drop cloths (page 21). Apply the base coat and let it dry completely.

2 Cut plastic garbage bags apart at the sides and bottom. You will need enough pieces to cover the entire wall. Stack the pieces where you can easily reach them as you work.

3 Put on rubber gloves. In a bucket, prepare the glaze, mixing one part paint with one part glazing liquid.

4 Beginning at an upper corner, apply glaze to the wall in an area slightly larger than one piece of plastic. Use the brush for cutting in and the paint roller for filling in the area.

5 Smooth a sheet of plastic directly into the wet glaze. Scrunch it slightly so there are a few wrinkles in the plastic.

6 Peel the plastic from the wall. The plastic will lift some of the glaze from the wall and leave a slightly wrinkled appearance. Dispose of the plastic.

7 Repeat steps 4 to 6 in adjacent areas until the entire wall is complete.

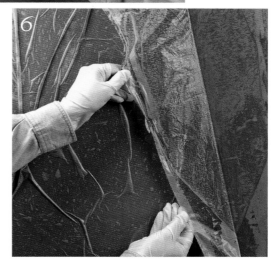

36 | Wood Graining

HANDSOME, REALISTIC wood-grain finishes can be painted with a specialty tool called a wood-graining rocker. Curved grooves in the rubber surface of the rocker create the characteristic whorls and lines as the tool is drawn through wet paint. Part of the charm of the technique is slight imperfections, which further enhance the authenticity.

Available craft stores and home improvement centers, the wood-graining tool requires a steady hand. It is important to practice on a sample board before graining the wall to get

a feel for the tool. Because you must work quickly on the wet surface, it is essential to limit the technique to small wall spaces, such as under the chair rail in a home library, home office, or dining room.

To achieve a realistic effect, use honey, tan, and other shades of brown found in golden oaks, light maples, dark cherry, and other real woods. Match the base-coat color to the underlying hue of thewood, and use a darker tone for the top coat. Unexpected bright hues or soft pastels create an offbeat, unconventional look.

MATERIALS & TOOLS

- ❖ Painter's masking tape
- ❖ Drop cloths
- ❖ Paint roller and tray
- ❖ Satin or semigloss latex paint for base coat
- ❖ Rubber gloves
- ❖ Satin or semigloss latex paint for top coat
- ❖ Wood-graining tool
- ❖ Clean rags

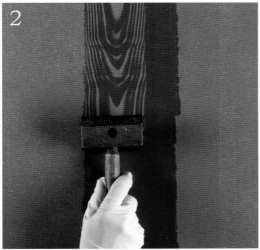

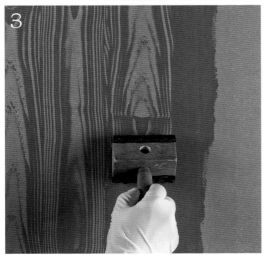

1 Prepare the walls for painting (page 17). Protect the area around the walls with painter's masking tape and drop cloths (page 21). Apply the base coat and let it dry completely.

2 Put on rubber gloves. Roll the top-coat paint onto the wall in a narrow strip (about the width of the roller) from top to bottom. Starting at the top, immediately slide the wood-graining tool downward through the paint, rocking it slowly back and forth in one continuous motion, to create oval markings. Wipe the excess paint from the tool onto clean rags after each full stroke.

3 Wood-grain the rest of the painted strip, working in continuous strokes that overlap slightly, varying the rocking rhythm to stagger the markings.

4 Repeat steps 2 and 3 in adjacent narrow strips until the entire area is complete.

37 | Granite

THE GRANITE TECHNIQUE combines a three-color sponging process with spattering to produce a multicolored, speckled surface that mimics natural granite stone.

The most effective color choices for this technique are those found in real granite. Traditional granite color combinations include black with gray flecks, dark green with gold flecks, and tan with dark brown and cinnamon flecks. It is recommended that you begin sponging with the darkest color first, as it is easier to adjust the depth of color by subsequently adding the lighter colors.

Natural granite is an increasingly popular surface in bathroom and kitchen spaces. The granite paint technique can be used to handsomely coordinate with natural granite back-splashes and countertops. The granite paint technique may be applied to a variety of styles of décor in spaces ranging from the master bathroom to the sunroom, craft room, or laundry room.

MATERIALS & TOOLS

- ❖ Painter's masking tape
- ❖ Drop cloths
- ❖ Paint roller and tray
- ❖ Satin latex paint for base coat
- ❖ Rubber gloves

- ❖ Satin water-based glazing liquid
- ❖ Latex paint in three colors (dark, medium, and light) and black for glazes
- ❖ Jars with lids for mixing glazes

- ❖ Disposable aluminum pans
- ❖ Large sea sponges
- ❖ Bucket of water
- ❖ Stiff-bristle brush, such as a toothbrush
- ❖ Spatter stick
- ❖ Semigloss varnish

1 Prepare the walls for painting (page 17). Protect the area around the walls with painter's masking tape and drop cloths (page 21). Apply the base coat and let it dry completely.

2 Put on rubber gloves. Mix the three colored glazes in separate jars, following the manufacturer's directions. Pour small amounts of each glaze into disposable pans. Dip a damp sea sponge into the darkest glaze. Sponge the glaze onto the wall lightly and evenly, working in a 3-ft. (1 m) square area. Allow much of the base coat to show through.

3 Dip the sponge into the medium glaze. Sponge the glaze onto the same area lightly and evenly, allowing some of the base coat and much of the first glaze to show through.

4 Dip the sponge into the light glaze. Sponge the glaze onto the same area lightly and evenly, allowing small peeks of the base coat and much of the first two glazes to show through. The colors will begin to blend together slightly.

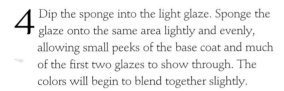
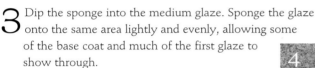

5 Stand back from the wall and decide where you would like to add darker or lighter areas of color. Sponge on more color as desired, adding the dark glaze first, then the medium glaze, and finally the light glaze. Let the glaze dry completely.

6 Repeat steps 2 to 5 in adjacent areas until the entire wall is finished.

7 Mix the black glaze. Spatter (page 54) it on sparingly using the stiff-bristle brush. Spatter any of the other color glazes, creating areas of greater and lesser density of color. Let the glaze dry completely.

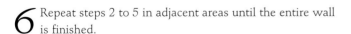
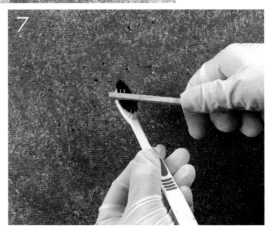

8 Apply several coats of varnish, allowing the wall to dry completely between coats.

38 | Stone Blocks

THIS APPLICATION CREATES the look of stone blocks separated by grout lines. Painted stone blocks can add interesting visual texture to a variety of interiors. Consider applying the technique to a front entry or surrounding a cozy breakfast nook. Irregular blocks produce a more authentic, rustic look for country-styled spaces. Additional detail can be achieved by hand painting cracks and fissure lines in the individual stone blocks.

Subtle colors that mimic the palette of natural stone are the best choices for this technique. Choose warm neutrals and natural stone colors such as sand, cream, and tan, as well as various shades of brown, gray, and putty.

The grout lines are created by first applying a grid of narrow masking tape to the wall and then painting over the entire surface. The lines are revealed when the tape is removed. Though the texture is mostly visual, there will be low ridges in the surface along the grout lines. Therefore, the wall will have to be sanded and primed before it can be repainted later.

- ❖ Painter's masking tape
- ❖ Drop cloths
- ❖ Paint roller and tray
- ❖ Cream flat latex paint for base coat
- ❖ Tape measure
- ❖ Pencil

- ❖ Carpenter's or laser level
- ❖ Painter's masking tape, ¼" (6 mm) wide
- ❖ Craft knife
- ❖ Rubber gloves
- ❖ Flat water-based glazing liquid

- ❖ Flat latex paint in three earth-tone colors
- ❖ Jars with lids for mixing glazes
- ❖ Foam applicator or paintbrush
- ❖ Newspaper

1 Prepare walls for painting (page 17). Protect the area around the walls with painter's masking tape and drop cloths (page 21). Apply the base coat and let it dry completely.

2 Mark a pattern of blocks with the tape measure, pencil, and carpenter's level or laser level. Apply narrow masking tape over the pencil lines, cutting ends and corners neatly with the craft knife.

3 Put on rubber gloves. Mix the three earth-tone glazes in separate jars, following the manufacturer's directions. Apply the earth-tone glazes in random strokes over a 3-ft. (1 m) square area, using the foam applicator or paintbrush. Allow some of the base coat to show through.

4 Fold a sheet of newspaper into several layers. Press it flat against the wall. Lift the paper, removing some of the glaze. Continue to press and lift the newspaper throughout the area, turning the paper in different directions to blend the colors. If the paper gets saturated, refold it so a fresh layer is exposed.

5 Add more color to an area by spreading glaze on the newspaper and pressing it against the wall. Repeat until the desired effect is achieved. Leave dark and light variations.

6 Repeat steps 3 to 5 in adjacent areas until the entire wall is finished.

7 Remove the tape, beginning at one end of the wall. The base-coat paint appears as the grout line.

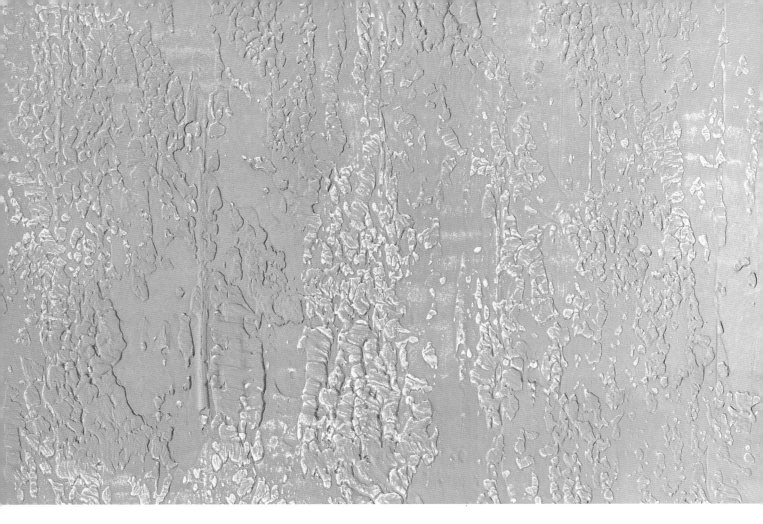

39 | Fossil Rock

THE FOSSIL ROCK finish is similar to a classic technique known as "knock down." It is a popular finish for ceilings but is increasingly used on interior walls as well. Drywall joint compound is roughly applied to the wall with a stippler. Then the rugged texture is flattened slightly by drawing a painter's spatula over the compound, leaving a surface that resembles weathered limestone.

Working with drywall compound has distinct advantages. The compound masks flaws and imperfections in the existing wall. It is a flexible medium that remains wet for approximately an hour, so you can remove or rework a section that doesn't look right. Once the compound dries, however, the only way to successfully remove it is to replace the plasterboard.

Color depth can be achieved with various decorative paint techniques, including color washing (page 26), overlaying of color (page 28), or double-roller painting (page 34).

While perfect in a home that proudly displays vintage collectibles and antiques or in a rustic-styled space, the fossil rock technique also provides the illusion of instant age for a new home that needs a few timeworn touches.

1. Prepare the walls for application of the drywall joint compound (page 17). Protect the area around the walls with painter's masking tape and drop cloths (page 21).

2. Put on rubber gloves. Dip the stippler into the bucket of joint compound and load it with a generous amount. Apply the compound to the wall surface as evenly as possible using the stippler.

3. Beginning at the top of the wall and working downward, gently drag the spatula over the compound, smoothing down the peaks of the stipples on the wall.

4. Clean the excess compound off the spatula by scraping it on the edge of the mud tray after each pass.

5. Overlap each section slightly and work in 2-ft. (0.6 m) sections downward on the wall. Continue until the wall surface is complete, and let the compound dry completely.

6. Prime the wall surface, and let the primer dry completely.

7. Apply the paint or glaze to the wall surface using one of the techniques mentioned opposite, and let it dry completely.

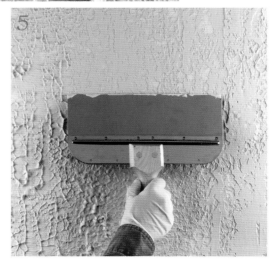

40 | Clouds

WHAT BETTER WAY to create a calming space for rest or relaxation than by applying gentle painted clouds to the wall? Although often used to portray an airplane or space theme in a nursery or child's bedroom, bathroom, or playroom, clouds can add instant whimsy to other spaces, such as a combination guest room/home office or front entrance.

You can use them near the top of a wall and extend to the ceiling. Sky blue or soft aqua for the base coat and various shades of white and pale grays for the clouds will create a natural

appearance. Vary the size and shape of the clouds, overlapping some and spacing them randomly for best effect. To add more depth to the sponged clouds, the background wall color can also be color washed (page 26) or double rolled (page 34).

For a unique twist in a cloud-inspired room, liven up the soothing space by introducing contrasting bold red accents in upholstered furnishings and fabrics. The powerful punch of red (when used in small doses) lends a zesty spirit to the area.

1 Prepare the walls for painting (page 17). Protect the area around the walls with painter's masking tape and drop cloths (page 21). Apply the base coat and let it dry completely.

2 Put on rubber gloves. Prepare the glazes, mixing equal amounts of glazing liquid and white paint in one container, and equal amounts of glazing liquid and gray paint in the other container.

3 Apply an arch of white glaze mixture to the wall, using the wide foam applicator. Apply a shorter arch of gray glaze mixture under the white one, using the narrow applicator.

4 Soak the sponge in water and squeeze tightly so the sponge is damp. Pat the sponge over the arches, softening the glaze into a cloud-like, translucent form. Blend the gray into the white to create natural-looking shadows.

5 Repeat steps 3 and 4 for each cloud, varying the sizes and shapes and scattering them randomly over the upper third of the walls. Rinse out the sponge as it becomes clogged with paint.

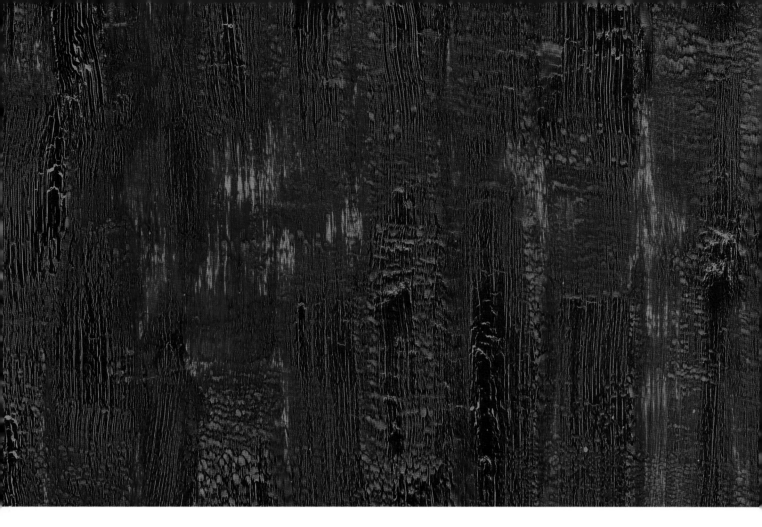

41 | Crackle

TIMEWORN, WEATHERED WALLS result from the crackle technique, which produces hairline cracks in a random pattern. Timing is very important with crackling, so be sure to read the manufacturer's directions carefully and test the technique before you begin. Crackling is most effective and easiest to accomplish on small, isolated wall areas. To remove or paint over a crackled finish, the wall has to be sanded smooth first.

Crackling can produce striking color combinations. To enhance the success of the finish, it is important to select a base-coat color that will show through the cracks and contrast with the top coat. The more dramatic the color contrast, the more dynamic the crackle effect will appear on the wall.

A wonderful complement to a Western-style ranch or rustic log home, the technique also comfortably fits into a historic home with vintage collections and antiques. Particularly suitable for a farmhouse kitchen, the technique can also be applied to coordinating furnishings.

- ❖ Painter's masking tape
- ❖ Drop cloths
- ❖ Paint roller and tray
- ❖ Paintbrush
- ❖ Satin latex paint for base coat
- ❖ Rubber gloves
- ❖ Crackle medium
- ❖ Wide paintbrush
- ❖ Latex paint for top coat
- ❖ Sealant recommended by manufacturer of crackle medium

1 Prepare the walls for painting (page 17). Protect the area around the walls with painter's masking tape and drop cloths (page 21). Apply the base coat and let it dry completely.

2 Using the crackle medium, cut in the edges of the wall with the paintbrush. Roll the crackle medium onto the remainder of the wall with the paint roller. Allow the wall to dry for the amount of time recommended by the crackle medium manufacturer (usually about 30 minutes).

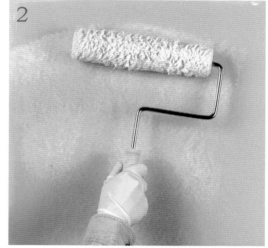

3 Apply the top coat of paint over the crackle medium, using the wide paintbrush. Work quickly, beginning at the ceiling and moving downward toward the floor. Apply the paint in segments. Be careful not to overlap the sections, which can result in removing the crackle finish from the wall surface.

4 Allow to dry completely. Seal the crackle finish with a sealant recommended by the crackle medium manufacturer.

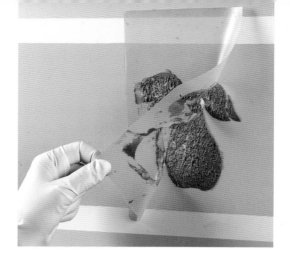

Wall
EMBELLISHMENTS

42 | Stamping

STAMPING PROVIDES an attractive accent in a wide range of decorating styles. Rubber stamps suitable for stamping walls are available in craft stores and decorating centers. Fruit and vegetable motifs can be stamped onto a prominent kitchen wall. Modern geometric designs can be stamped onto a wall that adjoins a staircase in a contemporary home. Stamping over a sponged, color-washed, or other background finish produces a subtle elegance in a formal dining room or master bedroom.

Stamping is fun and easy for even a beginning painter, and cleanup is a breeze. It is most effective on smooth wall surfaces. Designs can be applied in classic striped patterns, both horizontally and vertically. Motifs can also be stamped in polka-dot fashion on the wall. Used on the walls of an offbeat art studio or child's playroom, random stamping can be a memorable family project. An oversized, bold stamp, such as a musical note or an electric guitar, used with a vivid color produces an energetic effect when used in a music-loving teenager's bedroom.

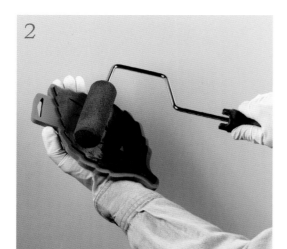

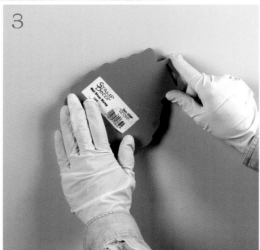

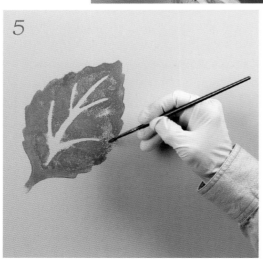

MATERIALS & TOOLS

❖ Painter's masking tape

❖ Drop cloths

❖ Paint roller and tray

❖ Latex paint for base coat

❖ Rubber gloves

❖ Paper plate

❖ Small foam roller

❖ Foam-mounted stamps in desired motifs

❖ Acrylic paint in desired colors for stamping

❖ Artist's paintbrush

1 Prepare the walls for painting (page 17). Protect the area around the walls with painter's masking tape and drop cloths (page 21). Apply the base coat and let it dry completely.

2 Put on rubber gloves. Pour some of the acrylic paint onto a paper plate. Using the small foam roller, apply an even layer of paint onto the raised surface of the stamp.

3 Press a stamp onto the wall, applying even pressure to the back of the stamp. Carefully lift the stamp from the wall.

4 Repeat steps 2 and 3 for each stamp.

5 Use the artist's paintbrush to touch up any areas that did not stamp completely as soon as you have finished stamping.

43 | Reverse Stamping

IN THE PROCESS of reverse stamping, a sponge shape is pressed into wet glaze, absorbing and lifting the glaze so the base coat shows through. A fun activity and suitable weekend project, reverse stamping may involve all members of the family.

Consider the existing color scheme in the space before selecting the colors for this technique. The most effective reverse-stamping color schemes use the darker hue for the base-coat color and a lighter color for the glaze.

Reverse stamping can easily be incorporated into any style of décor and in any area of a home. Stamps in any shape can be cut from compressed cellulose sponges, available at craft stores. Whimsical juvenile stamps can decorate the walls of a child's bedroom or bathroom. Stamps of fruits, vegetables, and other foods could enhance the walls of a walk-in kitchen pantry. The possibilities are endless.

MATERIALS & TOOLS

❖ Painter's masking tape
❖ Drop cloths
❖ Paint roller and tray
❖ Satin latex paint for base coat
❖ Compressed cellulose sponges
❖ Scissors

❖ Rubber gloves
❖ Latex paint for glaze mixture
❖ Water-based glazing liquid
❖ Paint bucket and mixing tool
❖ Bucket of water
❖ Paintbrush

1 Prepare the walls for painting (page 17). Protect the area around the walls with painter's masking tape and drop cloths (page 21). Apply the base coat and let it dry completely.

2 Draw the desired designs onto the compressed sponges and cut them out. Dip them in water to make them expand. Wring them out.

3 Put on rubber gloves. In the bucket, prepare the glaze, mixing one part latex paint with one part glazing liquid.

4 Beginning in an upper corner, apply glaze to the wall in a 4-ft. (1.2 m) square area using the paintbrush to cut in and the roller to fill in the area.

5 Press a sponge shape into the glaze and immediately lift it off. The sponge will pick up some of the glaze, leaving a slightly blurry negative image as the base coat comes through.

6 Repeat the reverse stamping with the sponge, flipping to the clean side when necessary, until it is too saturated with glaze to pick up more. Rinse the sponge in the bucket of water.

7 Repeat steps 4 to 6 until the wall is complete.

44 | Stenciling

STENCILS ADD a personal touch to a room. Decorator stencils are available in nearly every imaginable motif and can enhance many décors throughout the home.

Today's hottest stencils have popular design motifs like Mediterranean, Aztec, and English gardens. Stencils are often applied over decorative paint finishes, such as color washing. A stenciled design can define an architectural feature—highlighting a fireplace mantel—or can be repeated to make a border.

Quality supplies and proper care of stencils are key. Low-tack repositionable spray adhesive, quality stiff-bristle stencil brushes, and quick-drying and easy-to-clean acrylic paints are critical. Any mistakes made when stenciling can be quickly wiped away with a damp cloth. Then, simply allow the area to dry and restencil. Clean brushes with warm water right after use and allow them to air-dry. Store brushes in a container with their bristles up. Clean stencils right after use and dry them carefully with a towel. Store stencils flat to prevent bending.

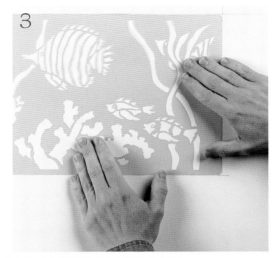

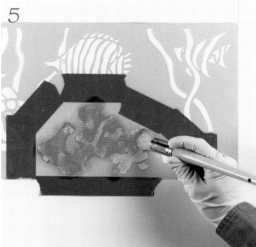

1 Prepare the walls for painting (page 17). Protect the area around the walls with painter's masking tape and drop cloths (page 21). Apply the base coat and let it dry completely.

2 If you are stenciling in a repeated motif, determine where you will begin to stencil. Use pencil marks to mark where the stencils will be placed.

3 Lightly spray adhesive on the back of the stencil and let it set for a few minutes, until it becomes tacky. Line up the center of the stencil with the center of the wall surface and press it against the wall in the desired position.

4 Mask off any design areas you don't want to stencil. Pour the first color of acrylic paint onto a paper plate. Gently dip the brush into the paint and dab off any excess.

5 Using a dabbing motion, lightly swirl the paint over the stencil's open portions. Work from one edge of the stencil toward the opposite edge. Reload the brush as necessary and complete the first stencil motif. To create shading, apply paint more heavily around the outer edges of each opening, leaving highlights in the centers.

6 Carefully remove the stencil and touch up any paint seepage. Allow the motif just painted to dry completely.

7 Reposition the stencil in the next location on the wall, using the pencil marks as a guide. Repeat steps 5 and 6 until you have achieved the desired look for your walls. Clean the stencil and reapply the adhesive as necessary.

45 | Dimensional Stenciling

DIMENSIONAL STENCILING creates a raised design through a plastic stencil and an embossing medium. The key is to apply the embossing material evenly over the stencil, building depth in thin layers. Stencils with large motifs and no fine details work best. Various embossing mediums can be used, including dimensional craft paint, as used above, and Venetian plaster (page 84). Both mediums are precolored, though dimensional craft paint can be purchased in much smaller quantities. Unpigmented mediums, such as artist's gels and modeling pastes, can also be used. Follow the manufacturer's directions for adding color.

Dimensional stenciling can be used in place of moldings near the ceiling or floor, under a chair rail, or above a backsplash. The flexibility of the stencil allows you to apply a design around a curve. Monochromatic looks with dimensional stencils that are similar in color to the base coat lend quiet elegance. Using an embossing medium that contrasts with the base coat accentuates the stenciled motif.

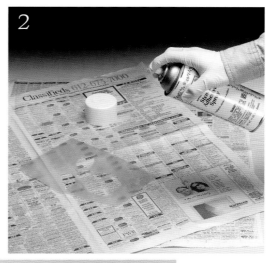

1 Prepare the walls for painting (page 17). Protect the area around the walls with painter's masking tape and drop cloths (page 21). Apply the base coat and let it dry completely. Lightly mark with a pencil where your stenciled designs will appear on the wall.

2 Holding the can of stencil spray adhesive at least 12" (30.5 cm) away, lightly mist the back of the stencil to ensure a tight seal around the edges of the design. Allow the adhesive to set up for a minute. Affix the stencil to the wall.

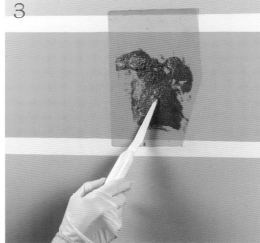

3 Apply a small amount of embossing medium to the trowel. Holding the trowel parallel to the wall surface, press a thin layer of embossing medium through the stencil using gentle pressure. Add more embossing medium to the trowel as needed, until all of the stencil openings are evenly filled.

4 If you want a low-relief design, stop after this layer is applied. If you want a heavy-relief design, add another layer of embossing medium, covering the entire stencil evenly.

5 Remove the stencil slowly, beginning at one corner and pulling it straight away from the wall.

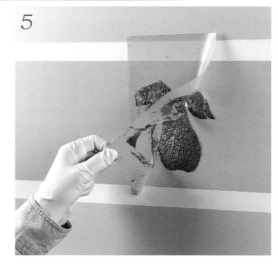

46 | Caulking

CAULK DESIGNS ARE limited only by the imagination! Designs consisting of lines and dots are drawn on the wall using tub and tile caulk. When the caulk designs are dry, the wall can be painted in any color desired. The shadows of the raised dots and lines produce subtle patterns.

Caulking can create cheerful flowers, graceful vines, trendy geometric patterns, and other exciting freehand motifs. Dots, swirls, and other simple figures are good for a beginner. This easy technique can add fanciful style to a child's bedroom or bathroom, a laundry room, game room, mudroom, or craft room.

The caulk adheres to the wall better if it is slightly cool when applied. The size of the dots and lines depends on the size of the opening cut in the tip of the caulk tube. For tiny dots and thin lines, cut the tip close to the end. For more substantial dots and lines, cut the tip off deeper. To remove the designs at a later date, scrape them off with a paint scraper, and patch and prime the walls again.

MATERIALS & TOOLS

- ❖ Painter's masking tape
- ❖ Drop cloths
- ❖ Paint roller and tray
- ❖ Latex primer
- ❖ Pencil
- ❖ Tub and tile caulk
- ❖ Scissors
- ❖ Satin latex paint for top coat
- ❖ Paintbrush

3

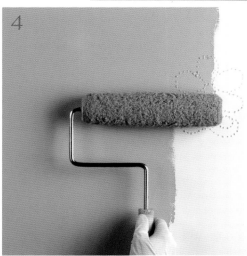

4

1 Prepare the walls for painting (page 17). Protect the area around the walls with painter's masking tape and drop cloths (page 21). Apply primer to the walls and let it dry completely.

2 Lightly pencil in the design of your choice onto the wall surface. Cut the tip off the caulk tube.

3 Apply dots and lines of caulk over the marked lines, squeezing the tube with even pressure. Stop squeezing and lift the tip from the surface at the end of each line. Using a wet fingertip, smooth down any bumps and tails after 30 minutes. Allow 24 hours for the caulk to dry completely.

4 Apply the top coat to the entire wall.

47 | Decoupage

A CENTURIES-OLD art, decoupage is cutting papers and sealing them to a surface. When applied over a beautifully painted base coat, decoupage can transform a wall.

Extremely effective when used in a compact area, decoupage can create a highpoint without overwhelming a space. In a large room, decoupage is a focal point. Black and white prints are traditional favorites for this technique and can be striking when placed over bold back-ground colors. For the background, consider decorative paint finishes such as color washing (page 26), overlaying color (page 28), or double rolling (page 34).

Decoupage must be applied to a smooth wall, as any texture or imperfections will show. Decoupage designs must be printed on lightweight paper so they lie as flat as possible on the wall. It is important that the images be cut out carefully and that all edges are sealed to the wall.

1 Prepare the walls for painting (page 17). Protect the area around the walls with painter's masking tape and drop cloths (page 21). Apply the base coat and let it dry completely.

2 Make photocopies of designs, enlarging them to the desired size. Cut out the designs using the scissors or the mat knife.

3 Put on rubber gloves. Dilute wallpaper adhesive with an equal amount of water. Apply an even coat of diluted adhesive to the back of a cutout using the foam applicator.

4 Affix the cutout to the wall, smoothing it from the center outward using a dry, stiff paintbrush. Allow to dry.

5 Repeat steps 3 and 4 with all the cutouts. If desired, mix the color-washing glaze and color wash the wall, as on page 26.

48 | Collage

COLLAGE TRANSFORMS a painted wall with thin, flat materials and sheer, light-colored paper. Water-based sealer coats the application and makes the paper more sheer, revealing the items layered underneath the paper. The result is a translucent, overlapping form and texture.

A great technique for hiding imperfections in walls, the collage process is usually limited to one focal area. The technique can change a bland wall into a personalized work of art!

The base-coat color should be carefully chosen. A muted version will show through after the layers of materials and water-based sealer have been applied. This application is permanent and cannot be successfully removed without damaging the wall. To repaint at a later date, you will need to replace the plasterboard.

MATERIALS & TOOLS

- ❖ Painter's masking tape
- ❖ Drop cloths
- ❖ Paint roller and tray
- ❖ Flat latex paint for base coat
- ❖ Rubber gloves
- ❖ Paintbrush
- ❖ Satin water-based sealer

- ❖ Skeletonized craft leaves, pressed flowers, torn pieces of tissue paper, or other thin, flat materials
- ❖ Sheer white or cream paper, such as Japanese mulberry paper, torn or cut into irregular, hand-size pieces
- ❖ Foam roller, 4" (10 cm) wide

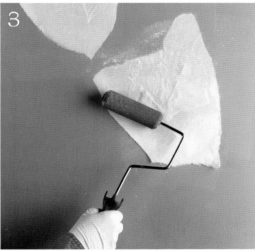

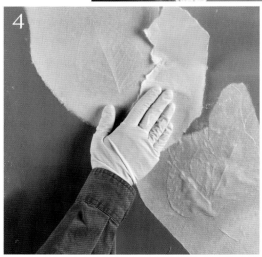

1 Prepare the walls for painting (page 17). Protect the area around the walls with painter's masking tape and drop cloths (page 21). Apply the base coat and allow it to dry completely.

2 Put on rubber gloves. Apply sealer to the wall in a 2-ft. (0.6 m) area using the foam roller. Smooth leaves or other flat materials into place over the wet sealer.

3 Smooth a piece of sheer paper over each collage item. Immediately apply more sealer over the paper using the foam roller.

4 Apply more pieces of paper in areas not already covered, overlapping the pieces and placing them at various angles, until the entire wall is covered. Allow to dry completely. The papers will nearly disappear, allowing the collage materials to show through.

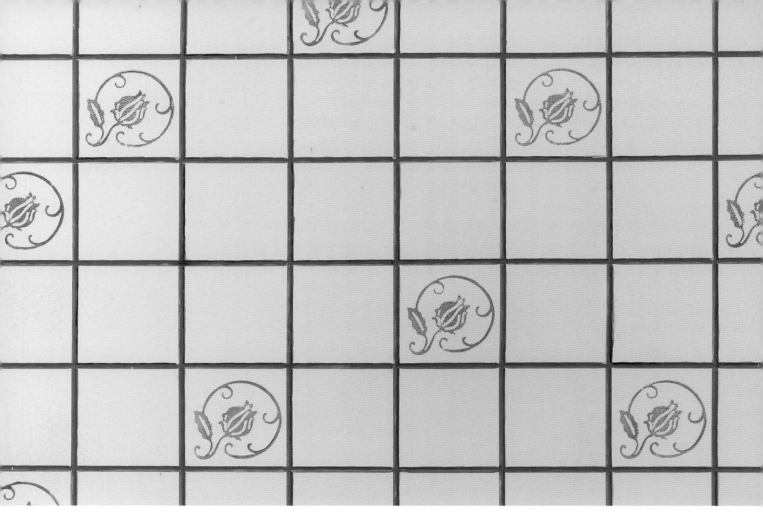

49 | Painted Tiles

FOR THE LOOK OF TILE without a large investment of time or money, this hand-painted tiles project is great for the absolute beginner. A square grid of narrow masking tape is secured over the base coat before painting the wall the color of the tiles. The grid becomes the grout between tiles when the tape is removed.

Painted tiles enhance the interior of a kitchen prep space or bathroom and can look festive in a laundry area. Design motifs can be hand painted or stamped onto the tiles to customize them.

Color selection is critical to creating a realistic appearance. Select a base-coat shade in the gray family, as it will become the grout lines between tiles. Various shades of white work well for the top-coat color, providing necessary contrast to the gray grout lines. White shades also help to provide the design contrast needed for the painted tiles to stand out on the wall surface. Bright hues, deep colors, and jewel tones are effective choices for the hand-painted, stamped, or stenciled designs in the centers of individual painted tiles.

MATERIALS & TOOLS

- ❖ Painter's masking tape
- ❖ Drop cloths
- ❖ Paint roller and tray
- ❖ Gray latex paint for base coat
- ❖ Carpenter's or laser level
- ❖ Pencil
- ❖ Masking tape, ¼" (6 mm) wide
- ❖ White latex paint for top coat

- ❖ Acrylic paints in black, white, and desired colors for designs
- ❖ Artist's flat paintbrush, ¼" (6 mm) wide
- ❖ Floating medium
- ❖ Artist's paintbrushes as needed for freehand designs, optional
- ❖ Stencils or stamps for designs, optional
- ❖ Clear sealer

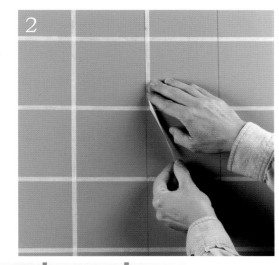

1 Prepare the walls for painting (page 17). Protect the area around the walls with painter's masking tape and drop cloths (page 21). Apply the gray base coat and let it dry completely.

2 Mark a pattern of 4" (10 cm) blocks using the carpenter's level or laser level, and pencil. Apply narrow masking tape over the pencil lines. Make sure the tape seals to the wall well.

3 Apply the white latex paint to the wall. Allow it to dry slightly. Carefully pull the tape off the wall, revealing the grout lines. Let the paint dry completely.

4 Dip the tip of an artist's flat paintbrush into the floating medium, then into the black paint, and again into the floating medium. Delicately underline the bottom and left side of each square.

5 Hand-paint, stamp (page 114), or stencil (page 118) a design of choice inside each square with the acrylic paints.

6 Apply four coats of clear sealer over the entire painted tile wall surface, allowing the wall to dry completely between coats.

Life is a journey. Travel it well. ~Charishma

50 | Words

LETTERS AND WORDS painted on a wall are the most personalized paint technique of all.

Thoughts, quotes, or words that have special meaning can be chosen. A baby's first words can be applied to the walls of a nursery. Quotes from a favorite children's book can be painted over a child's bed. Lettering styles are available in a wide range of options, from contemporary to old world.

The room's existing color scheme should be carefully considered when selecting the colors for the lettering. Monochromatic colors produce a more sophisticated look and can be a stylish accent in rooms with a formal ambience. High contrast between the base-coat color and the colors in the letters produces a bold look that works well for a child's play space or laundry room.

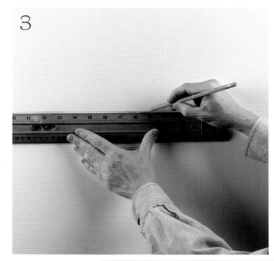

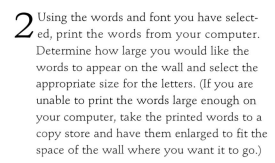

MATERIALS & TOOLS

- ❖ Painter's masking tape
- ❖ Drop cloths
- ❖ Paint roller and tray
- ❖ Latex paint for base coat
- ❖ Computer printout of available letter fonts
- ❖ Carpenter's or laser level
- ❖ Pencil
- ❖ Graphite transfer paper
- ❖ Acrylic paints in desired colors
- ❖ Artist's paintbrushes
- ❖ Aerosol flat clear acrylic sealer

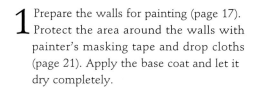

1 Prepare the walls for painting (page 17). Protect the area around the walls with painter's masking tape and drop cloths (page 21). Apply the base coat and let it dry completely.

2 Using the words and font you have selected, print the words from your computer. Determine how large you would like the words to appear on the wall and select the appropriate size for the letters. (If you are unable to print the words large enough on your computer, take the printed words to a copy store and have them enlarged to fit the space of the wall where you want it to go.)

3 Using the pencil and the carpenter's level or laser level, draw a guide line where the words will appear on the wall.

4 Tape a piece of graphite transfer paper to the wall. Place the photocopied words over the transfer paper, aligning them to the marked pencil line. Using the pencil, trace the letters and words.

5 Outline the letters with acrylic paint in the desired color using a narrow, flat artist's paintbrush. Then fill in the letters using a slightly wider flat brush. Complete one letter at a time.

6 If the words are in an area that may be touched frequently, spray on several coats of flat clear acrylic sealer, allowing the area to dry between coats.

Ceilings & Floors

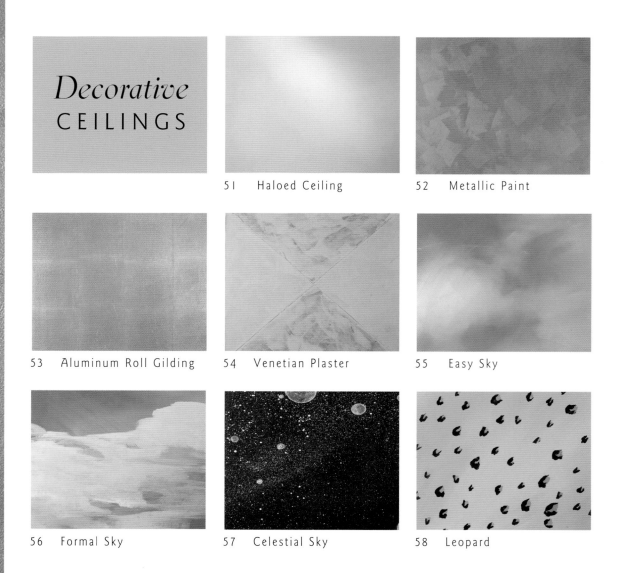

Decorative CEILINGS

51   Haloed Ceiling

52   Metallic Paint

53   Aluminum Roll Gilding

54   Venetian Plaster

55   Easy Sky

56   Formal Sky

57   Celestial Sky

58   Leopard

DECORATIVE PAINTING TECHNIQUES

59   Stamped Stars

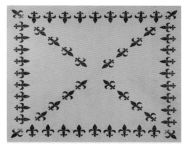

60   Stamped Motifs

61   Faux Drapery

62   Large Graphic

63   Applied Leaf Motifs

64   Elaborate Stencil

65   Decorative Molding

66   Faux Tin Ceiling

67   Antiqued Embossed Material

68   Ceiling Medallion

69   Cambric Cloth

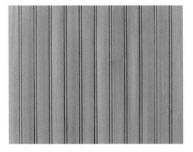

70   Weathered Beadboard

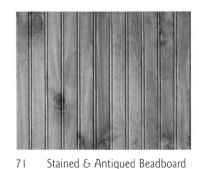

71   Stained & Antiqued Beadboard

72   Stained Knotty Pine

(continued)

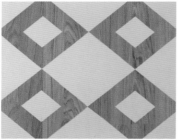

Decorative
FLOORS

73   Floor Cloth

74   Jute Monogram

75   Diamonds on the Floor

76   Bubbles

77   Distressed Painted Hardwood Floor

78   Center Star Medallion

79   Colored Japan Inlay

80   Distressed Fir Floor

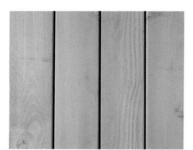

81   Decking Multi Paints

82   Decking Semitransparent Stains

83   Faux Bois Repair

84   Antiqued Brick Pavers

85   Freshened Sheet Vinyl
      B&W Squares

86   Awning Stripes

87 Arcs & Circles

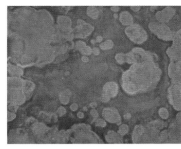

88 Faux Cement Stain

89 French Ironwork Stencil

90 Cement to Stone

91 Bluestone with Brick

92 Venetian Pavers

Molding, Doors & GLASS

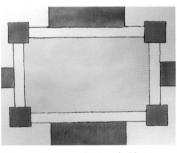

93 Faux Bois Door

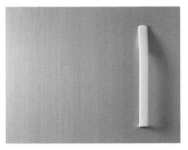

94 Faux Stainless Steel

95 Frosted Mirror

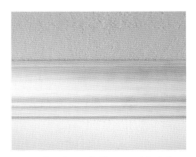

96 Imitation Stained Glass

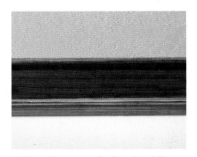

97 Antiqued Crown Molding

98 Aged Molding

99 Metallic Tiles

100 Reverse Color Molding

Ceiling & Floor Painting Basics

CEILINGS AND FLOORS are the largest surface areas found in a room and the least paid attention to!

It is time to pay attention to these areas. *Decorative Painting Techniques for Walls, Floors, Ceilings & Furniture* demonstrates many different techniques that will allow some justice to be brought to the oftentimes overlooked yet wonderful blank canvases that a ceiling and a floor can be.

The "More" demonstrations are intended to round off the repertoire of painted techniques of some other commonly overlooked surfaces that are indeed integral to the overall look and feel of a room.

Doors, windows, woodwork, and yes, even the refrigerator, can all become part of the design scheme.

Do not be shy about painting your ceiling or floor with any one of these techniques; keep in mind it is only paint. When a ceiling is painted with one of the simple techniques found in this book or merely painted in a wonderful and maybe even an unexpected color, the ceiling becomes a wonderful "lid," the finishing touch that caps off your entire room, a room that you have worked very hard on making beautiful.

Painting a floor likewise supports the overall design elements of the room and it is truly wonderful to discover that a floor has been asked to take part in the room's design. Imagine bubbles peeking out from underneath a plain or fanciful rug.

Painting floors can be a wonderfully inexpensive way to nudge that floor into a few more years of service and allows for your unique creative expression to take place.

Whenever you set forth to apply a painted finish, do so with confidence, wonder, and enjoyment and your work will look beautiful.

The demonstrations you find here are meant to employ and rely upon the philosophy of "The Economy of The Artist," which simply means: use the most efficient number of steps to arrive at your intended result. This concept is one that should be applied when painting the large surfaces of ceilings and floors; after all, painting these areas does take a bit of physical exertion due to their size and you really do not need to spend any more time than necessary to accomplish your creation.

Did you know that keeping your arms extended above your head for 20 minutes is equal to 1 hour of cardiovascular aerobic exercise? It is according to some, so you will also be getting the benefits of a great workout!

Enjoy the journey into the lesser-known areas of painting ceilings, floors, and more!

TIP

Every time an artist, a craftsperson, or a do-it-yourselfer starts a project, the aim is the same: SUCCESS. There is a secret to achieving that—always start at Step Zero.

Starting at Step Zero means reading all pertinent introductory sections and then reading through the project instructions before starting to paint. We suggest you buy high-quality equipment for the best project outcome. Being fully prepared by equipping yourself with knowledge and proper tools and materials helps you create the great finish you want.

All About Paint

A good basecoat of paint is extremely important for any of the techniques demonstrated in this book. Never use "ceiling white" or "ceiling" paint because the paint is just too absorbent and this will cause you trouble when attempting any of the outlined techniques. Instead use a high-quality latex or acrylic paint, just as you would for your walls.

A quick way to check to see if your ceiling paint is too absorbent is to take a wet rag and wipe it on your ceiling; if the water soaks in within 30 seconds, you should apply a proper coat of paint.

When it comes to painting floors, there are as many opinions as there are painters. The best advice to follow is that of a trusted clerk at your local paint store. New products are coming on the market as we speak and the clerk will be up to date on these new products.

Please be aware that companies are coming up with wonderful water-based products every day and most of the demonstrations shown in this book will use water-based products, except in a few cases. However, all of the demonstrations in this book can be done with a water-based product if you just take your time.

When preparing most floor surfaces first clean dirt, grease, and wax from the surface. Then, depending on what you are painting on the floor, you may be directed to apply a primer. Keep in mind that today some of the best primers are water-based.

A good primer should seal the surface below it and create a firm bonding film for subsequent layers of paint to follow; this is why you do not want to omit a primer coat if one is called for.

Floor paints today have made vast improvements in terms of color and durability. Some of the best products to use are the water-based variety, which are also better for you and the environment.

The question always comes up if a water-based polyurethane can be applied over oil-based stains. The answer is, yes, as long as the oil-based stain has had time to completely dry, which could take up to 30-plus days depending on temperature and humidity.

For topcoats, choose either a water-based polyurethane or an oil-based polyurethane. Always use the right tools for the right job. The photos show the appropriate applicators for water-based and oil-based polyurethanes.

Applicator Oil

Applicator Water

Specialty paints for masonry and decking are also available and, yes, these come in water-based formulas and are quite good. You will be surprised at the availability of the right paint for your job.

Okay, you have decided to paint your ceiling, but it has "popcorn" texture all over it. What to do? Remove it. If you are lucky, the texture has not been painted, in which case you can do one of two things:

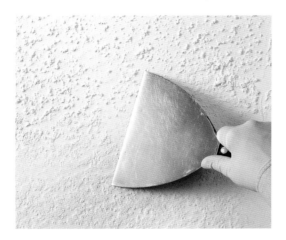

Scrape it down with a stiff 6" (15.2 cm) drywall blade. This will not remove everything, but will "knock down" the pebbly bumps to an acceptable finish. The semi-roughness can even be a positive aesthetic element on your ceiling. Always wear protective eyewear. Before any painting takes place you will need to prime the texture material; do so with latex-based primer. If the texture is of

a certain make-up, you may get very lucky and be able to simply take a wet wallpaper sponge and smooth the texture down to an almost perfect finish.

Popcorn Texture and Asbestos Safety

If your ceiling was applied prior to 1979, there is a very good likelihood that the material contains asbestos. You can buy a test kit at your local paint store to check for asbestos. Discuss the test kit and procedure with your paint store clerk. DO NOT scrape any ceiling texture until you carefully read and understand all of the directions. If your texture does contain asbestos, it is best to hire a company that specializes in the removal of asbestos.

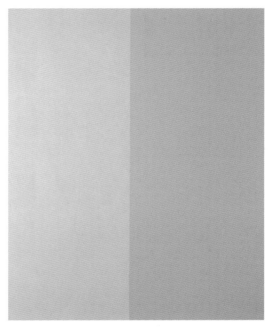

Always have the color of your primer tinted the same or very close to the color of your finish paint. This will make your job much easier and if you are a good painter, you will only need to apply one primer coat and one finish coat.

Painting Techniques

Universal Tinting Colorant (UTC)

UTC is not paint, but an additive used to tint all types of paint. In fact, it's used in the machine at the paint store to color paint. UTC comes in small tubes or pint sizes; buy the smallest tube, as it is a very powerful color agent. In addition to tinting paint, it also tints varnishes. UTCs never dry on their own, so wipe up spills quickly or the UTC will spread over everything. UTCs are transparent until added to paint.

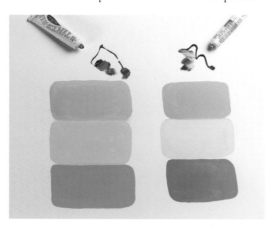

Blending

After applying a coat of oil-based or water-based paint, but before it sets up, use an off-loaded brush to gently brush in a cross-hatch pattern over the top of the paint. This softly blends paint and knocks down paintbrush ridges.

French Brush

This technique spreads the paint over the surface quickly with total coverage. Apply the paint in a crisscross fashion, arcing in and around and ending with an upstroke off the surface. Use either a straight or angled-edge paintbrush.

Pouncing

Apply glaze or paint using the French brush technique and while it's wet, tap perpendicularly on the surface with a 2" (5.1 cm) oval sash paintbrush using moderate pressure. This technique gives you a very tight "dotted" surface. The end result should look even, but a slight variation here and there is okay. This is a good way to blend two colors together.

Folding

To fold a glaze means to soften the texture and to reduce contrast and pattern, usually by lightly patting the surface with a pad of 90-weight cheesecloth.

Using Cheesecloth

The example shown below is the appropriate shape of a 90-weight cheesecloth pad. The side that touches the paint surface is fairly smooth, without wrinkles or little tails

Wet Edge

To keep a wet edge means that the outside section of the applied paint is not allowed to dry. Thus, when applying more paint, you may work wet paint into wet paint, which will create a smoother paint surface.

Caulking

It is always a more beautiful paint job if you take a minute to caulk along moldings and trim after priming and before applying the finish coat of paint. Run a bead of paintable caulk, dip your finger in some water, and smooth the caulk out with your wet finger.

Traditionally, natural woodwork is not caulked; only caulk a painted surface to a painted surface.

Pulling Tape

Always pull the tape away from the freshly painted surface at a 45° angle. If the fresh paint is wet, this will ensure that you do not pull the tape across the fresh paint; if the fresh paint is dry, this will put less "stress" on the paint.

Decorative
CEILINGS

51 | Haloed Ceiling

DON'T WANT TO PAINT your whole ceiling, but do want to give it a nudge toward interesting? Partially paint it.

Applying a soft painted finish to just the perimeter area of a ceiling is referred to as "haloing" the ceiling. This technique will give a softly faded color gradation around the edge of your room and subtly shade the outer edges and corners of the ceiling.

It's a great way to introduce just a blush of color in an otherwise continuous flat, solidly painted ceiling area.

Perfect for traditional homes or contemporary settings.

If for some reason your ceiling is painted in oil-based paint, merely switch the following directions to use oil-based products.

If your ceiling is painted in sheen paint, use the same sheen paint for the haloing paint.

1 Using the French brush technique of paint application, apply the halo paint color to the ceiling starting at the outside edge of the ceiling, where the wall meets the ceiling. Start just slightly left or right of a corner.

2 Immediately apply the existing ceiling paint color with a clean brush. Work the paint that is the ceiling color into the color of the halo paint using the French brush technique.

3 Blend the two colors together using the brush of the haloed color. Fade the haloed color out into the existing ceiling paint color.

Blend and soften the two colors while all paint is wet. Continue around the room until you are done.

Note: If you work fast enough you will not have to use any water to loosen the paints up. However, if you find that the paints are drying way too quickly, first try to loosen the paints up by adding a third amount of water. If this does not help and the paints are merely being sucked into the surface, you probably are trying to paint over "ceiling paint." You will have to stop and repaint the ceiling in a high-quality latex or acrylic paint before continuing.

52 | Metallic Paint

METALLIC PAINT can add drama and a touch of reflectivity to a ceiling. The nature of any metallic coating is to reflect light slightly; this is good news and this is bad news. What usually happens is that roller or brush marks are revealed in an undesirable way. This demonstration relies on the French brush method of application to create interest and beauty on a metallic surface by allowing you more control of the paint's movement during application.

Because you will be hand-brushing a ceiling area, another way to make your job easier is to first basecoat the ceiling in a flat latex paint that is very close in color to the metallic you have selected. The basecoat is applied in the conventional manner of cutting in the corners with a brush and rolling out the rest. This will save you from having to apply multiple coats of the metallic paint to achieve an opaque metallic finish coat.

Coverage of the basecoat should be adequate but does not need to be perfect.

You may use a flat-edge paintbrush scaled to the size of your working area.

1 Notice how close the basecoat color is to the copper metallic.

Start to apply the copper metallic paint using the French brush technique.

2 Continue across your surface. It is always best to apply the metallic paint rather heavily and simply brush out without going over too much of what you have already painted on. Keep a wet edge.

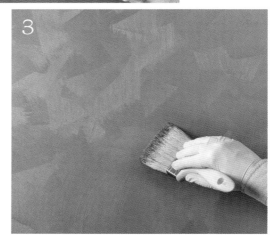

3 Mix a few drops of equal amounts of Burnt Umber and Raw Umber UTC into satin oil varnish.

Apply in the same French brush manner a coat of tinted satin sheen oil varnish.

This varnish coat will help tone down the copper paint and will help even out some of the uneven sheen from your first application.

Remember, if you like your work without the tinted varnish applied, it is perfectly acceptable to not apply the tinted varnish.

Water-based varnishes will tend to crawl when applied over a metallic paint. That is why oil varnish is used.

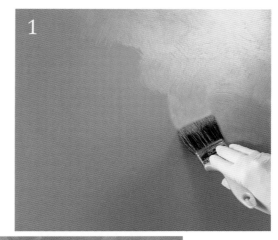

53 | Aluminum Roll Gilding

IF YOU do not want to apply many single sheets of aluminum leaf over your head to a ceiling in the traditional manner, there is an easier way: aluminum leaf comes on a roll! It is made just for this type of large, continuous surface application.

An aluminum-leafed ceiling is a spectacular finish.

It's wonderful for intimate rooms or even a large dining room where the lights from the chandelier can dance across this marvelous finish.

As with any gilding process, the final look is only as good as your prep, so make sure that your ceiling surface is smooth and free of any blemishes and cracks. The leaf will hide nothing.

Basecoat the ceiling to be leafed in a pale warm gray, eggshell-sheen latex paint applied with a foam roller to keep roller stipple to a minimum. The eggshell sheen will ensure proper sealing of the surface.

- ❖ Water-based gold-leaf size
- ❖ Flat latex paintbrush, 4" (10.2 cm)
- ❖ Roller handles, 7" (17.8 cm)
- ❖ Aluminum leaf on a roll
- ❖ Spreading knife, 6" (15.25 cm)
- ❖ Wallpaper blade
- ❖ Lamb's wool pad
- ❖ Denatured alcohol
- ❖ Lint-free rag
- ❖ Satin acrylic varnish

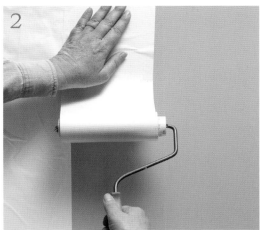

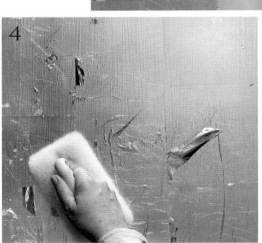

1 With a latex brush apply the size to an area of ceiling that you can comfortably gild in one day. Do not leave any skips.

Follow the instructions on the size bottle to know how long to wait before applying the leaf.

2 Start along the edge where the ceiling meets the wall to keep the roll of leaf straight.

With a 6" (15.25 cm) spreading knife, tuck the narrow side of the roll into the edge. Allow ½" (1.3 cm) excess to fall onto wall.

With mild tension, pull the roll of leaf at a 45° angle to the opposite side of the ceiling using your free hand to lightly press leaf to ceiling as you go.

When you are at the opposite wall, cut the leaf with a sharp wallpaper knife into the corner.

Overlap the previous row by ¼" (6 mm) and repeat until ceiling is covered.

3 With a lamb's wool pad, softly brush over the paper and the leaf. This will adhere the leaf, and the paper will fall off at this time.

4 Continue softly cleaning until all excess leaf is removed.

5 With a rag dampened with denatured alcohol, gently wipe the entire gilded surface down. This removes the wax on the surface of the leaf and allows your topcoat to be applied. Topcoat cannot be applied over the wax film.

6 With a good latex brush, apply a coat of satin acrylic varnish.

54 | Venetian Plaster

THE BEAUTY OF Venetian Plaster is the rich, smooth, polished surface that results from the application and the burnishing. Multiple thin layers of the material applied with a special blade achieve the finish.

There are many good Venetian Plaster products on the market, just ask at your favorite paint store. The paint store should also sell the special blades with which to apply the material.

The demonstration shown here is the simple, basic technique with the added twist of using a second color to create a geometric pattern.

Picture this gleaming finish on a powder room ceiling.

❖ Venetian Plaster, colors of your choice

❖ Venetian Plaster spatulas (spreading blades)

❖ Chalk line

❖ Metal straightedge

❖ Wet/dry sandpaper, 800-grit (optional)

It is a good idea to generally apply a color close to the color of your plaster for your basecoat color.

The ceiling surface should be smooth and without any imperfections as this plaster product will not cover imperfections due to the thinness of the application.

Follow the instructions found on the product that you buy, but know that basically you will be applying multiple thin coats of plaster and burnishing with a blade to create the polished look.

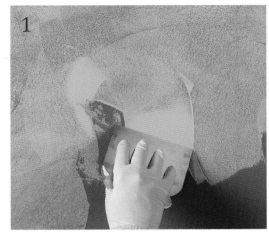

1 Apply the first coat of Venetian Plaster to the entire surface.

Using the special spreading blade, apply the material thinly and in short arched strokes that crisscross one another. Do not leave ridges; do not have all the blade strokes going the same direction.

Work quickly and do not go back over what you have already laid down.

2 Allow the first application to dry. Lightly run the blade over the surface to remove any burrs and apply a second application just as you did in step 1.

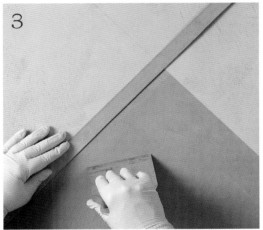

3 Allow the second coat to dry. With a chalk line make 2 diagonals from each corner of the ceiling.

You cannot tape Venetian Plaster, so hold a metal straightedge as your guide flat to the ceiling. Apply the darker material in the same manner you did the previous two applications.

You will have to keep moving the straightedge to create the line.

4 After the darker material has dried, apply a final coat of the light-colored Venetian Plaster to the entire surface.

The darker color will become softly buried under the lighter plaster.

5 Allow to fully dry. Polish the plaster with the blade held flat against the surface or sand with 800-grit wet/dry sandpaper to produce a beautiful polished stone look.

Tip: Practice your application on a sample board first. The plaster should go on thinly and smoothly in many layers to achieve the beauty of this product.

55 | Easy Sky

NOTHING SAYS "sky" like blue and white. If you are unsure of your cloud-making abilities, relax; you can achieve a believable sky-like painted ceiling in very quick fashion by simply using the French brush technique, outlined on page 140, by painting blue and white together.

Really, it is this easy. Remember that there are many types of natural skies and cloud formations so yours will indeed look like one found somewhere in nature.

When applying the colors always bring the white off the ceiling by having it appear to continue beyond the surface you are painting. This will give a more believable look of motion and expanse.

Due to the nature of the French brush technique you can generally paint over any well-painted ceiling as long as the color is not too far from white or blue. If you want to basecoat first, a coat of the light blue paint you will use can be applied. One coat should be sufficient, as you will be painting the surface again.

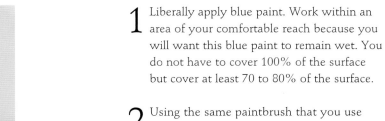

MATERIALS & TOOLS

- ❖ Flat latex paint, blue
- ❖ Flat latex paint, white
- ❖ Flat latex paintbrush, 3" (7.6 cm)

1 Liberally apply blue paint. Work within an area of your comfortable reach because you will want this blue paint to remain wet. You do not have to cover 100% of the surface but cover at least 70 to 80% of the surface.

2 Using the same paintbrush that you use to apply the blue paint, liberally apply the white paint, starting in the voids of the blue paint and brush into the wet blue paint. You may apply more blue too. Keep all paint wet.

3 While the blue and white colors are still wet, blend and soften the two paint colors together with the same paintbrush you have used to apply the blue and white.

Continue over the entire surface until complete. When you are done you will have a predominantly blue ceiling with softly folded-in areas of white that will suggest clouds.

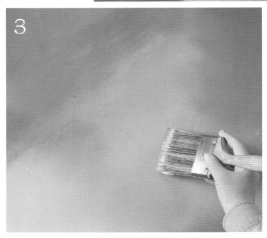

56 | Formal Sky

REALLY, it can be this easy! Just like the natural sky above us, there are all different kinds of clouds and skies. A windy day, a big billowy summer afternoon, even a dark and foreboding stormy sky.

This demonstration is for a windy day. If you can do the Easy Sky on page 152, then you can do this technique because it is simply taking the Easy Sky a couple of steps further.

The only specific advice to remember is to take your clouds off the edges of the ceiling so they will look like they are passing through.

You may wish to clump a large cloud bank just slightly off-center or create a circular cloud pattern around your room.

You may want to add a few clouds cutting across the room at a slight angle in just one corner. The choice is yours.

Relax and picture yourself outside, or if it is a cloudy day, look outside for your inspiration!

❖ Medium value flat latex paint, blue

❖ Flat latex paint, white

❖ Flat latex paintbrush, 4" (10.2 cm)

❖ Pail of water

1 French brush the blue and white together quickly.

2 Using the same paintbrush that you used to apply the blue and white paint, keep brushing the wet blue and white paint together to soften down any harsh brushstrokes, creating a softly mottled blue and white appearance.

3 When your blue and white paint has dried, look at the ceiling and see if you can start to see clouds. Focus on the light areas.

With the paintbrush, pounce in cloud formations.

Work within an area of your reach.

4 You may loosen the paint up a bit by dipping the brush into water.

Go back into your cloud formations and soften the brushwork down.

Remember, clouds generally have a bottom, so apply some of the blue paint to the bottom side and watch a cloud take shape.

Create voluminous clouds or soft wispy ones; anything goes. Give your cloud very white highlights to suggest the sun.

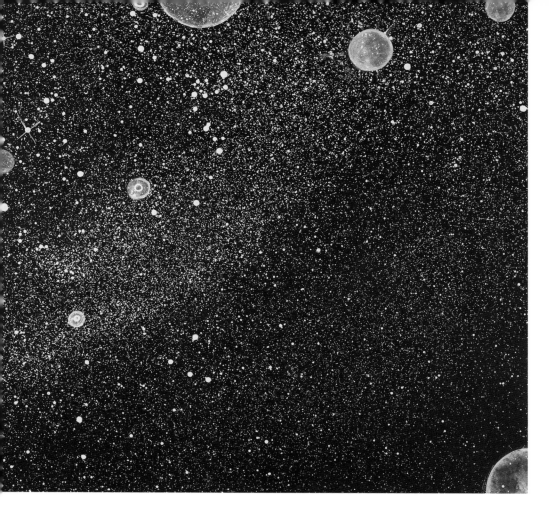

57 | Celestial Sky

THE MYSTERY of a night sky painted right onto your ceiling can be a wonderful technique for children's rooms, libraries, powder rooms, or entry hall—just about anywhere you would want to see the stars.

For inspiration, look up "planetary and night sky images" on the Internet and you will soon discover that the sky is indeed the limit.

This can be a messy finish to apply so be sure to mask your room off with plastic and wear safety glasses and old paint clothes. Have fun creating the stars above and, oh, don't forget to wear a baseball cap!

- Roller, 9" (23 cm)
- Flat latex paint, deep midnight blue
- Straight latex paintbrush, 4" (10.2 cm)
- Spray bottle with adjustable nozzle

- Flat latex paint, white
- Paint pail
- Flat latex paintbrush, 1" (2.5 cm)
- Flat latex paintbrush, ¼" (6 mm)
- Soft lint-free rag

You will have to do 2 coats of the midnight blue in preparation for the stars. The first coat may be rolled on, but the second coat you will brush on.

1 After you have rolled out the first coat of blue paint and that coat has dried, apply the second coat with a brush.

Using a 4" (10.2 cm) flat latex brush, apply the second coat of blue paint using the French brush technique (page 140). The blue basecoat will be almost opaque, but not quite.

2 Mix a mixture of 60% flat white latex paint and 40% water in a paint pail and pour into a spray bottle.

Begin to apply the star matter. Set your spray bottle on the mist or spray setting, stand directly under the ceiling and softly squeeze the trigger until you get the feel of how the paint comes out.

You want a soft misting of star matter over entire surface.

3 Move a little closer to the surface, set your spray bottle to the stream setting, and gently squeeze the trigger to get a larger dot of paint.

You do not want a full stream of paint to come out; rather by squeezing gently you will get just a few larger dots of paint.

Coverage should be about 20 to 30% of entire surface area.

4 Use a ¼" (6 mm) paintbrush dipped into white paint and paint in a small planet.

Immediately press a lint-free rag into the center of the white paint to remove some of the paint, which will create the translucent quality.

Repeat with a 1" (2.5 cm) flat latex brush for larger planets.

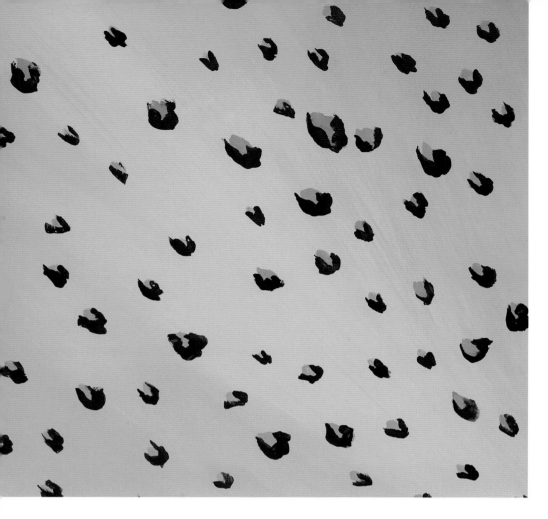

58 | Leopard

YOU CAN PAINT LEOPARD, oh yes you can … and what fun you can have with it!

It is easy! It's basically blobs of paint going in a certain direction. We will call this direction: the growth direction, how the fur grows.

Imagine this technique on just about any ceiling. Whimsical and fanciful for a porch, kitchen, child's room, or even the master bedroom.

Read the description to #73, Floor Cloth, and make up a few of these to scatter throughout your home.

Do as many or as few "rosettes" as you wish. Make many smaller ones or fewer great big ones for a fantasy of leopard.

This technique is to have fun with, so pull out the paints, roll up your sleeves, and get wild.

❖ Latex flat paint, light beige/crème

❖ Flat latex paintbrush, 3" (7.6 cm)

❖ Flat latex paint, medium tawny beige

❖ Flat paint, darker tawny beige

❖ Angle-edged artist acrylic paintbrush, ¼" (6 mm)

❖ Flat latex paint, black

1 Create the "undercoat." Down the middle, apply the light beige paint in a slight radial pattern.

　While the light beige paint is still wet, apply the medium tawny beige paint alongside and blend, keeping the slight radial pattern.

　Let the undercoat dry.

2 Apply the center of the rosettes by merely tapping the side of a ¼" (6 mm) brush that has been loaded with the dark tawny beige against the surface.

　Following the radial pattern, place more and smaller rosettes closer to the narrow portion of the undercoat and open fewer larger ones out toward the end.

　Mix in a few larger centers along the way. Allow the paint to dry completely.

3 With the ¼" (6 mm) paintbrush apply black paint around the dark tawny centers.

　Sort of "blob" the paint around the center portion.

　Leave one end open. Continue until you have your masterpiece.

Note: Practice a bit on paper to get the feel of your brush applying the black. It will come to you quickly.

59 | Stamped Stars

LET CERTAIN MATERIALS and tools make your life easier! There are many great stamps on the market today, go out and find yourself a good star.

A random placement has been selected for this demonstration, but you may follow a pattern if you wish. Select any basecoat color you want, but a deeper color seems to work best for this technique.

Always use solvent-based inkpads so that your beautiful work is permanent. You may apply as many or as few stars as you would like, but I would caution against a 50/50 distribution. Imbalance and an asymmetrical distribution make for a more interesting total effect.

What makes this mere stamping of stars onto a ceiling more elegant is the addition of a shadow. The shadow will add depth and interest to the gold star on top of it. Usually a consistent light source is applied to the placement of a shadow, but in this application you do not have to concern yourself with this directional shading; just go forth, stamp away, and enjoy yourself.

1 Start wherever you feel comfortable and apply all of the black star shadows first.
   The stamp should be solid and opaque.

2 Continue until you have a nice placement and are happy with it.

3 Allow the black stars to dry at least 4 hours. When the black stars are dry apply the gold stars.
   Make sure the stamp is replicating the black star's orientation.
   Offset the position of the gold star stamp slightly and stamp.
   Continue until all the black shadow stars have their top gold star.

60 | Stamped Motifs

THE USE OF a stamp motif is a wonderful and easy way to see the beauty of a repetitive pattern.

Since stamps tend to be small, you may want to try this finish in a small powder room.

The inks for stamps come in a variety of beautiful colors and the only thing to keep in mind is to use a solvent-based inkpad. This will ensure a permanent pigment.

You will be using a chalk line here because you do not want a pencil mark. The chalk wipes off with a slightly water-dampened soft rag, although do not attempt to do so until all inks have been given an overnight dry.

The hardest thing for me when stamping is knowing where to put my next stamp so that everything comes out evenly spaced. I know that some stamps sometimes have little dots on them to indicate orientation, but I have never really come up with a good way to do even spacing, so I cannot tell you.

I just eyeball it and it seems to work pretty well for me. Remember: we are not machines.

The center was left blank in this demonstration, indicating where a light fixture would be.

- Chalk line
- Stamp with motif of your choice
- Solvent-based inkpad, color of your choice
- Water-based satin varnish
- UTC, Burnt Umber
- UTC, Raw Umber
- Flat latex paintbrush, 4" (10.6 cm)
- Cheesecloth, 90-weight

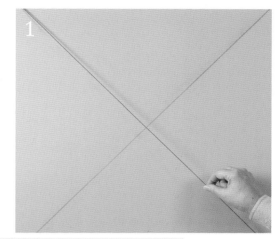

1 Find the center of the ceiling by snapping two diagonals chalk lines. Where they intersect is the middle.

Determine your border size and snap in chalk lines for those.

2 Begin in the center of the outside borderline and work to your left or right.

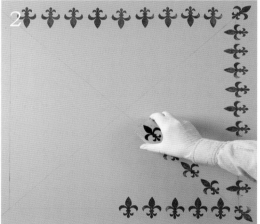

3 Allow the ink to dry overnight. To quietly soften the contrast and to protect your work, apply a coat of latex satin varnish tinted just a bit with UTC Burnt Umber and Raw Umber.

Brush on with the paintbrush and fold back with a pad of 90-weight cheesecloth. Remember to work quickly and keep a wet edge.

61 | Faux Drapery

THINGS THAT APPEAR difficult often-times are not.

This technique is wonderful for powder room ceilings, entries, or any other intimate ceiling. Yes, it can be done on a large ceiling, but practice first on a smaller ceiling.

The colors used in the demonstration are neutral, but you can always use a color such as red or deep blue if you choose. When selecting your color palette just remember that you will have three colors: the darkest, the medium, and the lightest.

Select a brush that is the appropriate size for the ceiling. In a powder room,

a 2" (5.1 cm) or 3" (7.6 cm) angle-edged latex paintbrush would be an appropriate choice.

The drapery will come out of the center in a radial pattern and will be wider at the wall line and narrow at the center. Think of pie wedges. How wide you choose to make the drapery is up to you.

It is always easier to work the paints together when they are wet, so work in sections and then pull everything together at the end. Yes, you can go back into and over your work until you are satisfied.

MATERIALS & TOOLS

- ❖ Angle-edged latex paint-brush, size appropriate to surface area
- ❖ Flat latex paint, almost black or warm black
- ❖ Flat latex paint, medium warm black
- ❖ Flat latex paint, white
- ❖ Small pail of water

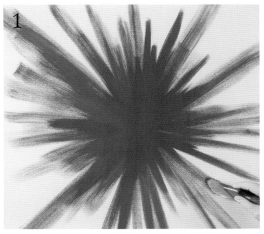

1 The darkest color radiates out from the center.

Brush in the undiluted warm black paint in a radial pattern.

The bulk of this color remains toward the center, but do pull some all the way out to the wall.

2 While the darkest color is still wet, and using the same paintbrush, paint the medium color into and alongside the dark color.

Do not completely cover the dark color.

Taper the medium color into the dark color.

Pull the medium color out to the wall edge more than you did the darkest color.

3 The white is applied with the same paint brush into the wet medium color and up into the darkest color.

Taper the paint into the center.

The application of the white into the other two darker colors will blend all three colors together.

Do not over-blend, as you do want to see some highlights from the white and some very deep lowlights from the darker colors.

Note: If you are having a difficult time keeping all the paints wet, you may set in the darkest so you have your pattern and go back and work in sections following the above steps.

The pail of water is used to "loosen" any of the paints by dipping your brush into the water just a bit and picking up your paint.

You do not need to nor should you clean the brush between colors.

62 | Large Graphic

WHAT DOESN'T look like much can become much. A large graphic applied to a large, otherwise blank ceiling can add interest and "architecture" to a room. The demonstration outlined on these pages is rendered in a soft color palette suggesting "shadows." This design features a very close color palette, which in effect slowly pulls the viewer's eye upward.

If you would like to use a very bold color palette, feel free to do so. Consider mimicking the pattern onto your floor in one of the other techniques outlined in this book. Picture, if you will, this ceiling graphic applied and then you stencil large floor designs onto your floor using the same design, or copy the ceiling's design to relate the two surfaces of floor and ceiling together.

This can create a very understated impact of the pattern.

The key to this technique is finding the center of the ceiling and building the design out from that point, as walls are generally never perfectly straight and you want the center to indeed be the center of the ceiling.

❖ Chalk line

❖ Measuring tape

❖ Painter's masking tape and paper

❖ Flat latex paint, very pale blue

❖ Flat latex paint, very pale green

❖ Paint roller appropriate to size of pattern

1 To find the center of your ceiling, snap a chalk line diagonally from corner to corner.
  Using the center point, define the center square or rectangle if your room is rectangular. Simply measure out from the center point the same distance on all 4 diagonals and connect the dots with the chalk line.

2 Set in the very pale blue corners by again measuring from the diagonals an equal distance on all 4 diagonals and make the squares the size you wish. Generally the design looks better if you leave a border of base color between the edge of the square and the wall.

3 Mask off the center square and apply the very pale green to the center.
  Wait for all paint to dry and wash off or brush off the remaining chalk lines.

Tip: When taping off the chalk lines, run the tape just along the outside of the chalk line, leaving the chalk line on the inside of the tape so that when you paint, the chalk line is erased by the paint.

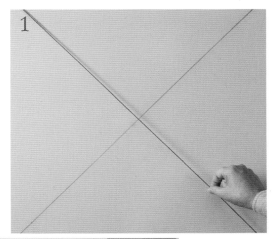

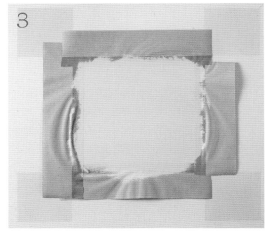

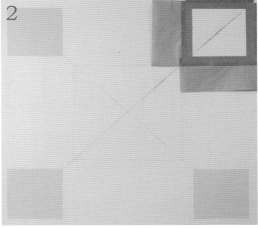

63 | Applied Leaf Motifs

UNLESS YOU ARE a wonderful pictorial artist and can merely freehand paint these leaves in, you might not think that you can get a pictorial to look as nice as this. But you can. You can use stamps, handmade stencils, and a little bit of painting in to do the job easily and beautifully.

This demonstration will provide you with a quick and easy way to paint a leaf canopy peeking out of the corners onto the ceiling.

To make this job effortless, use stamps and stencils to quickly determine where you want your leaves to go. A composition will always look better if it looks random. Think in terms of asymmetrical placement. You might want to bunch up more leaves in only one corner of the room and allow the other corners to have fewer leaves painted in. You do not have to cover each of the four edges of your ceiling; instead let the motifs meander and roam and suddenly appear.

Remember to have on hand some of the basecoat paint just in case you might want to "erase" an errant leaf.

Some brushwork will be involved and will be demonstrated to show you quickly how to use your brush to paint in the stamped and stenciled leaves.

MATERIALS & TOOLS

- ❖ Stamp of leaves
- ❖ Solvent-based inkpad, dark green
- ❖ Stencil material
- ❖ X-Acto knife
- ❖ Stencil brush
- ❖ Angle-edged artist acrylic paintbrush, ¼" (6 mm)
- ❖ Flat latex paint, dark green
- ❖ Flat latex paint, black
- ❖ Flat latex paint, white

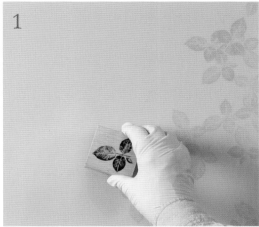

1 Use the leaf stamp to start the design of your foliage.

Stamp as many or as few as you wish.

2 Add the stenciled leaves. Cut out 3 leaves from a good blank piece of stencil material: a large one, medium one, and small one.

Apply the leaf stencils randomly and over the stamped leaves.

3 On a piece of paper, practice making the small strokes that you will use to paint in your leaves. This stroke will work for the larger leaves too; you will just have to paint in more.

Color mix your black, green, and white paint with your paintbrush as you go to vary the tones of green.

Do this by merely picking up some black and green for the darkest, just green for the mid-tone, and green with some white for the lightest leaves.

4 When you are comfortable, proceed to the ceiling.

Remember to vary the colors of green leaves. Some leaves will be dark while others will be pale. This will create depth and interest.

64 | Elaborate Stencil

THE LOOK of a hand-painted ceiling corner, border, or center embellishment can be achieved by using a stencil as a guide.

Remember that a stencil is broken up only to form bridges that hold the stencil together. You will simply be mending some of those bridges to create a more hand-painted look. Positive space is simply the space that is filled in.

You will notice in this demonstration that the stencil is a light and "feathery" one. If this were to be applied just as is to a ceiling, the beautiful design might become lost. Remember that artwork applied to a ceiling tends to disappear due to the overhead position of the ceiling. Therefore, this type of stencil would lend itself to a bit of "beefing up" so the pattern becomes more distinguishable.

By filling in certain areas within the stencil, this positive (filled in) space becomes an important element of the design and composition. Look for those that have an interesting shape.

Even the most intricate or minimal stencil can benefit from this technique.

The following demonstration is for use of the stencil as a border along the outside edge of the ceiling.

❖ Pencil

❖ Large wall or ceiling stencil

❖ Spray can of temporary fixative

❖ Measuring tape

❖ Flat latex paint

❖ Foam roller brush and roller handle, 4" (10.2 cm)

❖ Small paint tray

❖ Stencil brush

❖ Artist angle-edged acrylic paintbrush, ½" (1.3 cm)

❖ Small round artist detail paintbrush

1 Determine the middle of your border. Do this by finding the middle of the ceiling as it runs along the wall.

2 Draw a perpendicular line the depth of the stencil to the wall line in pencil.

3 Spray the back of the stencil with a low-tack temporary adhesive. This will help keep the stencil in place on the ceiling. You will have to periodically reapply.

4 Line up the center of the stencil along the perpendicular line you drew designating the center and begin to paint. The use of a small foam roller to apply the paint over the stencil will make your job easier.

   Load the roller, off-roll a couple of times, and gently roll over the stencil with the loaded roller.

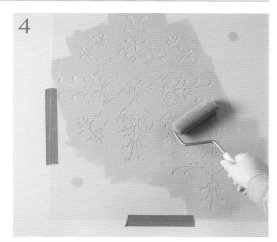

5 Continue applying the stencil along the perimeter of your ceiling until you have finished. Make sure to mark the registration marks that are found on most high-quality stencils.

   When you have completed the border, look at the design and if you like it, you are done! If you would like to liven it up a bit, begin to paint in logical sections. Do the same sections around the entire border.

   Notice how filling in and connecting lines changes the attitude of the stencil.

Note: I oftentimes buy two stencils so that, if need be, I can cut one for the corners.

Note: If you do not want to spend all this time on a ladder, simply make your own border as done in Cambric Cloth (page 180).

65 | Decorative Molding

ANY CEILING likes a little pick-me-up. Simply adding a decorative piece of molding to a ceiling and exercising some color changes can take a simple plain ceiling to a sophisticated statement.

This technique is beautiful on large living room and/or dining room ceilings.

It softens a bedroom ceiling and gives you something to look at while you are lying in bed.

You might want someone who is really good at measuring and sawing wood to do the cutting. A chop saw is handy for the cutting part. Simple miter cuts are what you need to make and the seams can be filled with caulk if they do not fit perfectly. But once the molding is up and the nails holes filled, it is time to dress the ceiling up.

Prime the wood molding before you apply it to the ceiling. This will make painting it easier.

This technique is based on a color formula to get different shades of the same color, which will give depth and interest to the ceiling area and still maintain an overall color palette.

❖ Decorative ceiling molding, cut and installed

❖ Appropriate amount of the darkest color flat latex paint

❖ Equal amount of flat white paint

❖ Paint pail

❖ Angle-edged latex paintbrush, 2" (5.1 cm)

❖ Angle-edged latex paintbrush, 2½" (6.4 cm)

❖ Paint rollers for larger areas

1 Take the darkest paint and pour some into a separate pail. Add an equal part of the white paint. This will be your molding color and the lightest color.

   Paint the molding first, as it is detailed, and do not worry if you get some paint on the ceiling, as you will be painting that, too.

2 Apply the darkest color to the outside perimeter of the ceiling. Practice cutting in so you have no need for tape.

3 Pour some of the darkest color into a pail and add one-quarter of the amount of white paint. This will be the center of the ceiling color. Apply to center of ceiling.

   You can see that you will use mostly the dark color, so purchase accordingly and always use the same white paint to mix your colors with, as there are many different whites in a paint line.

   You could just buy the three colors that are next to one another on a color deck, but doing the color mixing this way creates a softer, less discernible sophisticated color shift on your ceiling.

66 | Faux Tin Ceiling

THERE ARE A FEW heavily embossed wall coverings on the market today that have patterns resembling tin ceilings. These wall coverings are usually made from a paper pulp material and need to be painted with a flat latex paint.

The embossed material is hung like most wall coverings. Always follow manufacturer's instructions for proper installation and priming.

These heavily embossed textures will not hide a horrible ceiling surface, but will cover up minor imperfections and truly give a very elegant and special look to a ceiling.

Try it in a small powder room or a smaller entry for that special touch of importance to an otherwise ignored ceiling surface. Or, feel free to apply to larger areas. The choice is yours!

- ❖ Deeply embossed wall covering
- ❖ Flat latex paint for basecoat, pale gray
- ❖ Flat latex paintbrush, 4" (10.2 cm)
- ❖ Metallic latex paint, silver or aluminum-colored

- ❖ Satin oil-based varnish
- ❖ UTC, Burnt Umber
- ❖ UTC, Raw Umber
- ❖ UTC, Raw Sienna
- ❖ Flat oil paintbrush, 4" (10.2 cm)

- ❖ Small flat block
- ❖ Mineral spirits
- ❖ Cheesecloth, 90-weight
- ❖ Respirator(s) for vapors and fumes

1 Basecoat the material according to manufacturer's instructions in a pale gray color.

2 Select one of the many high-quality silver or aluminum-colored latex metallic paints available on today's market.

   Brush on liberally to get into all the low points. Metallic paint should be opaque and solid covering.

3 Tint satin oil varnish with mostly Burnt Umber, half of that amount with Raw Umber, and half of that amount with Raw Sienna UTCs. Add about a quarter amount of mineral spirits to loosen the varnish up. Add tint slowly. The color should be transparent.

4 You cannot remove the varnish glaze while it is wet. Let the varnish dry just until it loses its high sheen. When it has, usually within half an hour, you are ready to remove the glaze from the high points of the embossed pattern.

   To do so, wrap a block that you can comfortably hold in your hand in a few layers of 90-weight cheesecloth. You want the surface that you use to remove the glaze to be firm and flat so that it only removes the glaze from the high points.

   Carefully rub the cheesecloth-wrapped block over the surface, removing glaze from high points, adjusting the pressure as necessary to remove the glaze. When your cloth gets too dirty, simply re-wrap to a cleaner side.

Note: Wear a respirator when you work with the oil-based varnish because you will be very close to the ceiling where the fumes like to collect!

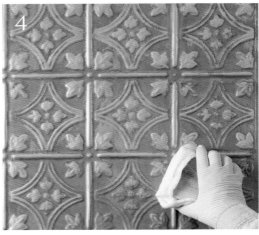

67 | Antiqued Embossed Material

THE MAIN difference between this technique and the Faux Tin Ceiling (page 174) is that you will be using a flat latex paint instead of a metallic latex paint. Think in terms of color with this technique. By adding color and texture to your ceiling, you can add interest and even depth to an otherwise overlooked ceiling surface.

Always follow the manufacturer's installation instructions.

Picture this technique elegantly enhancing a small yet special powder room or even an open and otherwise blank kitchen ceiling.

Another difference with this technique as opposed to the tin ceiling technique is that in step 2 you will be "folding" the satin oil-based varnish glaze back into the surface by texturing with a cheesecloth rag.

You will be using UTCs to tint the varnish glaze, so remember that UTCs go a long way, as does the varnish when you brush it out.

For 1 quart (1 liter) of the tinted varnish, start with a small squirt of the green UTC and about a third of that of Raw Umber UTC. Always add colorant slowly so you do not over-tint.

MATERIALS & TOOLS

- ❖ Deeply embossed wall covering
- ❖ Flat latex paint for basecoat
- ❖ Flat latex paintbrush, 4" (10.2 cm)
- ❖ Satin oil-based varnish
- ❖ UTC, Permanent Green
- ❖ UTC, Raw Umber
- ❖ Flat oil paintbrush, 4" (10.2 cm)
- ❖ Cheesecloth, 90-weight
- ❖ Small flat block
- ❖ Mineral spirits
- ❖ Respirator(s) for vapors and fumes

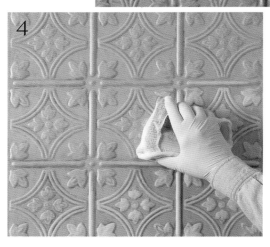

1 Apply the flat latex basecoat paint with the latex paintbrush. Generally lighter colors work best for basecoat, darker colors for glazing medium.

2 Mix your satin varnish glaze by adding a small amount of UTC Permanent Green tint to oil-based satin oil varnish and "dull" the green down a bit by adding a smaller amount of UTC Raw Umber. Add a shy quarter amount of mineral spirits to the varnish.

Apply tinted varnish to a workable area of the ceiling. Remember to keep a wet edge.

3 To remove brushstrokes and fold the varnish into the surface, pounce softly with a pad of 90-weight cheesecloth. Continue to brush on tinted varnish and pounce to soften until the whole area is covered.

This will help even out the varnish and help it set up.

4 Once the varnish has lost its high-gloss sheen and has dulled out, you may start to remove the varnish glaze from the high points. Carefully rub the cheesecloth-wrapped block over the surface, removing glaze from high points and adjusting the pressure as necessary to remove the glaze. When your cloth gets too dirty, simply re-wrap to a cleaner side.

Note: Wear a respirator that is approved for vapors and fumes.

68 | Ceiling Medallion

THINK OF THESE as jewelry for your ceiling. Adding a ceiling medallion around a light fixture can be the perfect added accessory that finishes the "outfit." Once painted, these Styrofoam medallions certainly can be impressive. A visitor would be hard pressed to distinguish it from an old plaster medallion.

The good news is, you can sit and watch television while you make this wonderful little treasure. Patience and a fairly steady hand, along with a couple of good brushes, is all it takes.

The color palette chosen for this demonstration is a subtle one, but yours could be as festive as colorful Italian pottery if you so desire. In the example shown here there is also a play of sheens happening. The base-coat is flat, the acanthus leaves (the big beige leaves) are eggshell, and the metallic rope is semigloss. When the medallion is hung with a light in the center, this interplay of sheens will be lovely.

Putting the medallion on a lazy Susan helps. You will get familiar with painting in with one stroke, using the shape of the brush.

1 Apply the green basecoat to the entire piece. Use the oval sash paintbrush and pounce the flat green latex paint on, making sure to get all crevices. The coat does not have to be opaque and solid covering; if you see a bit of the white factory basecoat coming through, that is desirable. Allow to dry.

2 Apply the eggshell sheen latex beige paint to the acanthus leaves. Coat should be solid covering.

3 Apply the latex metallic champagne color to the rope section. Coat should be solid.

4 Paint in the deep green to the grape leaves. Coat should be solid.

5 Paint the rust onto the grapes.

69 | Cambric Cloth

IT REALLY CAN be this simple...

Cambric cloth is the material most window shades are made out of. This cloth makes a wonderful material to cut and apply to a ceiling, just as you would any wallpaper. The material may be first painted, gilded, stenciled, or anything else you may think of. The nice thing about this technique is that you can do the majority of your artwork down on a worktable, because you will install the final product, as you would wallpaper.

Ask at your local paint store which of the wallpaper adhesives would be the best to use.

Another wonderful attribute is that the material is extremely easy to remove when you want to change.

The technique outlined here is a free-form approach using cutouts of squares and rectangles. You may want to sketch out a basic design on paper first, but this technique is much more fun if you just "go for it." In other words: don't think too much and you'll find that a beautiful design begins to take shape.

Consistent inconsistency along with the contemporary use of shape and color is what this technique is all about.

1 The cambric cloth will come on a roll most likely 36" (91.4 cm) wide by however long you request, so the first thing you want to do is cut the material down into manageable sizes. Once you have done that, simply paint your different colors on with a paintbrush.

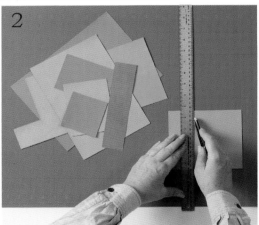

2 When the pieces are dry, you may begin to cut up the material into sizes and shapes you like. Sometimes it helps to set your corners in first as a mild form of direction. If you want pieces of the same size but different colors, simply put one piece over the other and double-cut.

3 Use tape to test-fit the pieces to the ceiling to map out your design if you wish. Paste the pieces into their final position. Use a wallpaper knife to flatten the pieces to the ceiling.

70 | Weathered Beadboard

THIS FINISH is perfect for the boat-house—if you are lucky enough to have one! If not, this is a lovely finish for a porch ceiling or a dado in your kitchen.

This technique demonstrates blending deep colors together with lighter colors to create depth and interest in the final result.

If the beadboard surface is not painted, no need to prime first. If the beadboard surface is painted and you do not know with what, apply a latex bonding primer before applying your colors.

The influence of the deeper colors may not be all that apparent in the final photo, but rest assured that on a larger surface area you will see the influence. You can control the amount of that influence by how much and how heavily you apply the lighter colors.

The deeper underneath colors will produce a subtle shading and depth to the final lighter colors.

MATERIALS & TOOLS

- ❖ Flat latex paint, dark green
- ❖ Flat latex paint, brick red
- ❖ Flat latex paint, medium blue
- ❖ Flat latex paint, white
- ❖ Flat latex paintbrush, 3" (7.6 cm)
- ❖ Flat latex paintbrush, 4" (10.2 cm)

1 Apply the green and red with a 3" (7.6 cm) brush and blend together a bit. Do not think too much. Leave the grooves the darkest.

Paint is used straight from the can, but occasionally dip your brush in some water to loosen everything up a bit if your paint is drying too quickly.

2 When the green and red paint are dry, use a 3" (7.6 cm) brush to apply the blue and white together.

The more often you dip your brush in the water, the looser the paints will be. The looser the paints, the more transparent they are. Use the water to vary the degree of transparency of the blue and white.

3 When all paints are dry, prepare a "white-wash" by mixing 1 part white paint to 2 parts water. With a 4" (10.2 cm) brush, apply the wash for a slightly "chalky" look.

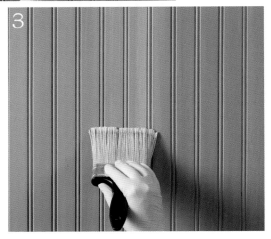

71 | Stained & Antiqued Beadboard

IF YOU ARE FACED with a large expanse of a beadboard installation, this is a quick and painless way to achieve a beautifully stained and antiqued look, which will bring a warm coloration and interest to the room.

Woodworker's stores and high-quality paint stores now carry interesting lines of water-soluble dyes that come in colors other than just the standard browns. Simply mix the dye solution with water to make your solution.

These dyes will work only over unfinished wood surfaces.

Due to the intensity of the colors, this demonstration shows you how to tone down the color and give a slight suggestion of age. Remember that color on the ceiling tends to appear darker so the richness of the tinted varnish will help to deepen and add richness to the bright vibrant color dye.

The products used in this demonstration are all water-based.

Be sure to follow manufacturer's instructions.

MATERIALS & TOOLS

- ❖ Water-soluble dye
- ❖ Measuring cup
- ❖ Flat latex paintbrush, 3" (7.6 cm)
- ❖ Water-based satin polyurethane
- ❖ UTC, Raw Umber
- ❖ UTC, Burnt Umber
- ❖ UTC, Raw Sienna

1 Mix the dye with water according to manufacturer's instructions. If you want a deeper color you may mix with less water. It is always wise to have a sample piece of wood handy to test color.

Start at the top if you are working on a slanted ceiling and be careful not to drip dye onto surfaces below you. Brush in a back-and-forth manner to evenly distribute the material. Work the length of the surface; do not skip around. Brush from end to end. Simply brush on and feather into completed section as you continue.

2 Continue applying the dye. Let the grooves work for you. Cut into the grooves as you proceed, using the groove to guide your paintbrush.

3 Allow an overnight dry period to make sure everything is dry. Then apply a water-based satin polyurethane tinted with just a few drops of UTC Raw Umber, a little less of UTC Burnt Umber, and even less UTC Raw Sienna.

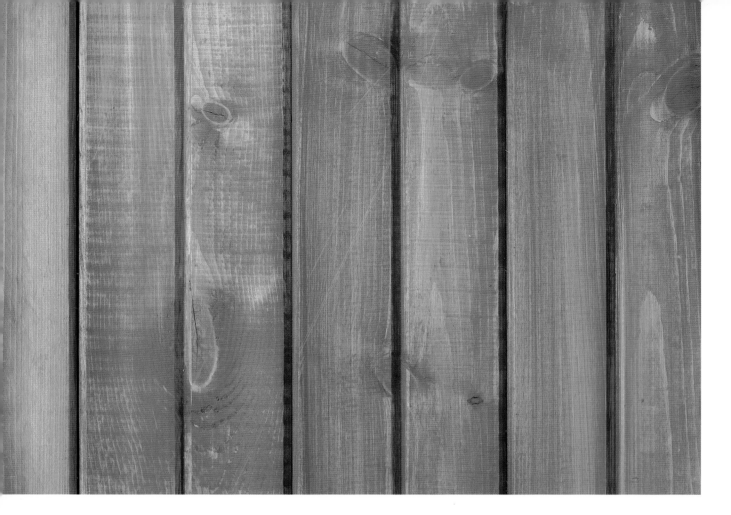

72 | Stained Knotty Pine

KNOTTY PINE PLANKS are often used for and make a lovely ceiling material. Found in cabins and even urban homes, it makes for a good ceiling material where installing sheetrock would be difficult and time-consuming, as the planks fit together with a tongue-and-groove assemblage and the thickness hides a myriad of unfinished area difficulties.

Try installing in that third floor you have been meaning to finish off.

If the wood is slightly stained or just clear-coated, the look is fresh and clean. However, if it is the look of age you are after, this technique will make you happy.

Picture a final result that looks as if it has been there awhile. With the warm glow of time, you can see this finish complementing a beautiful wood floor with a warm rug and an inviting fire in the fireplace beckoning you to bring your book and curl up.

MATERIALS & TOOLS

- ❖ Flat oil paint, Raw Sienna
- ❖ Mineral spirits
- ❖ 2 flat oil paintbrushes, 3" (7.6 cm)
- ❖ Gel stain, Dark Walnut
- ❖ Lint-free rags
- ❖ Airtight water-filled container

1 Thin the Raw Sienna oil paint with one-third mineral spirits. Apply the Raw Sienna-colored flat oil paint to the flat portion of the plank with the paintbrush. Be liberal with the amount of paint.

2 Along the still-wet Raw Sienna oil paint, tuck the Dark Walnut gel stain into the groves of the plank.

3 While everything is still wet, blend the paint and stain together, allowing the darker gel stain to hold in the crevices. Continue until all surface area is done. Apply a satin oil varnish topcoat if so desired for a beautiful gleam or just leave for a more rustic look.

Tip: You do not want the materials to dry out, so work along the whole length of a couple of planks. As you continue, the oil paint will blend into the finished area, but it is best to keep your work neat and end with the Dark Walnut wiped out of a crevice; then move on with the Raw Sienna-colored paint.

Note: Dispose of staining rags in an airtight water-filled container so they do not spontaneously combust.

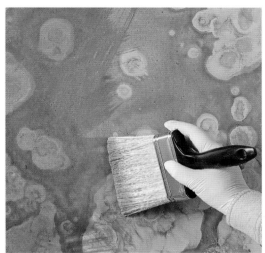

Decorative FLOORS

73 | Floor Cloth

THIS DEMONSTRATION will show you how to make a floor cloth out of basic, everyday sheet vinyl.

Home improvement stores sell large and small pre-cut rolls of vinyl and what's on the face of this vinyl does not matter, as you will be using the back of it!

The historical way of making a floor cloth out of canvas can be believably emulated by simply using the backside of vinyl. No pasting edges down and "blocking" canvas.

Vinyl is easy to cut, has a crisp edge that will not fray, and is easy to find.

You could even try hot-gluing some fringe to the underside edge if you want. Place a rug gripper pad under your floor cloth when you are done and it will really stay in place.

The stencil used in this demonstration is for a medallion motif. When selecting a floor stencil, look for the images that would lend themselves to a medallion design.

This floor cloth is perfect for outdoor or indoor use; just be sure to use the appropriate paints and topcoats.

MATERIALS & TOOLS

- Vinyl sheet
- Utility knife
- Metal straightedge
- Latex bonding primer
- Flat latex paint, black
- Flat latex paint, green

- Medium value flat latex paint, beige
- Flat latex paintbrush, 4" (10.2 cm)
- Floor stencil
- White chalk pencil

- Foam roller brush, 4" (10.2 cm)
- Roller handle, 4" (10.2 cm)
- Small circle stencil
- Flat stencil brush, ½" (1.3 cm)
- latex satin polyurethane

1 Cut your vinyl to the desired size with a very sharp utility knife and a metal straightedge.

2 Prime the backside of the vinyl sheet with a white latex-bonding primer.

3 Apply your background color using the French brush technique. Try to keep the center area of your "canvas" lighter and the edges darker. This application will give you a slightly mottled background that will make your overall result look a bit more mysterious.

4 Find the center of your "canvas" and draw a line with a white chalk pencil through it in each direction.
   Your canvas will now have 4 sections.

5 Begin to apply the stencil by lining up the registration mark with the center point and line you have drawn.
   Use the foam roller to apply the paint. Load the roller and off-load a bit. You do not want a heavily loaded roller when you apply to the stencil. Roll from the bottom up and out. Be sure you have transferred the registration marks and continue until all 4 sections are painted in.

6 Once the medallion stencil is painted, it is nice to add a little something to the center and to the corners. A circle will be used to do so. Use a small circle stencil and small stencil brush to apply. With a water-dampened rag, remove any visible pencil lines.

7 Apply two coats of latex satin sheen polyurethane for floors.

74 | Jute Monogram

WANT TO MAKE a statement on your rug? You can use stencils to say whatever you might want to express; this demonstration outlines a traditional monogram.

Fabric paint is used on the jute material. Fabric paint comes in heat-sensitive and nonheat-sensitive; use the nonheat sensitive. This simply means that you do not have to apply heat to set the paint. Explore your craft store for fabric paint and look for a fuller-bodied paint as opposed to a fabric paint that is very thin.

This technique may also be applied to cotton rugs or sisal and is a great way to have some fun and or sophistication.

The only thing to keep in mind is that you really have only one chance to make your statement, so think before you speak. Take the time to make a mock-up first to check placement, measurements and spacing. This will save you any surprises on your rug.

1 Make a mock-up of the monogram.

2 Measure where you want the bottom line of your letters to be. This line should not be dead center, rather make the bottom space an extra ¼" (6 mm) to ½" (1.3 cm) larger. Just as you would in matting a picture, do so here, as the slightly more space at the bottom will visually allow the monogram to appear more centered.

Also set a side line where your letter will begin. Use a triangle to make sure the bottom and side line create a 90° angle.

Use your mock-up to make sure everything will be where you want it to be.

3 Begin to apply the letters one letter at a time. Line the edge of letter stencil along the edge of side line. Line the bottom of letter stencil along edge of bottom line. Use green tape to hold stencil in place.

Softly pounce the paint on with the stencil brush, starting in the center and off-loading a bit before moving to the edges. Stencil in all the letters one at a time.

4 After you have all the letters applied, you may or may not like the look of a stenciled letter. If you do you are done; if not you may use the edge of a stencil to fill in.

Simply lay the stencil along a letter edge and stencil in gap to about half the letter's thickness.

Be careful not to extend paint too far into center at interior angles.

Hold the stencil edge along the opposite edge of letter and complete the filling in. Fill in all gaps and you are now complete. Allow paint to fully dry before use.

75 | Diamonds on the Floor

IT'S ALL ABOUT the tape! Let the tape work for you. This demonstration is done over a pre-fabricated floor and the wood showing will be part of the design.

If you have a tired old wood floor and want to freshen it up and change the look of the room, this technique will do just that.

It's good for porches, kitchens, anywhere where you will be seeing the whole, or most of, the floor, because this technique is an all-over pattern. After you have spent all that time on your knees, you will want to see your lovely work.

The color in the demonstration is a light neutral color, suggesting informality, but as an alternative, imagine this design done in warm black with small white squares for a more formal feel.

MATERIALS & TOOLS

- Ruler
- Chalk line
- Black marker or white pencil
- Lacquer thinner (if using black marker)

- Painter's masking tape, 2" (5.1 cm)
- Latex bonding primer
- Latex floor paint in color of your choice

- Foam roller brush
- Roller extension pole
- Straight paintbrush appropriate for topcoat
- Satin polyurethane for topcoat

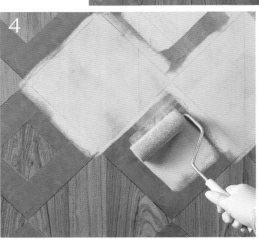

1 Find the center of your floor. Begin in the center and mark off the desired size of the diamond. Be sure you center the first diamond over the center.

Mark your measurement off all the way around the room and draw connecting lines from each one.

To form the diamond, draw in on the diagonal the measurement you want. Connect all the diagonals.

2 Erase the unnecessary lines. Lacquer thinner will remove permanent marker if that is what you used. Always do a test first to make sure whatever you used to make the lines can be easily removed from the exposed wood floor.

3 Tape off all the diamonds you want to paint. Mark them with a little bit of tape.

Your tape should be placed so that the line will be painted over.

Lay the tape down fairly smoothly and you will see your smaller diamond form.

Be sure to burnish down all tape edges securely, using an old credit card (saves your fingernails).

4 Apply your primer. The best way is to use a foam roller. Attach the roller handle to a roller extension pole or a broom handle so you can stand up and paint.

Allow to dry.

5 Apply your paint coat. Once the paint has dried, carefully remove the tape. If the paint is pulling the paint off the floor, put a straightedge down and first score the paint along the tape edge.

6 After all paint has dried, apply one or two coats of satin polyurethane.

76 | Bubbles

WHY NOT HAVE bubbles on your floor? This amusing technique is as fun to do as the result. There is no pattern to follow; just let your eye lead you. Consideration of where furniture and rugs may go would be the only thing you might want to pay attention to.

It is easy to give a bit of volume to a circle by adding a highlight. Voilà, a flat circle becomes a dimensional "bubble."

When you are done applying all the bubbles, topcoat the entire floor. This will not only protect your artwork, but something else very interesting happens as well. When you look at the floor from a distance and at an angle you might not see much, but when you get above the bubbles and look down you certainly will. The topcoat enhances the dimensional allusion.

1 Prime in your circles using the different size circles. Allow the primer to dry.

2 Apply a "crescent" of white paint over the primed circle.

3 While the black and white paints are still wet, blend the black into and softly over the white. Do not obliterate the white, but rather softly blend the two colors together to have a light spot.

Note: It is always easier to apply dark into light. Practice a bit first with the shading; you will get it. The use of a stencil will help you to not load your brush too much and this will make the blending easier.

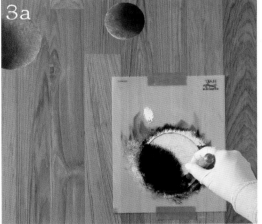

77 | Distressed Painted Hardwood Floor

THE WARMTH AND BEAUTY of age is what this demonstration reveals. This finish may be applied over an old and worn hardwood floor or a new and shiny prefabricated floor, changing either of them into a beautiful old and worn look that says, "I have been here a longtime."

This is a great fix for hardwood floors you do not want to refinish just yet, or to make a prefabricated floor far more interesting. This technique is a delightful way to alter the look of your floor to fit in better with your décor and bring a change of attitude to your room.

Before any paint is applied, the surface must be clean and free of any wax buildup and scuff-sanded.

Because this finish requires the use of paint stripper, work in a well-ventilated room and always use gloves and safety glasses. There are some very good water-based low-odor paint strippers on the market today; be sure to find one.

MATERIALS & TOOLS

- ❖ Flat latex paint, beige
- ❖ Hair dryer (optional)
- ❖ Flat latex paint, white
- ❖ Flat latex paintbrush, 4" (10.2 cm)

- ❖ Flat latex paintbrush, 3" (7.6 cm)
- ❖ Paint stripper
- ❖ Gloves
- ❖ Lint-free rag

- ❖ Low-sheen water-based floor polyurethane
- ❖ UTC, Raw Umber
- ❖ UTC, Burnt Umber
- ❖ Lamb's wool applicator

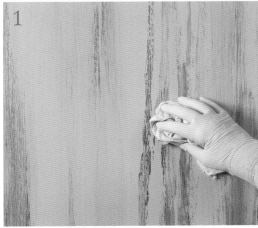

1 Selectively brush on some of the beige paint. Do not paint beige paint on 100% of the surface.

Work in an area you are comfortable with. When the beige paint has begun to dry out and is matte (paint can be forced dry with a hairdryer), use your smaller brush to selectively brush on some of the paint stripper.

Begin to wipe out the stripper, selectively removing some of the paint.

You want the stripper and paint to be able to be rubbed slightly off, leaving paint residue.

Continue to treat the entire surface in this manner.

2 Repeat step 1 only with the white paint. You want some of the beige color to show through and you want some of the white to remain.

3 Tint water-based polyurethane with a little Raw Umber and Burnt Umber.

After all paints have dried, apply a coat of the lowest sheen water-based polyurethane you can find for floors.

If the area to be topcoated is not large, use the 4" (10.2 cm) flat latex paintbrush; if the area is large, apply polyurethane with a lint-free lamb's wool applicator.

Note: Why not just put both colors selectively on and then use the paint stripper? The reason each coat is treated separately is because you want the floor to look like layers of different colors of paint have worn through and you do not want the stripper to be applied to paint that is too dry. You may certainly try to do it that way. But the outlined way will create a more subtle final appearance.

78 | Center Star Medallion

WOOD MEDALLION inlays on a floor are beautiful, but the real thing is pretty costly. With this demonstration you can achieve a believable look for a fraction of the cost and you get to entirely customize your medallion.

If you are at a loss for a motif, simply search "hardwood floor inlays" on the Internet and you will find many lovely examples or make up your own!

Entrance halls, libraries, and sun porches can all benefit from this technique.

Remember that you are painting on a floor, so it is best to use floor paints and polyurethanes made especially for floors.

There is no need to apply a topcoat to your entire floor but rather you may simply apply a fresh topcoat to your new beautiful hand-painted medallion. I caution you, neatness counts with this one.

Yes, this medallion is a circle and yes, you can paint a circle if you just remember to breathe. If you really do not want to try to paint a circle, change it to a square.

- ❖ Large adjustable compass
- ❖ Sandpaper, 220-grit
- ❖ Latex bonding primer, tinted dark gray
- ❖ High-quality angle-edged acrylic artist paintbrush, ¼" (6 mm)
- ❖ Flat latex floor paint, black
- ❖ Clear ruler, 2" (5 cm)
- ❖ White pencil
- ❖ Painter's masking tape
- ❖ Angle-edged latex paintbrush appropriate for medallion size
- ❖ Metallic latex paint, brass-colored
- ❖ Oval sash paintbrush, 2" (5 cm)
- ❖ Stencil of alphabet
- ❖ Small stencil brush
- ❖ Water-based floor polyurethane

1 Determine the placement and size of your star and the background circle. It is best to make a drawing first and lay it on the floor to see if any adjustments are needed.

2 With a compass large enough to make your circle, draw in the circle directly on the floor.

3 Make sure the floor surface you are painting is clean and free of any wax. You may want to sand lightly with 220-grit sandpaper. Apply the dark gray-tinted primer. With the ¼" (6 mm) artist acrylic paintbrush, paint in the outline of your circle. If you are very comfortable with a larger brush, please feel free to use one. Taping a circle never looks good; take your time and you will be able to paint the outline.

4 Once the primer is dry, repeat step 3 with the black floor paint.

5 Draw in the star. The star pattern is made up of two 4-cornered stars with the smaller one drawn in first.

6 Tape off the outline of the star and pounce on the latex metallic paint.

7 When the brass metallic paint is dry, stencil in the compass points and add the smaller black circle to center of star.

8 When all paint is dry, apply water-based floor polyurethane to just your design. You can apply to just the letters using a small brush.

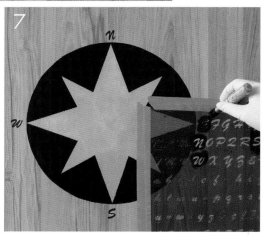

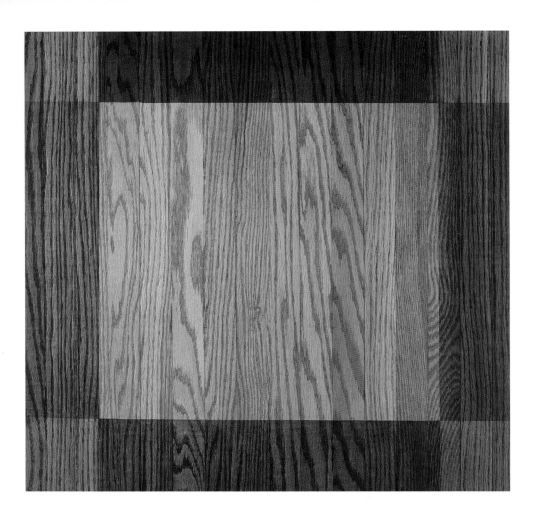

79 | Colored Japan Inlay

THE JAPAN paint color Prussian Blue was used in the following demonstration because of the color's beauty and intensity.

Japan paints may be used either as a stain on an unfinished wood floor surface or as a slightly translucent paint over a sealed wood floor surface.

Never overlook the opportunity to use Japan paints as a stain because the colors are so extraordinarily intense and beautiful. This demonstration outlines the Japan paint over an unsealed wood floor surface to create a lovely and soft-colored border and, utilizing the potential of an oil-based paint, simply wiping out more of the paint to create a soft square.

The Japan paint is applied much like a stain. It is thinned down with mineral spirits to a skim-milk consistency and brushed on and wiped off.

If you are applying over a sealed wood floor, do not wipe out the paint, but instead softly brush the color on, blend to eliminate brushstrokes, and then topcoat with an oil-based polyurethane when dry.

Japan paints may be found at good woodworker's stores and online.

MATERIALS & TOOLS

- ❖ Painter's masking tape, 2" (5.1 cm)
- ❖ Japan oil paint, Prussian Blue
- ❖ Flat oil paintbrush, 3" (7.6 cm)
- ❖ Lint-free rag
- ❖ Mineral spirits

1 Lay out your border design.

2 With mineral spirits, thin the Japan paint slightly to a skim-milk consistency and brush on, making sure to get into all the cracks.

3 Before the paint is dry, tape off the square made at the border's corners and wipe off yet more of the paint with a rag slightly dampened with mineral spirits.

    Do not let the paint dry too long. It's best to do the corner squares as soon as you have applied the two sides. This will create a soft inset square without any fuss and muss.

80 | Distressed Fir Floor

ARGUABLY fir is not the loveliest of wood grains, so obliterate it! The good news is that fir is very soft so you can distress it with a minimum of effort.

I have even seen where a homeowner had a fir floor installed in a kitchen very early on in the construction process and she wanted the raw fir left uncovered so that all the workers and activity would purposefully mar and distress the floor. When all the work was done, the floor was stained a very dark stain and the result was that she had a floor that looked like it had been there forever.

Pine is also a soft wood that can be distressed easily.

Marring and distressing a floor gives it a worn warmth. If you like this distressing and aged look, read on!

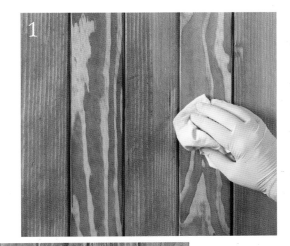

1 Very lightly stain the floor with a thinned-down gel stain and mineral spirit mixture, 1 to 1. This will allow you to see your distressing. You do not have to let it completely dry before you begin.

2 Distress the floor. Use a hammer to scratch and dent the surface. Use a wood chisel to gouge out areas along the joints. Pound a nail in to create holes. Use the nail to scratch and mar the surface. Have fun!

3 Heavily apply the mahogany and walnut stains together with the paintbrush. Use the brush more than a rag to blend and distribute the gel stain. Wipe very little stain off with the rag. If the first stain coat is not dark enough, apply a second stain coat when the first coat has dried.

   When the stain has dried, seal the surface with a coat or two of satin oil polyurethane.

Note: Always dispose of staining rags according to instructions found on label of stain can—never leave them in the sun or sitting out.

Note: Every day the market improves the water-based stains and dyes, so if you do not want to use oil-based products, try water-based products.

81 | Decking Multi Paints

INSTEAD OF just a solid coating of exterior deck paint, try using more than one color to create interest.

It is not that much more difficult to apply the paint as outlined in the following demonstration and it does allow for some of the grain to show through and will give a softer looking finish to your deck.

This demonstration would also work for the semitransparent stains that you may now find in any good paint store. Follow the same steps if you use the semitransparent stains.

The following demonstration outlines the use of an exterior deck and floor paint.

MATERIALS & TOOLS

❖ Latex deck paint, warm gray

❖ Flat latex paintbrush, 4" (10.2 cm)

❖ Latex deck paint, white

❖ Lint-free rag

1 Clean your deck surface thoroughly and then allow it to dry.

2 With the paintbrush, brush on some of the warm gray paint.

3 While the gray paint is still wet, apply the white paint next to and into the gray paint with the paintbrush.

4 While all paint is wet, softly pull a lint-free rag through the paint. This will further blend the two colors and remove some of the paint, revealing some of the wood underneath.

Tip: All paints must be wet before you rag off any, so work in an area comfortable to manipulate and always work end to end to avoid stops and starts in the middle.

Deck paints are fairly "loose" to start with, but you may add a bit of water to your brush to keep the paint a little looser. Do not add too much water.

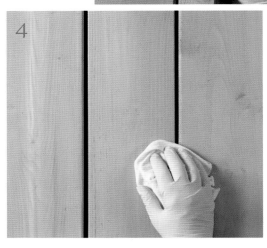

82 | Decking Semitransparent Stains

THERE REALLY ARE some wonderful new semitransparent colored stains coming onto the market these days. We are no longer limited to the standard wood tones.

The exterior areas of homes are now being paid attention to like never before and the public has asked for the same color versatility outside as they have inside. Luckily the manufacturers have responded.

Exterior spaces are now becoming "outside rooms" with all the attention to detail the interiors have enjoyed all these years.

Which means—don't be afraid of color!

The nice thing about the semitransparent stains is that they are just that—stains. A stain will penetrate the wood as opposed to a paint that will sit more on top of the wood surface.

MATERIALS & TOOLS

- ❖ Inexpensive flat oil paintbrush, 4" (10.2 cm)
- ❖ Semitransparent stain, blue
- ❖ Lint-free rag

1 Make sure the deck surface is clean and completely dry.

2 With the paintbrush, apply the blue stain. If you like the darker blue version as seen in photo 2b, apply a second coat of the stain once the first one has dried completely.

3 Softly wipe stain off with a lint-free rag to remove excess stain. This evens out the stain and distributes the material evenly.

Note: If you use an oil-based semitransparent stain, always dispose of staining rags according to the manufacturer's instructions—do not let the rags sit out!

83 | Faux Bois Repair

WOOD IS ALWAYS all about the color! To have wood graining say wood, it is primarily the color that speaks the loudest and most convincingly. Match the color, add a bit of graining, and you will have a match.

This is a good demonstration to know if you have taken out a wall, have a malfunctioning radiator or a misbehaving pet, and do not want to wait for the repair person to come and patch your floor.

Yes, you could use this technique to cover an entire floor area, in which case just keep going with the instructions outlined here.

- ❖ Sandpaper, 150-grit (optional)
- ❖ Latex bonding primer
- ❖ UTC, Burnt Umber
- ❖ UTC, Raw Umber
- ❖ UTC, Raw Sienna
- ❖ UTC, Permanent Green
- ❖ UTC, Thalo Blue
- ❖ Flat oil paintbrush, 3" (7.6 cm)
- ❖ Satin oil-based floor polyurethane
- ❖ Lint-free rag
- ❖ Hair dryer (optional)
- ❖ Painter's masking tape, 2" (5.1 cm)

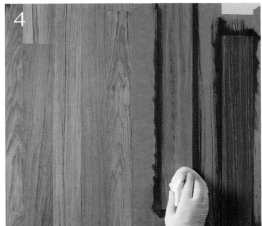

1 Make sure the section you need to repair is clean and dry. You may have to sand it with 150-grit sandpaper first.

2 Tint your primer to the lightest color found in the wood you are matching.

Apply to the section you need to repair.

Keep brushstrokes in the pattern of the existing wood grain.

3 Draw in your new wood planks. Mask off alternating planks to give a look of realism.

The UTC list above is large, but you will find that those are generally the tints that will you get you where you need to go with the basecoat and the graining solution.

Apply two coats of basecoat and allow them each to completely dry.

Have brushstrokes of the basecoat follow the grain pattern.

4 Slowly add UTC drops to satin oil polyurethane, matching the existing wood color. Match the medium/dark coloration.

Brush the woodgrain-tinted polyurethane onto the taped-off exposed "planks."

Take a lint-free rag and gently pull through the graining material a few times to create a grain.

Play with it a bit; you will get a believable grain.

5 You can use a hair dryer to force-dry the oil polyurethane so you may continue. Force-dry until the sheen has dulled down; then you can apply tape without smearing your work and continue until you are finished.

Make sure your tape is securely pressed down.

6 After a 24-hour dry, apply a coat of polyurethane that matches the sheen of the rest of the floor.

84 | Antiqued Brick Pavers

IF YOU WOULD like to change the look of dark red brick (or in this case, dark red brick pavers) to something else altogether, you may do so! You are not stuck with this color if you do not want it and you do not have to go through the expense of removal and putting in something new.

At least try this demonstration as a way to have the color you want before you go ripping everything out.

If you have interior bricks of this nature, follow the same steps to help those along too.

The antiquing of the new color will lend yet another layer of interest and realism to your new pavers.

MATERIALS & TOOLS

- ❖ Masonry paint, medium gray
- ❖ Flat latex paintbrush, 4" (10.2 cm)
- ❖ Foam roller brush (optional)
- ❖ Masonry paint, black
- ❖ Masonry paint, white
- ❖ UTC, Burnt Umber
- ❖ UTC, Raw Umber
- ❖ Lint-free rag

1 Clean the pavers. The basecoat could be almost solid covering, but doesn't need to be.

   If you use a roller, do not leave roller marks. A brush is easier to control.

2 After the basecoat has completely dried, mix the dark "dirt" color.

   If you have black paint, turn it to dirt by adding ¼ of the white paint and a healthy squirt of UTC Burnt Umber with a dash of UTC Raw Umber. You do not want it black but rather dirty looking.

   Apply dark paint with the paintbrush.

   Dip brush into water, then into paint, and then onto surface.

3 While the dark paint is still wet, remove some with a wet rag.

   Look to see where dirt and age would build up and take your lead from these areas. You do not have to cover with the gray basecoat 100%.

   You may leave the dark color on as heavy as you want or remove as much as you want. You may thin the dark paint down with water if you want a less dramatic look.

   Just be sure that you do not let the dark paint dry out before you have had a chance to remove.

   Work in an area that you can comfortably reach and blend the wet paint into dried paint carefully.

85 | Freshened Sheet Vinyl B&W Squares

SICK OF YOUR same old vinyl? Don't want to replace it, but want something more interesting? You can paint it with this simple yet effective technique.

This demonstration will show you how you can freshen up what is probably a perfectly good vinyl floor that you are just a little tired of.

Always try to make your job easier for yourself by not doing the whole area but just punching the floor up in selected areas with selected colors. You can sit on your floor, relaxed, and have fun transforming what is old into what is new.

Remember to always strip off any wax buildup and dirt before applying any paint.

MATERIALS & TOOLS

- ❖ Flat artist acrylic paint-brush, 1" (2.5 cm)

- ❖ Latex bonding primer, white

- ❖ Latex bonding primer, darkly tinted

- ❖ Semigloss latex paint, white

- ❖ Semigloss latex paint, black

- ❖ Semigloss latex floor polyurethane

1 Decide which squares you want to paint.

2 Prime with white latex bonding primer the squares you want white.

Prime with dark latex bonding primer the squares you want black.

You will notice that the embossing on the surface of the linoleum is not straight, so you do not even need to paint a straight line.

Simply hold the brush flat to the surface and follow the embossed edge around the squares and try not to get a paint ridge along the edges. Holding your brush flat to the surface will help with this.

3 After drying, apply the white semigloss latex paint to the primed white squares.

Do the same with the black semigloss painted over the darker primed squares.

4 To protect your paint, apply a coat or two of semigloss floor polyurethane to the squares that have been painted.

86 | Awning Stripes

REMEMBER THE OLD flecked vinyl tile floors that maybe you had in your bedroom or playroom as a child, the floors that were popular because they are easy to install and wear amazingly well? Unfortunately, these vinyl tiles did not come in any impressive array of colors.

It is always a pity to have to replace a perfectly good vinyl floor when it is in good condition, securely adhered, or otherwise in perfectly good shape and has served you well.

Maybe you do not have to replace it—just yet.

This demonstration will show how you can spiff up that tired yet still serviceable vinyl floor.

Stripes are fun and easy to paint and will give your room a sense of casualness.

Render in a muted color palette for a more sophisticated appearance or have a bit of fun with color, as this demonstration shows.

Take your inspiration from an awning perhaps seen out of a window or even your favorite striped bedding.

Exaggerate the size of the stripe and you will add visual space and direction to the room.

MATERIALS & TOOLS

- ❖ Painter's masking tape
- ❖ Flat latex paintbrushes appropriate to size
- ❖ Foam roller brush (optional)
- ❖ Latex bonding primer
- ❖ Flat latex paint, color of your choice
- ❖ Latex floor polyurethane, sheen of your choice

1 Completely clean any and all wax and dirt off the floor. Use a wax stripper, if need be. The floor surface must be clean.

2 Use the tape to create the stripes. You can lay out your design before you begin or you can just begin to put in the stripe.

Use the areas under the tape to reveal the original floor and become a stripe. Because of this, tape should always be laid down straight, keeping in mind what is underneath is also a stripe.

3 Burnish the tape edges down very well. With a brush or roller, apply a coat of primer to the exposed stripes.

Note: It is easier if you allow some of the blue tape to show, as this will help you see where the stripes are if you have taped off a large area.

4 Apply your colors. Stripe should be opaque, so depending upon your color(s) apply one or two coats after first coat is completely dry.

5 Pull the tape as soon as you can and always pull tape at a 45° angle away from the painted surface. Apply 2 coats of latex polyurethane in the sheen of your choice.

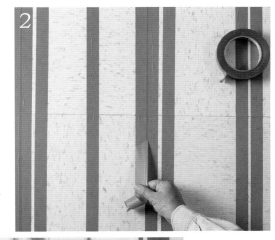

87 | Arcs & Circles

THIS DEMONSTRATION is about the imagery more than what you put it on. These arcs and circles would look beautiful over just about any floor surface. Always remember to use compatible paints with the right surface.

Imagine very soft Japan paints over a previously sealed hardwood floor.

Instead of solidly painting the arcs and circles, you could use stains on a raw wood floor, creating softly colored shapes.

Feel free to make the arcs and circles as big or small as you want. You will have fun drawing in your patterns—just remember that less is probably more.

❖ String

❖ Pencil

❖ Latex enamel floor paint

❖ Angle-edged artist acrylic paintbrush, ½" (1.3 cm)

❖ Angle-edged latex paintbrush, 3" (7.6 cm)

❖ Latex floor polyurethane (optional)

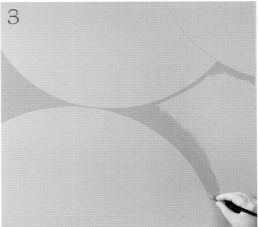

1 Tie an arm's length of string around a pencil. To make an arc, hold one end of the string down tightly to the floor, extend your arm and hand until the string is very tight, and making sure the hand that is holding down the string does not let the string go loose. Place the pencil to the floor and draw from side to side, always keeping tension on the string—voilà—a perfect arc!

It is that simple. You can do even larger arcs if you have someone else hold the other end.

2 Continue with step 1 and remember to turn your body now and then to change arc direction.

To make circles, simply have someone hold one end while you move around with the pencil or make smaller ones you can complete.

3 When outlines are complete, begin to paint in the inside angle portions first.

Use the smaller paintbrush to paint in the outline; then use the larger paintbrush to fill in.

It is always easier to follow an outside curve with a paintbrush as opposed to an inside angle.

Use the smaller angle-edged brush to fit into the tight angles.

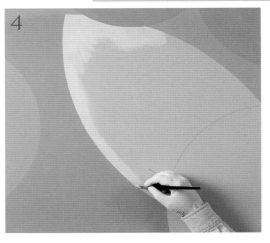

4 Paint in the outside curved shapes.

5 Keep going until you are done. You may want to topcoat your work of art with the appropriate polyurethane.

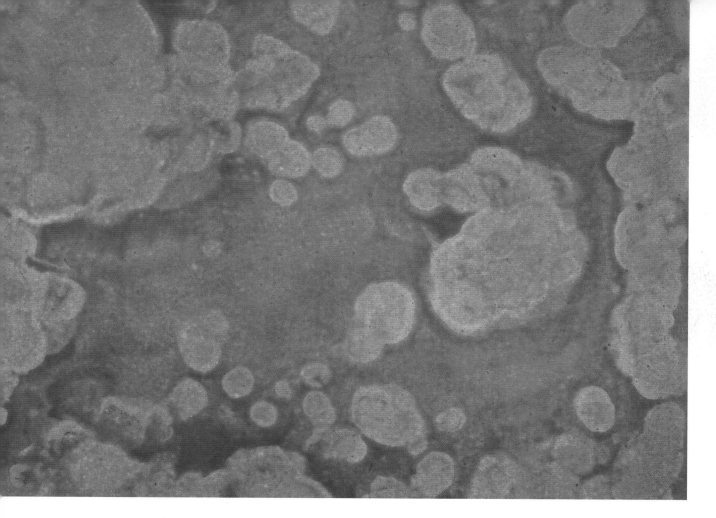

88 | Faux Cement Stain

DO YOU HAVE a cement floor somewhere in your house that you would like to have look more interesting? If you have seen the cement stains available on today's market, you know the beauty that can be achieved on a plain old cement floor. However, the cement floor in your home is perhaps already painted or sealed, which means you cannot apply one of these lovely cement stains, as they go either into wet or onto unsealed cement.

Good news! You can achieve a very similar look by merely tinting a floor topcoat.

This demonstration is for water-based floor polyurethane only, which can be applied over previously painted latex floor paint or a yet unpainted but sealed cement floor.

If the technique looks too difficult for a large floor, always remember that you can mask off the floor into manageable sections. The larger, the better, but work an area you are comfortable with. You should not start and stop this finish in the middle of an area.

Generally the cement stains tend to be earth-tone colors of warm browns and greens and that is why these colors have been selected for this demonstration.

MATERIALS & TOOLS

- ❖ UTC, Burnt Umber
- ❖ Water-based satin floor polyurethane
- ❖ Gloves
- ❖ UTC, Yellow
- ❖ UTC, Permanent Green
- ❖ Flat latex paintbrush, 4" (10.2 cm)
- ❖ Denatured alcohol
- ❖ UTC, Black

1 Mix UTC Burnt Umber into the polyurethane. Mix UTC Yellow and Permanent Green together in another container of polyurethane in equal amounts.

2 With your brush and working in small sections, French brush (page 140) the two tinted polyurethanes together. Do not add water to your poly; rather dip your brush into water every third load or so. You want the poly to remain wet and rather soupy on the floor.

3 Before polyurethane begins to set up and while it is still very wet, dip your hand in denatured alcohol and let some drop off your fingers. Stay close to the floor surface; this will allow larger "puddles" to form. The application of the alcohol will break up any brushstrokes, ooze the colors together, and add an interesting element.

Allow to dry completely.

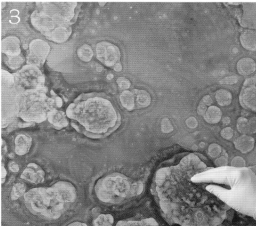

4 After you have applied the two colors of poly and the alcohol to the entire surface and it has dried completely, maybe even overnight, you will now apply a coat of the same two polyurethane colors with the addition of a third: black-tinted poly.

Apply quickly in the French brush manner. You may use the same brush and you may dip the brush into water every now and then to keep brushstrokes down.

Do not over-brush the poly and it will level out better.

You want this coat to bury the previous work and cut down the contrast of the light areas.

You may have to repeat this step to further bury and reduce contrast once the previous coat of poly is dry.

Tip: Have someone help you by applying the alcohol as you apply the poly.

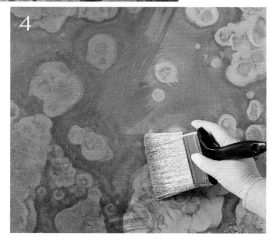

89 | French Ironwork Stencil

A BEAUTIFUL WAY to treat a large unbroken slab of cement flooring (or any other type of flooring for that matter) is with a general overall pattern. The pattern chosen for this demonstration is that of French ironwork because the delicacy of the pattern plays out over a large surface in a lovely way.

Light and airy in design, yet due to the receptiveness, substantial and interesting underfoot.

No need for a throw rug here.

As with any stencil, always use the same side and directional orientation throughout your application and always remember to put in the registration marks!

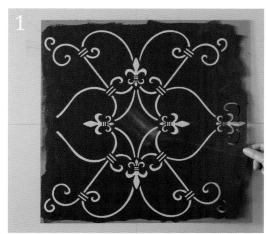

1 Determine the middle of the floor using a chalk line.

Have someone hold the line in one corner while you pull it out to the diagonally opposite corner. Pull the line taut and snap it against the floor. Repeat for the other corners. Where the two lines intersect is your center.

To be sure you are going straight (or level), use a triangle and make a square from the diagonals. You are now centered and true.

This is important because all the other stencils will come off of this very first one.

Line stencil up on center.

2 Load the roller with the paint and, moving from center out, roll over the stencil.

You may wish to use a temporary fix-it spray on the back of the stencil to hold it in position, but as it is on the floor, usually just one or two pieces of tape will hold the stencil in place.

3 Force the paint dry with the hair dryer if it is not already and match up the registration marks and continue as you did in step 2 until the area is complete.

Note: If you are applying the stencil over a painted cement floor, there is no need to apply a topcoat, as you are using the same type of floor paint. Be careful with the fresh stencil floor paint for at least a week while the paint cures.

If you are applying the stencil over unpainted (raw) cement, talk to your paint store clerk to see if you would need to apply a cement sealer first.

If your raw cement floor is not damp and has no moisture problem and if you use a good cement floor paint, you should not need to seal the entire floor first, but ask.

90 | Cement to Stone

THIS IS AN amazingly versatile technique. The material you will be using has many different surface applications, from exterior pavers to interior linoleum.

You may now find in your local paint stores this spreading stone material. If your paint store doesn't carry this product, you can find it online; search for "spreadable stone."

Keep in mind that you will want to follow the manufacturer's instructions and use all their products found in the system, even the grout tape, to ensure a compatible result. I have found the spreading stone systems to be all quite good and they are products of high quality.

This is a demonstration of how you can make a regular old interior cement floor look like a beautiful stone floor in a very easy manner.

A white spreading stone material was used because the material can be color washed with water mixed with powder dyes provided by the manufacturer. The look and manipulation of these dyes gives a more believable stone finish.

This finish has texture, which also lends itself to a true stone look.

Dark gray floor paint was used as the basecoat color, which will show through in random places, becoming part of the stone finish.

MATERIALS & TOOLS	
❖ Spreading stone material system from paint store	❖ Pail of water
❖ Spreading blade, 6" (15.2 cm)	❖ Lint-free rag

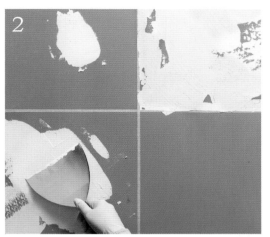

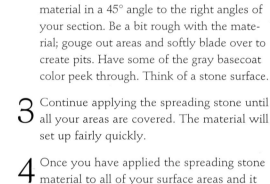

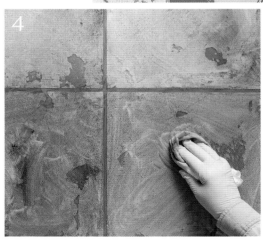

1 Determine your pattern. Apply the grout line tape provided by manufacturer. Do not substitute regular ¼" (6 mm) tape, as the manufacturer's has a fiber content that allows you to be able to remove it.

2 Place a small amount of spreading stone onto a section. You do not want the depth of the material to exceed ⅟₁₆" (1.6 mm).

Using your spreading blade, pull the material in a 45° angle to the right angles of your section. Be a bit rough with the material; gouge out areas and softly blade over to create pits. Have some of the gray basecoat color peek through. Think of a stone surface.

3 Continue applying the spreading stone until all your areas are covered. The material will set up fairly quickly.

4 Once you have applied the spreading stone material to all of your surface areas and it has dried, pull the grout tape off.

With the spreading blade, softly burnish over the surface to remove any burrs or little chunks.

Mix the powder dyes with water according to the manufacturer's instructions.

Rag on the two colors of golden brown and darker brown.

Blend together to remove rag marks. Allow to dry a bit, and then with a water-dampened rag remove some of the color from the high parts while leaving color to remain in the crevices.

Tip: If you are doing a large surface in this fashion you do not need to do each "stone" individually. You may cover more than one 12" x 12" (30.5 x 30.5 cm) section at a time. Change direction every now and then to create a realistic result—just like Mother Nature.

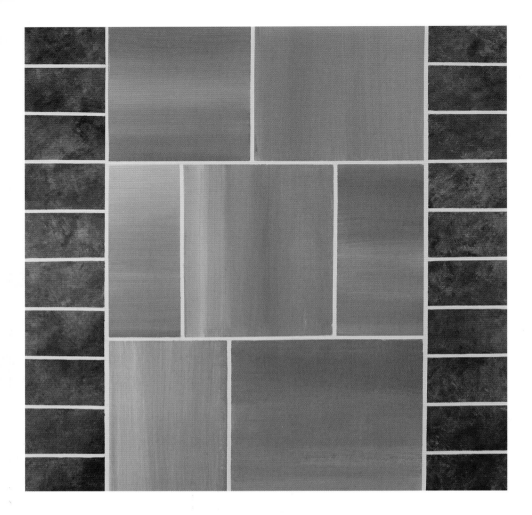

91 | Bluestone with Brick

TIRED OF THE concrete or cement patio slab? Think concrete or cement can't be painted? Oh, it can. At the paint store ask for a paint that will go on concrete or cement. Be sure to look at paint specific to either interiors or exteriors depending on your application. There are paints for masonry, cement, and concrete—and they are often water-based. So the sky is the limit when plotting your new patio.

The most important part is that your concrete or cement is very clean and very dry before you begin any applications.

If you get a bit of wear in your artwork you can either fix it or let the wear become part of the overall look.

Be brave and have fun turning the slab into something beautiful.

- ❖ Latex paint suitable for concrete, dark gray
- ❖ Medium value latex paint suitable for concrete, beige
- ❖ Latex paint suitable for concrete, black
- ❖ Latex paint suitable for concrete, brick red
- ❖ Painter's masking tape
- ❖ Flat latex paintbrush, 3" (7.6 cm)
- ❖ Lint-free rag
- ❖ Pail of water

1 Lay out your design.

2 Tape off what will be your grout lines and begin to apply paint to create the bluestone.

Dip the 3" (7.6 cm) brush into dark gray paint generously and paint in a couple of "rows."

Before the dark gray paint is dry, dip the same brush into the beige paint and apply paint next to and over the dark gray, lightly blending the two together.

To create texture, turn the brush sideways and pounce some of the paints together.

While all paints are still wet, stroke the paintbrush over the surface, blending and softening even further.

You could just tip your paintbrush into water to help with the blending.

The key is to keep all the paints wet so that you may soften and blend the colors together.

3 Continue until all bluestone is complete. Notice that the direction alters for the different pieces.

4 Paint in the brick. Pounce some black paint on. Pounce some brick red paint on and over and next to the black. Blend the two colors. While paint is wet, texture with a rag. Continue to use the rag to soften out the texture a bit.

Tip: Work only in an area you can reach at one time so you can keep the paints wet. The bluestone has a soft striation as its grain, so change the direction of the pieces for more interest.

92 | Venetian Pavers

TIRED OF YOUR existing pavers? Want to add some pizzazz or fun surprises? You can change the color of pavers.

This demonstration uses a "Venetian color palette," the brightly colored blues, reds, and yellows that you will find underfoot as you stroll through Venice. However, as is always the case, feel free to create your own palette!

Always use exterior paints if your pavers are outside and discuss with your paint salesperson the best paint to use for masonry. Remember, you can change the colors and make up colors by using your UTCs.

You will be applying and removing the paint, so if over time your painted areas show wear, relax and appreciate the natural wear and tear. The paint is supposed to look a bit old and worn!

MATERIALS & TOOLS

❖ Exterior latex masonry paint

❖ Angle-edged latex paintbrush, 2" (5.1 cm)

❖ UTCs (optional) to alter color

❖ Lint-free rag

1 Decide your pattern.

2 Apply your first color. Simply brush on, but do not get too far ahead of yourself, as you want to keep the paint wet to be able to rag some off.

If the paint seems too thick, or if you are in the sun and the paint is drying too quickly, dip your brush in water every other time before you load the brush with paint.

3 Before the yellow paint has dried, water-wash it by dipping the brush into water and wash over the applied yellow paint.

Immediately take a lint-free rag and rag off as much paint as you desire.

4 Continue the above steps—and sequence of paint, water, and rag—with your other colors until complete.

Tip: Do not dilute the paint too much with water, as this will weaken it. Instead try to apply it full-bodied and use a little water to just help rag off some paint.

Molding, Doors & GLASS

93 | Faux Bois Door

THIS TECHNIQUE IS wonderful for that fire door between your kitchen and garage or just anytime you might want to add a wood-grained door or match a door to existing woodwork found in a room.

If your woodwork is painted and you have a beautiful raised paneled door that is also painted, no need to go through the mess and fuss of stripping—merely wood-grain the door! A wood door set into painted frames and within a room where the woodwork has been painted are absolutely acceptable in terms of good design. Actually

quite a traditional approach was to highlight the beautiful wood of the door by leaving that the only element not painted.

Remember, you may choose any color for your door, deepen the color, and add a bit of antiquing to the wood graining once it has dried for a rich look. Or, you can lighten the wood graining once it has dried with a white color wash for a contemporary look.

Please read the demonstration for Faux Bois Repair, as the information will be helpful.

1 Primer and basecoat the door to be wood-grained. If you are matching existing wood, the basecoat should match the lightest color found in the wood you are matching.

Use a white, eggshell-sheen paint and color it with your UTCs if you do not want to buy a quart of paint.

2 Mix the desired wood-graining glaze by adding UTC colorant to satin oil varnish to achieve the desired color. If the varnish is too "sticky," you may add a small amount of mineral spirits to loosen the varnish up.

3 Apply the wood-graining glaze with a chip brush to the interior panels first.

4 Softly wipe through the glaze with a lint-free rag to create a wood pattern. Leave the recessed panel portion less textured.

5 With your flogger brush, start at the top of the panel and lightly flog downward. The pressure is light and the brush should be held almost parallel to the door surface.

Try not to hit the completed raised panel portion.

With a rag dampened with a bit of mineral spirits, wipe off excess glaze from around the panel.

6 Repeat steps 3, 4, and 5 along the rails doing one section at a time.

You may lightly tape over a glazed section (to get a nice crisp edge) once the varnish has dulled down. You may use a hair dryer to force-dry the varnish if you need to. Do not get fresh varnish on previously varnished surfaces.

94 | Faux Stainless Steel

HAVE A PERFECTLY good refrigerator, large or small, that no longer matches your décor? You do not have to look at it and not like it—paint it!

Great for wet bars, dorm rooms, or even the kitchen refrigerator.

Choose a latex-based metallic paint close to the color of your existing stainless. You may add a few drops of UTC to tweak the color if you need to. Or you might find that a warm champagne metallic mixed with a silver metallic will match the coloration.

Obviously this finish does not go well over the pebbly textured appliance fronts. But it does work well over flat fronts.

Dishwashers and trash compactors can both benefit from this technique.

You will want to prime the surface to be painted with a high-quality latex bonding primer tinted to a color close to your metallic color. The primer should be painted in the same fashion as described below for the metallic.

The reason being: stainless has a slight grain in it and you want to simulate that grain, so a slight linear pattern to your brushwork is desirable.

MATERIALS & TOOLS

- ❖ High-quality latex bonding primer, tinted to a color close to metallic color
- ❖ Metallic latex paint
- ❖ Flat latex paintbrush, 3" (7.6 cm) or 4" (10.2 cm)
- ❖ Metal straightedge
- ❖ Satin latex polyurethane

1 Prime your surface and allow to completely dry.

2 Apply the metallic paint in a very straight up-and-down manner with the paintbrush. To keep your strokes straight, place a straightedge onto the surface and use as a guide for your brush.

3 After the first coat of metallic paint has completely dried, apply a second coat in the same manner.

4 Clearcoat your artwork with durable latex polyurethane.

95 | Frosted Mirror

DO YOU HAVE a wall of mirrors that you want to freshen up? The use of an interesting stencil pattern and a can of "frosted glass" can add interest and a pattern to a room.

This pattern will bring a soft contemporary feel to any mirror.

This demonstration shows an overall coverage, but certainly feel free to mask off and apply as a border only if you so wish.

Make your job easier by using a simple design stencil. A larger and more simplistic design works best. The "frosted glass" used here was created with a spray can, which is an effective and easy application for simple designs.

Because you are working on a glass surface you should not use a low-tack stencil adhesive to keep in place, as it will transfer to the surface. A larger stencil is heavier and will lie flatter.

If you get tired of the look or wish to fix a mistake, simply scrape off with a safety razor, being careful not to scratch the glass, and wipe clean with some denatured alcohol.

Use the aerosol-frosted glass in a well-ventilated area and always follow the manufacturer's instructions.

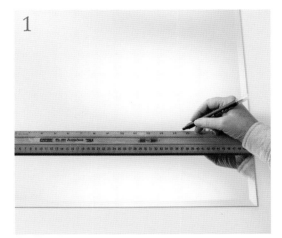

1 Before starting anything, make sure that your surface is clean and dry.

It is important to have the first stencil centered and straight, as you will be working from the stencil register marks after the first stencil is made.

Start in the middle of the wall, lining up the stencil on the centerline. Bubble rulers have a level on them and are very handy for keeping your work level.

2 Mark the face of the stencil with a piece of tape indicating the top.

Position the first stencil directly over the centerline and tape into place at the top corners.

Use the white paper to mask off all surrounding areas against overspray. Apply masking paper to the stencil, not the mirrored surface. You may keep this paper attached if it is not in your way.

Keeping one hand on the bottom of the stencil, spray on the frosted glass material. Use gloves because the frosted glass will get on your hands.

Spray the material in short bursts; do not apply heavily. Less is better.

Make sure to mark register marks with black water-based marker.

3 You may proceed horizontally or vertically, whichever you would prefer. Always make sure that the face of the stencil is toward you.

Always make sure your register marks are lined up.

Always make sure you have masked the surrounding area against overspray.

Continue until all the surface area is covered.

Allow to dry overnight and the next day you may clean up any mistakes or overspray carefully with a safety razor.

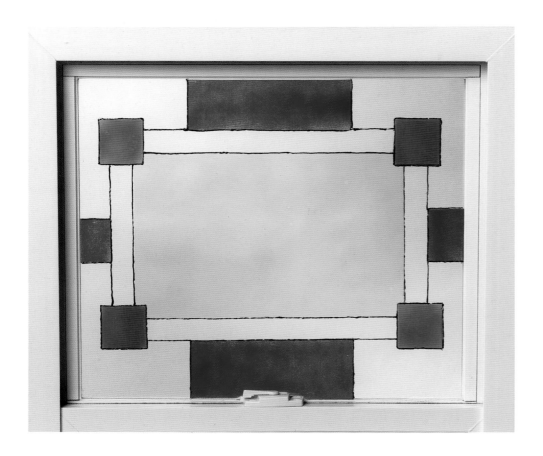

96 | Imitation Stained Glass

THIS DEMONSTRATION OUTLINES how to make any window look like a stained glass window. Use it to jazz up the boring sidelight windows to doors, or add something fun to your child's windows.

For those of us who do not know how to construct stained glass, this is an easy alternative and a versatile look to our windows.

If you get tired of the look, the paints and faux leading may be removed with a safety razor and/or lacquer thinner.

Follow a monochromatic color palette for a sophisticated look or add color and whimsy to any environment with this fun application.

There are many stained glass pattern books on the market from arts-and-crafts style to free form. Search and execute!

❖ White paper

❖ Clear plastic ruler, 2" (5.1 cm)

❖ Felt-tip marker

❖ Spray Stained Glass (found in crafts stores)

❖ Painter's masking tape, 6" (15.2 cm)

❖ Handheld masking machine

❖ Blue painter's tape

❖ Liquid leading

1 Lay out your pattern on a piece of paper first and when you are satisfied, transfer the pattern to the window by placing the drawn layout behind the glass surface you will be painting.

Using your marker, draw the pattern onto the front of the glass.

Mask off the area you will be spraying with the Spray Stained Glass and apply in short sweeping motions. Make sure all surrounding areas are masked off and protected from the Spray Stained Glass.

Do not spray too heavily, as the paint will run.

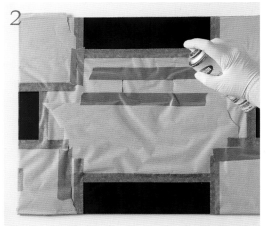

2 Repeat the masking and spraying of the red and blue Spray Stained Glass colors, allowing the dry time suggestions found on the label.

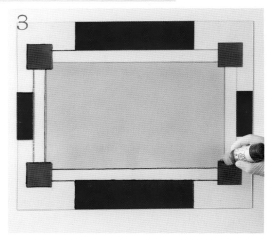

3 When all the colors have been applied and dried, apply the liquid leading material following the lines you made with your marker.

Note: You may do more intricate patterns if your glass is not installed. Simply find a pattern and set it underneath a piece of glass, sort of like a "paint by number." There are also stained glass paints that come in a liquid form which are better for the more intricate designs that you can do with your glass flat in front of you.

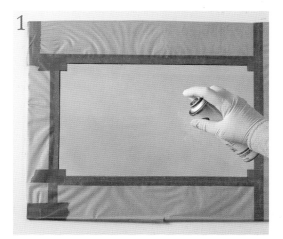

97 | Antiqued Crown Molding

THE QUESTION IS always: is the crown molding part of the wall or part of the ceiling? If the crown moldings are incorporated into the ceiling, you get a lovely "cap" or "lid" to your walls, so please, experiment with making the crown molding part of the ceiling.

The finish described here is a standard and easy antiquing demonstration. In fact, it's so easy that you may want to continue it onto all the painted woodwork in the room for a truly special look.

Soft and subtle, the slight antiquing gives interest and shading to white woodwork and softens the contrast between walls and ceilings.

The demonstration shows latex antiquing glaze over latex enamel. However, if your woodwork is painted in an oil enamel, please use an oil paint for the antiquing glaze mixed with the same proportions, but use alkyl glazing liquid, instead of water-based glazing liquid, and mineral spirits instead of water.

MATERIALS & TOOLS

- ❖ Flat latex paint, soft gray
- ❖ Glazing liquid
- ❖ Water
- ❖ Angle-edged latex paint-brush, 3" (7.6 cm)
- ❖ Lint-free rag

1 Mix the antiquing glaze: 1 part paint, 1 part glazing liquid, and 1 part water.

2 Brush the antiquing glaze into the recesses of the molding.

3 Load the brush with the glaze and draw over the entire surface with just one continuous stroke.

4 Immediately take a soft lint-free rag and with one stroke remove some of the glaze from the high points of the molding, leaving a heavier deposit in the low points. The trick is to keep working before the paint dries out, but you should have plenty of time. If you remove too much from certain areas, continue around the room; then go back and gently touch up.

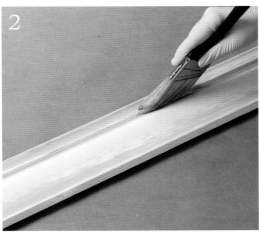

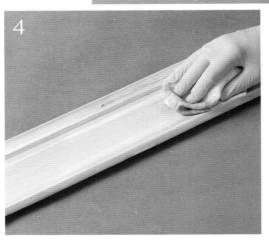

98 | Aged Molding

WHEN YOU WANT the look of aged and darkening varnish, this simple technique works well and is very easy.

A beautiful baseboard complement to a distressed floor, the molding will enhance the richness of the floor and create a unified design element within the room.

The technique is purposefully done to appear old and dark. It's a beautiful way to have a dark colored molding without having to paint it.

We are all accustomed to seeing light-colored moldings in a room, but for a dramatic change try going to the dark side—the result can be quite stunning and handsome.

This treatment will warm a room up and speak of a long life.

No glaze is mixed in this demonstration because the black paint is used full-bodied.

This finish is for use on raw wood.

1 Apply the Golden Oak gel stain to 100% of the surface with a lint-free rag.

2 Immediately apply the Dark Walnut gel stain with a lint-free rag, not all over but rather selectively, into the crevices and along the edges, pulling some onto the flat face portion of the board and blend together with the Golden Oak.

Work the two stains together with a lint-free rag.

Allow the gel stains to dry, following the label instructions.

3 Thinly apply the black paint into the recesses and along the edges and some of the face.

Immediately wipe with a soft water-dampened rag to remove, blend into, and soften the black paint.

If the paint feels too thick, dip your brush in a bit of water—not too much, just a tip.

Do not apply too much black paint; you want to be able to pull the black paint out onto the surface and remove.

Tip: Work quickly so that the black paint remains wet and able to be removed and blended.

Remember that if the black latex paint dries out on you, denatured alcohol on a rag will remove it.

Note: The rags from the gel stains are flammable; follow manufacturer's label instructions on proper disposal. Do NOT leave the rags lying out after use.

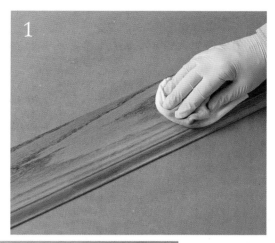

99 | Metallic Tiles

HAVE YOU EVER tried to dig out just a few tiles? Not very easy… Want to add a bit of something new to your tile walls?

Metallic tiles are quite popular now and are not cheap, so this demonstration will show you how you can simply paint your own right onto your existing tiles.

Consider using an existing pattern that also might be in the room. Couple the metallic look with a frosted mirror (page 236) or complement a stained glass window that you have made for the window (page 238). Or simply randomly decide to make certain tiles metallic. No need to limit yourself to just one metallic color—consider copper, gold, and aluminum!

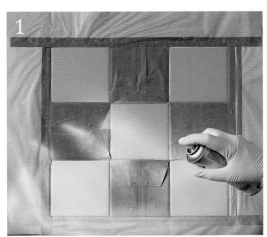

1 Mask off the surrounding tiles from the ones you want to apply the metallic paint to.

Run the tape just along the edge of the grout where it meets the tile.

Make sure everything around the area to be sprayed is well masked. Spray the primer on.

2 Immediately remove all tape and masking paper. When primer is dry, re-tape the tiles that are to receive the metallic paint.

Cut a small 2" x 2" (5.1 x 5.1 cm) piece of sponge from a larger wallpaper sponge.

Apply the metallic paint to the primed tiles with the sponge.

Dab the paint straight up and down until you have eliminated the air bubbles.

Immediately pull the tape before the metallic paint dries; otherwise the tape will most likely pull the dried metallic paint off along the edges.

100 | Reverse Color Molding

PEOPLE ALWAYS PAINT their moldings white—why not do the opposite and paint them black? A black molding is a dramatic molding and really is a lovely touch to any color scheme. Black, just like white, goes with anything—it is merely the opposite end of the spectrum.

To further add a touch of intrigue and mystery to the color black, this demonstration will show you how a few extra steps will really make the black molding a special and sophisticated element.

While this demonstration shows the high contrast of beige against black in the early stages, if you like the appearance of your molding with just these colors painted on, feel free to consider yourself finished!

You may also use a color other than beige and merely use that color in place of the beige as outlined in the following instructions.

1 The molding has been primed first in a color very close to the beige eggshell enamel paint.

Paint the narrow section of the molding with the beige enamel paint.

2 When the beige paint is dry, paint on the black eggshell enamel paint.

Note: No need to tape, merely cut in the black paint. The line does not have to be perfect—but close.

Also, the black paint does not have to be 100% opaque—but close.

3 When all paint is dry, mix a black glaze (⅓ black paint, ⅓ latex glazing liquid, and ⅓ water) and carefully brush over the beige paint.

Before the paint is dry, wipe with a lint-free rag to lightly antique the beige paint.

If you like the molding at this point, you are done.

4 Once the beige paint has dried, apply beige glaze (⅓ beige paint, ⅓ latex glazing liquid, and ⅓ water) over the black portion of the molding.

Before the beige paint is dry, rag off as much as you want of the beige paint.

Note: When moving from one section to the next, do not apply the glaze right where you left off. Instead start a little ahead and feather the paint back into the previously painted area.

If the glaze seems too "wet," add more paint and glazing liquid in equal amounts to thicken up.

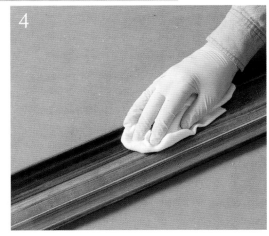

Furniture

Creative FURNITURE EFFECTS

101   Negoro Nuri

102   Steel Wool Stria

103   Mottled

104   Textured Plaster

105   Photo Montage

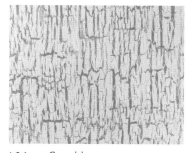
106   Crackle

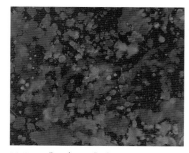
107   Broken Paint

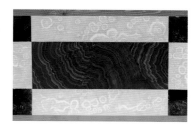
108   Intarsia

109   Striping

110   Soft Geometry

111   Torn Paper

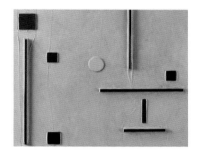

112   Words & Numbers

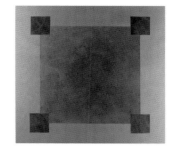

113   From the Can

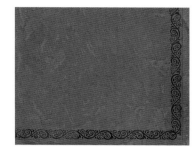

114   Stamping

115   Found Objects

116   Magnetic Paint

117   Chalkboard Paint

118   Checkerboard Tabletop

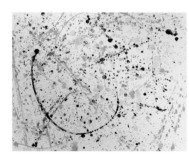

119   Drip & Spill

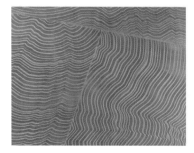

120   Squeegee Combing

Fabulous
FURNITURE
FAKES

121   Faux Tiles

122   Parchment

123   Faux Marquetry

124   Faux Leather

125   Shagreen

126   Faux Goatskin

127   Malachite

128   Faux Stone

129   Marble

130   Shaker Finish

131   Burled Wood

132   Basic Wood Graining

133   Mahogany

134   Rust

135   Bronze

136   Verdigris Patina

137   Provincial Lapis

DECORATIVE PAINTING TECHNIQUES

Antiquing & GILDING

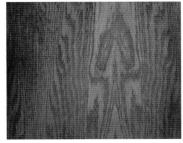

138   Stain Antiquing

139   Staining & Distressing

140   Distressed Latex

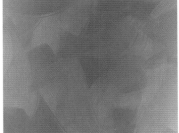

141   Oil Paint Antiquing

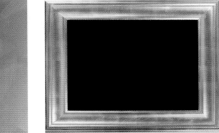

142   Aluminum Gilding

143   Copper Gilding

144   Burnished Metal

145   Carved Surface Gilding

146   Tarnished Patina

147   Noton

148   Antiqued Gold

149   Pickling

150   Trompe L'oeil Panel

Furniture Painting Basics

Furniture Finishes

Paints offer versatility in color, composition, and opacity. They bring finishes to life or serve as a base for glazes.

Latex

Buy latex paint from a paint store, not a craft store; it's less expensive and comes in larger containers. It comes in four sheens: flat, very dull when dry; eggshell, very low sheen; semigloss, and gloss. Eggshell, semi-gloss, and gloss are poor choices for the techniques in this book as they are too "slippery."

Oil-based

Oil-based paint is also purchased at a paint or home store and available in the same four sheen levels. Oil-based eggshell sheen is called "low luster." Low luster is the only sheen used in the techniques, although gloss is recommended as a topcoat on some finishes.

Japan Color

This is a super finely ground color pigment mixed with a drying agent. An oil-based paint, it comes premixed in small containers and is available in a wide variety of colors. Japan Color paint dries completely flat and is desirable owing to the radiance of its colors. Japan Colors can be found online or at good woodworking stores.

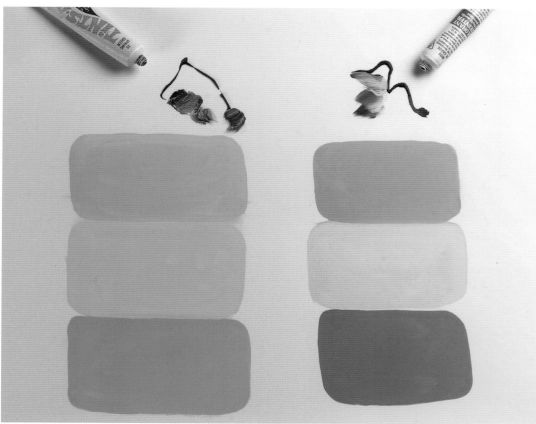

Artist Tube Paints

Either acrylic- or oil-based tube paints can be used when you need only a small amount of a color. They cost more per ounce than any other paint. If you use artist oils, mix two- or three-parts paint with one-part alkyd glazing liquid and a small amount of mineral spirits to promote drying.

Milk Paint

This paint is also called casein paint. It is truly milk-based. Milk paint comes as a dry powder to be mixed with water. It's very good for certain finishes, but is the weakest and least durable of all the paints.

Universal Tinting Colorant (UTC)

UTC is not paint, but an additive used to tint all types of paint. In fact, it's used in the machine at the paint store to color paint. UTC comes in small tubes or pint sizes; buy the smallest tube, as it is a very powerful color agent. In addition to tinting paint, it also tints varnishes. UTCs never dry on their own, so wipe up spills quickly or the UTC will spread over everything. UTCs are transparent until added to paint.

All About Product Compatibility

Latex (water-based) paint may be put over any latex product but not over an oil-based product. Water is the solvent for latex products, and is used to remove or thin the paint.

Oil-based paints may be put over oil-based and latex products. Mineral spirits or paint thinner are the solvents for oil-based products, and are used to remove or thin the paint.

Acrylic-based varnishes may be applied over latex products. Oil-based varnishes may be applied over oil-based and latex products. Lower-sheen varnishes go over higher-sheen varnishes as the higher the sheen, the stronger the varnish. It is common to apply the first varnish coat in a gloss and then the sheen of choice.

Polishing waxes may be applied over latex or oil-based products.

Caution: Although there are a number of good spray varnishes and topcoats on the market, some of these may be incompatible with certain paints and cause lifting or cracking (called crazing). Always ask at the paint store if a spray product may be applied over your paint. An incompatibility could destroy your work. Never use spray lacquers as they are dangerous to your health and the environment.

Equipment

The instructions for all finishes in this book assume you have a basic painting kit when you begin a project. Always buy high-quality tools and materials (both for your kit and for your project supplies), as they help you achieve the best results.

- 220-grit sandpaper (used whenever a grit is not specified in the materials list)
- 400- and 600-grit wet/dry sandpaper
- Tack cloths to remove sanding dust and to prepare the surface for topcoating
- Drop cloths to protect work area floors
- Stir sticks for mixing
- Empty paint containers (with lids) for mixing and dirty rag disposal
- Foam roller, 5" (12.7 cm)
- Roller handle to use with the roller
- Paint tray
- Dust masks
- Gloves
- Safety glasses
- Blue painter's masking tape
- Craft knife
- Tape machine (this makes taping a breeze)

All About Glazes

A glaze is paint thinned to a slightly transparent quality and the consistency of whole milk. The binding agent in paint loses strength when thinned with a solvent, but glazing liquid restores strength to paint. Glazing liquid is clear, flat, and does not affect the color of the paint.

Varnish tinted with a small amount of paint also acts as a glaze. UTC may be used to tint a varnish for a very transparent glaze.

The basic recipe for a latex paint glaze is one-part paint, one-part acrylic glazing liquid, and one-part water. Add the water slowly to avoid thinning the glaze too far (add more paint and glazing liquid if this occurs). If the glaze appears too thick, add more water.

The basic recipe for an oil glaze is one-part paint, one-part alkyd glazing liquid, and two-parts mineral spirits. Add the mineral spirits slowly to avoid thinning the glaze too far (add more paint and glazing liquid if this oc-curs). If the glaze appears too thick, add more mineral spirits.

Many standard glazes are used with the finishes in this book. Two fun variations are tinted oil-based varnish and stained overglaze.

Tinted Oil Varnish

Tint oil varnish slightly with UTC burnt umber and UTC raw umber. Apply using a paintbrush or foam roller. This offers a lovely, slightly aged transparent quality.

Stained Overglaze

For oil-based paints, mix one-part paint, one-part alkyd glazing liquid, and eight-parts mineral spirits. For latex paints, mix one-part paint, one-part acrylic glazing liquid, and eight-parts water. Apply using a paintbrush or foam roller. The glaze will be skim milk consistency. Overglazes help reduce contrast and also add translucent beauty to surfaces.

All About Stains

Use stains to add color to wood. There are many colors and types, and compatible types may be mixed to make custom colors. Whatever type of stain you choose, wipe it on with one lint-free T-shirt rag and wipe it off with a clean one.

Always wear safety glasses, dust masks, and gloves, as necessary, to protect yourself when sanding and working with paints and solvents. Always read manufacturer's instructions for proper cleanup and disposal information. Always work in well-ventilated areas to avoid build-up of fumes.

Stains and rags used for staining are combustible. Linseed oil (found in most staining materials) causes them to give off heat as they dry, enabling them to self-combust. *Never* throw a dirty staining rag in your trash. Fill an empty gallon-size paint container with water. When finished staining, immerse the rags in the water and tightly seal the lids. Dispose of the materials properly.

Gel Stains

Full-bodied gel stains are easy to work with and can be used as an overglaze right from the can. You can find them in paint stores. In the top example, a red mahogany was applied over birch wood.

Pure Color Stains

Pure color stains come in vivid colors. You can find them at woodworkers' stores. In the middle example, a bright cheerful green was applied over birch wood. Mix the Japan Color to a skim milk consistency with mineral spirits; wipe it on and then immediately wipe off the project surface. Unlike gels or pure color stains, paint-based Japan Color is compatible with all oil paints, so any oil paint may easily be applied over it. In the bottom example, a Prussian blue was applied over birch wood.

All About Topcoats

"Topcoat" refers to any medium that protects a furniture surface. Varnish and wax are used on the projects featured in this book as they are good topcoats and the easiest to apply.

Varnish

Oil-based varnishes tend to level out (flow together) better than water-base varnishes, and they offer a richer appearance. Never apply a water-based varnish over an oil-based varnish.

Always use the highest quality paintbrush possible to apply varnish, and keep that paintbrush exclusively for varnishing. Load your brush with roughly 1" (1.3 cm) of varnish, and lay-off (apply) quickly, always ending in a full top-to-bottom or side-to-side stroke and continuing until the project surface is evenly coated. Never over-brush varnish; it will set too quickly and refuse to level out. Good varnishing takes practice and the more you do it, the better you will become.

Do not thin varnish. You may gently heat oil varnish to help it level out. Put the amount you need in a clean container. Set the container in a pot of *previously* boiled water.

The higher the gloss level, the stronger a varnish dries. Apply a gloss varnish as the first topcoat; then apply subsequent layers in the sheen of choice. Lightly wet-sand the dry gloss varnish with 400-grit wet/dry sandpaper before applying a lower sheen. The three sheen levels (shown in the top example) for either oil-based or water-based varnishes are gloss, satin, and dull/flat.

Wax

Wax gives a beautiful hand-rubbed gleam to surfaces. Paste wax with a high carnauba content produces a very strong finish. The bottom example shown is a pecan-stained pine board finished with three coats of paste wax.

Basecoat Techniques

A good basecoat takes a finish from just okay to "oh-my-gosh" extraordinary. It's important to properly clean and prime surfaces to be painted not only to provide a smooth, even surface for the paint but also to get the most life out of your finish paint. A proper basecoat allows your finish paint to cover more surface and last longer.

Cleaning

This is the simplest of all the basecoats. Clean the entire furniture piece with denatured alcohol using #000 steel wool; then wipe the entire surface with a lint-free rag and denatured alcohol. Sand with 150-grit sandpaper and wipe again. The denatured alcohol will remove old wax, polishing product residue, grease, and grime. If a furniture piece requires stripping of layers of stain or paint, refer to the manufacturer's instructions for any product you choose to use.

Priming

If you will be painting on raw wood, or if the surface is already painted with an unknown type of paint, repaint the surface with a primer. A good primer seals the surface, covers undesirable stains, stops bleed-through, and prevents paint adhesion problems.

Primers come in latex and oil-based formulas, but use acrylic bonding primer as it is better for the environment and for you. For small pieces such as chairs and for carved items such as picture or mirror frames, spray primers are a sensible choice.

TIP FROM THE AUTHOR

The Base of Success
The success of the basecoat dictates the success of the finish. Before basecoating a previously stained or painted surface, thoroughly clean the surface to be painted. Unless otherwise specified, apply painted basecoats with a 5" (12.7 cm) foam roller. Allow the paint to dry; then sand with 220-grit sandpaper. Remove the sanding dust with a tack cloth.

Brushing

On the example shown, primer is being applied with a 2" (5.1 cm) angled-edge latex paintbrush. Paint the interior of an inset before other areas, and always follow the grain of the wood when applying primer. Be as neat as if applying a finish paint coat.

Rolling

If the area is large or you are unsure of your brushing ability, use a combination of brushing and rolling. First, brush primer neatly into recesses, corners, and edges, and then using a 5" (12.7) foam roller, apply primer to the remaining surface.

Avoid overloading the foam roller. Load the foam roller in the roller tray; then roll off some of the primer on scrap wood or in a clean area of the tray. It's best to apply a thin coat of primer on your project surface. The beauty of using a foam roller is it leaves very little "roller stipple." Keep rolling the primer, with a light pressure, until you have a very smooth application with low roller stipple. Practice loading and rolling, as it will save you irritation when priming large surfaces.

Spraying

Zinsser B-I-N® is a white shellac-based primer. It is an extremely effective sealant for most surfaces and may be sprayed on. Follow the manufacturer's label instructions.

Tip: Shellac-based products are alcohol based. If you get a big drip or paint sag, allow it to dry, then rub it smooth with a little denatured alcohol. Most sags and drips flatten on their own.

DECORATIVE PAINTING TECHNIQUES

Painting Techniques

These are the methods of removing, adding, or manipulating paints and glazes used in this book.

Tufbacking

Tufbacking is also known as wet sanding. The technique works best on oil-based paints and sprayed enamels.

This technique takes a surface from nice to knockout. Tufback after the final oil-based paint basecoat, after the final basecoat before gilding, and after the second-to-last coat of varnish.

After the final coat of paint or varnish is dry, spray a workable area of the project surface with water using a spray bottle. Use 400-grit wet/dry sandpaper, and sand using a small circular motion. Wipe the water off frequently with paper towels to check your progress. Be patient; there is no way to hurry this process. Do the final sanding with the 600-grit wet/dry sandpaper. When are you done? Dry the surface and look at it sideways and on an angle. The surface should have an even sheen and be as smooth as glass.

Laying Off

There is a proper stroking method to achieve an even coat of paint. Use short up-and-down, then back-and-forth strokes, ending with one soft, long pull end to end. This evenly distributes the paint, producing a smooth paint layer. This needs to be done quickly to allow the wet paint areas to blend together readily.

Blending

After applying a coat of oil-based paint, but before it sets up, use a dry oil paintbrush to gently brush in a crosshatch pattern over the top of the paint. This softly blends the paint and knocks down paintbrush ridges.

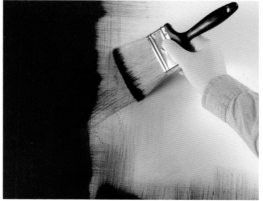

Distressing and Aging: Techniques and Tools

Distressing a surface means to physically mar it to suggest the wear and tear of age. To distress paint means making it appear rubbed off or worn away. Physical distressing can be a lot of fun.

Hammer

You simply pound the surface. Wear will happen in predictable places, so examine the furniture piece to decide where wear might have occurred. Then go for it!

Nail

Lay a nail on its side and pound the nail head with a hammer. Create small holes by pounding only the point of the nail into the project surface. Press and drag a nail along the surface to make a deep scratch.

Chisel

Use a wood chisel to make factory-fresh surfaces look like they've been around for a while. Carve off corners and crisp edges, and gouge deep into the surface for extreme wear.

Sandpaper

Use 100-grit sandpaper to pull paint off edges and corners revealing the wood underneath. Sand paint off larger areas to simulate wear. A bonus to using sandpaper to distress is that you have also sanded the surface smooth.

Antiquing: Positive Method

To antique a surface using the positive method means to apply paint, varnish, or stain, to suggest age.

When you antique, allow the antiquing glaze to remain heavier in the corners and the recesses of the surface where dirt and dust would normally build up. Apply the antiquing glaze with a paintbrush, wipe the surface with a soft lint-free T-shirt rag, and then softly blend with a clean paint-brush to remove obvious brushstrokes.

In the example shown, a warm, almost dusty, colored gray glaze was applied over a red basecoat.

Antiquing: Negative Method

Antiquing with the negative method means to remove paint—it simulates wear that rubbed the paint down to the base over years of use.

To remove oil paint, use sandpaper. To remove latex paint, dip a T-shirt rag into denatured alcohol and rub the area where you want to remove the paint, using both circular and up-and-down motions. A believable and soft aging occurs with no need for sanding.

In the example shown, a coat of flat blue latex was applied over a primer coat and allowed to dry. Denatured alcohol was then used to remove the paint in logical "wear" areas.

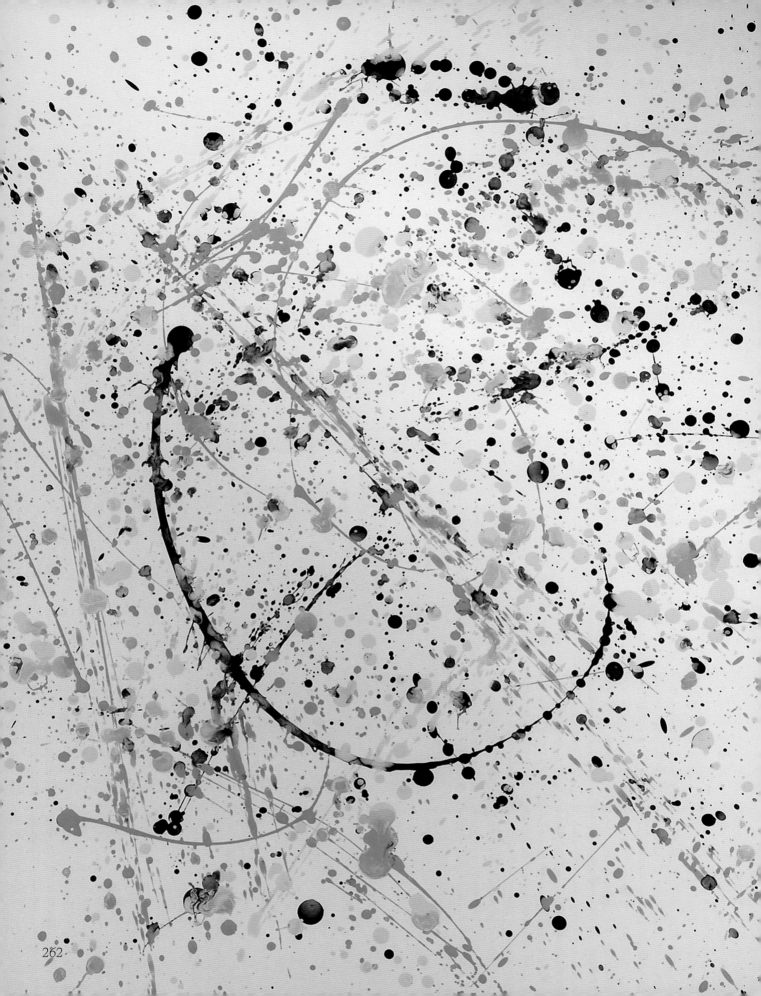

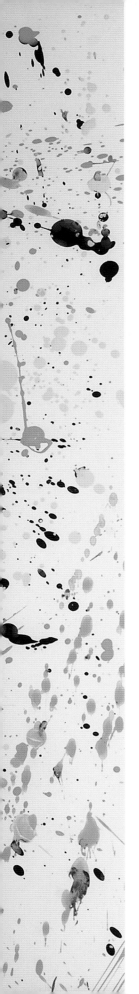

Creative FURNITURE EFFECTS

THIS ELEGANT FINISH reproduces the lacquerware techniques used by Japanese monks since the fourteenth century. They first applied a black lacquer basecoat followed by a red lacquer coat. As the objects were used, the red wore away revealing the black underneath. The Negoro Nuri finish requires a bit of patience, restraint, and thoughtfulness but the dramatic result is very rewarding.

For best results, choose furniture with straight lines and objects of simple design. Study your furniture piece and imagine where the natural wear patterns will be. Edges, corners, legs, and tops are the most common. The appearance will be most believable and graceful if the wear pattern is asymmetrical.

101 | Negoro Nuri

Pick a bright red with a slight orangey undertone. The traditional colors of this finish are red over black, but experiment if you're a rebel.

Because the finish is achieved by "tufbacking" (page 259), it is necessary to use oil-based paints. Numerous coats of the black and the red also must be evenly applied, with overnight drying times. This is where the patience comes in. Take your time and enjoy watching the finish emerge.

Refer to Tufbacking (page 259).

MATERIALS & TOOLS

- ❖ Flat/matte oil-based or spray paint, black
- ❖ Flat* oil-based paint, red/ orange

  *satin may be substituted if necessary

- ❖ Mineral spirits
- ❖ Flat oil paintbrush, 3" (7.6 cm)
- ❖ Paper towels or clean rags

- ❖ Spray bottle
- ❖ Wet/dry sandpaper, 400- and 600-grit
- ❖ Gloss oil-based varnish

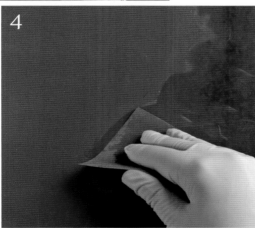

1 Basecoat the project surface with three coats of black paint using the paintbrush, or spray paint applied carefully in very thin coats. Avoid sags and drips. Sand between coats with 220-grit sandpaper. Allow it to dry.

2 Apply at least three thin coats of red/orange paint, alternating the direction of brushing with each one and allowing each to dry overnight. Aim for an even coverage without many brushstrokes. If the paint is difficult to spread, thin it slightly with no more than 20 percent mineral spirits. The thinner the paint, the more coats you will need to apply. Allow the final coat to dry for at least 24 hours.

3 Wet the surface slightly by misting water over the surface with the spray bottle before beginning to sand. Keep the surface wet while sanding. Work in small circular patterns using the 400-wet/dry sandpaper to remove all brushstrokes and imperfections. Wipe the surface frequently. The red should look and feel mirror smooth. Some of the black will begin to shadow through. Take your time, and slowly reveal the beauty.

4 After determining the natural wear patterns, use the 600-wet/dry sandpaper to "pull out" the black. Use a back-and-forth sanding motion until the black begins to appear; then use a combination of circular and back-and-forth sanding patterns for the most natural look. Create irregular black areas with tapering tops and bottoms. The black will come through an already shadowed area easier, and more believably.

5 When you are satisfied with your result, clean the surface with a soft cloth, and allow it to dry. Topcoat with one or two coats of varnish.

102 | Steel Wool Stria

THIS VERSATILE TECHNIQUE
gives you a soft, linear, textural pattern. It's appropriate for any piece
of furniture, whether traditional or
contemporary.

Although it stands on its own merit,
try it as a background for painted embellishments or other finishes. Achieve an
interesting look by stamping or painting
a freehand design and then using the
Steel Wool Stria technique over it.

Adjust the degree of transparency
by mixing more or less paint to glazing
liquid. Mix more glazing liquid into the
paint for a more transparent glaze.

Here's a general rule of thumb for
choosing your colors: if your basecoat
is light, use a darker glaze; if it's dark,
use a lighter glaze; and with a medium
value basecoat, either way works.

1 Basecoat the project surface with the medium gray paint until opaque; allow the paint to dry after each coat.

Note: You may use any type of paint, but if the basecoat is an oil-based paint, you *must* use an oil-based glaze. You may apply an oil-based glaze over latex paint.

2 Mix a glaze using one-part white paint, one-part glazing liquid, and slightly less than one-part water. Apply the glaze to an area small enough to allow you to complete the next two steps easily. Do *not* allow the glaze to dry as you work.

3 Pull through the glaze lightly using a small wad of cheesecloth, and taking care not to remove all the glaze.

Tip: If you remove too much glaze and your surface is still wet, brush on some more.

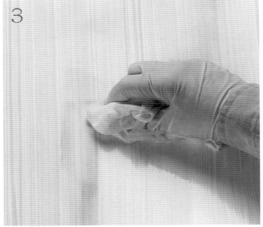

4 Drag the steel wool pad through the glaze using a medium steady pressure. Pull straight down or across the surface. You may do this more than once.

5 Topcoat with one or two coats of varnish.

103 | Mottled

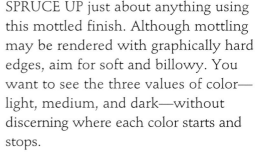

SPRUCE UP just about anything using this mottled finish. Although mottling may be rendered with graphically hard edges, aim for soft and billowy. You want to see the three values of color—light, medium, and dark—without discerning where each color starts and stops.

With this easy finish, you apply paint straight from the can—no mixing glazes! Latex paint is most often used, but if you choose oil-based paint, a very softly blended look develops.

This finish is flexible and adaptable. To give this highly contemporary finish an antique feel, use deep browns. For a self-sealed surface, use paints with different sheens. It's even easy to touch up bangs and bumps if you record the paint colors used when you apply the finish.

The paint must stay wet while you work this finish. The finish develops in a sequence. You'll apply light, then medium, then dark paint, covering a smaller area, and then you'll repeat the sequence. Simply wipe, no need to clean, the brush between paint colors.

Refer to French Brush (page 140).

1 Basecoat the project surface with the primer.

2 Load the paintbrush generously with the white paint and apply using the French brush technique over about 75 percent of the surface (if small) or not larger than a 12" × 12" (30.5 × 30.5 cm) area. Wipe the paintbrush on a rag or paper towel, but do not clean. Load the paintbrush generously with the beige paint and apply in and around the white paint, covering approximately 40 percent of the project surface.

3 Load the paintbrush with the gray paint (use less than the other colors), and apply in and around the beige and white areas, covering about 15 percent of the surface.

Tip: Imagine the gray as a shadow and the most buried color. It is the gray that allows the finish to have depth and it should move through the surface.

4 Apply more white and blend it into the gray; pick up the beige and blend; pick up the gray and blend. Continue this rhythm until the entire piece is painted.

Tip: Try to avoid blotches. Think of working back and forth among the colors and in and out of various areas.

5 Topcoat with one or two coats of varnish.

104 | Textured Plaster

SOMETIMES THE MOST common object creates an uncommon look. This very textural finish appears much more sophisticated than the material used to achieve it—an ordinary fiberglass window screen.

Although especially suitable for contemporary designs and flat surfaces, the Textured Plaster technique can be used on a traditional piece for an interesting visual contrast.

This piece was created using a random pattern to apply and to remove the plastering compound. You can achieve other looks by using an even application or removing in an all-over pattern. Make sure the piece of screen you use is slightly larger than the project surface for ease when handling. Screening comes in many widths, giving you the opportunity to work on almost any size project.

MATERIALS & TOOLS

- ❖ All-purpose joint compound
- ❖ White glue, Elmer's® Glue-all
- ❖ Spreading knife, 6" (15.2 cm)
- ❖ Screen material, fiberglass
- ❖ Sandpaper, 150-grit
- ❖ Eggshell latex paint

- ❖ Latex paintbrush, 4" (10.2 cm)
- ❖ Flat oil-based paint, light beige
- ❖ Mineral spirits
- ❖ Flat oil paintbrush, 3" (7.6 cm)
- ❖ Cheesecloth, 90-weight
- ❖ Flat oil-based varnish

1 No basecoat is necessary with this technique. The wood may be unfinished, painted, or varnished. If varnished or painted, sand with 150-grit sandpaper to roughen.

2 Mix nine-parts all-purpose joint compound with *exactly* one-part white glue. Apply randomly to the surface leaving some voids and low spots.

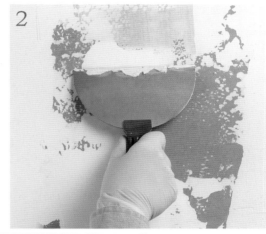

3 Place a flat piece of fiberglass screen over the wet joint compound. Press the screen into the wet compound with the spreading blade; then remove the excess compound from the back of the screen. Remove the screen and allow the surface to dry completely.

4 Sand lightly to remove any burrs and nubs. Apply two coats of latex paint to the entire surface using the latex paintbrush. Avoid flooding the screen indentations with paint. Allow the paint to dry.

5 Thin the oil-based paint to skim milk consistency with mineral spirits, and apply using the oil paintbrush. Allow the paint to dry only until it takes on a matte look (usually 10 to 20 minutes). Do not allow it to dry completely. With a piece of cheesecloth slightly dampened with mineral spirits, remove the oil-based paint from the surface, leaving paint in the recessed areas.

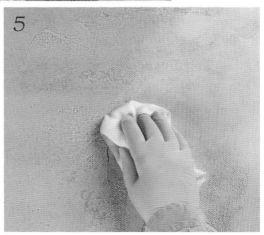

6 Topcoat with one or two coats of varnish.

WONDERING WHAT TO DO with the many photographs stored in your computer? Take them beyond a scrapbook or a silver frame set on a table—let them become the table! Imagine a child's headboard covered with favorite images. This finish is not decoupage, but a modern application of paper to a piece of furniture. Whether following a theme or choosing random much-loved photos, your work is sure to be a conversation piece.

A computer, a basic photo-editing program, and a printer allow flexibility, as you can manipulate the size and color of the images, but photocopies can be used as long as they are produced on matte-finish photo-grade paper. Photocopying allows you to change color into black and white,

105 | Photo Montage

and alter the size of the image to fit the surface as well. Stiffer magazine covers also work, offering themes for teens to toddlers.

When working with photographic images, never use your originals. Store them in a safe place and use copies.

The images used in this project started as color photographs. After duplicating the image in an editing program, the copy was converted to a sepia tone to add a bit of age.

For best results, print your images on matte-finish photo-grade computer printing paper.

❖ Flat latex paint, black

❖ Matte finish photo-grade computer printing paper

❖ Wallpaper cutting blade

❖ Metal straightedge or ruler

❖ Chalk, white

❖ Painter's masking tape

❖ Smooth, acid-free artist sketchbook pad, 18" × 24" (45.7 × 61 cm)

❖ Spray adhesive, 3M Spray 77®

❖ Wax paper

❖ Rubber roller

❖ Satin oil-based varnish

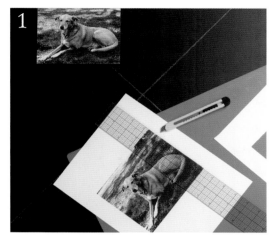

1 Basecoat the project surface with the black paint. Trim the white borders from all images using the cutting blade and a metal straightedge or clear acrylic ruler.

Tip: Determine the size of the area your photocopies will cover and which photos will be placed "portrait" or "landscape." Size your images appropriately before printing.

2 Draw two diagonal lines with chalk to find the center intersection of the surface. Locating the center helps facilitate a balanced composition.

3 Place a number of images on the surface and move them around until you find a pleasing composition. Keep your composition in place by sticking a loop of painter's tape *very lightly* to the back of one image, then replace it. Repeat with all the photos.

4 Lift one image and remove its tape. Lay the image back side up on a clean sketchbook page. Lightly apply an even coat of spray adhesive across the entire back. Place the image back carefully, for you will *not* be able to reposition it.

5 Place a sheet of wax paper over the image. Roll it smooth using the rubber roller and flatten any bubbles or air pockets. Smooth with clean fingers, if necessary. Repeat steps 4 and 5 with all images. Allow the surface to dry for 24 hours.

6 Topcoat with one or two coats of satin oil-based varnish.

Tip: When applying the varnish, the photo paper may bubble. Don't worry. Press the image flat with a fingertip once the varnish is dry.

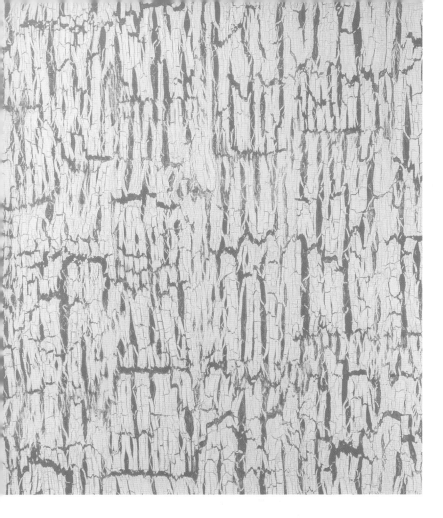

106 | Crackle

A CRACKLED FINISH is fun on just about anything. The weathered look rescues even battered furniture, giving it shabby chic style.

Crackles can be as large as in the example shown or as fine as the cracks in porcelain. You control the size of the crackle by the type of crackle product used and by varying the thickness of the overcoat paint.

There are many crackle products; however, the best choice is crackle from a paint store rather than a craft store. The containers are larger and the medium is less expensive. Check the label to find out if you are purchasing a large- or small-crackle material.

An overglaze of dark gel stain antiques the finish further. It's a lovely option, especially if you are using small porcelain crackle material.

❖ Eggshell latex paint, gray
❖ Flat latex paintbrush, 4" (10.2 cm)
❖ Crackle medium, Modern Masters® Crackle
❖ Flat latex paint, white
❖ Hair dryer (optional)
❖ Gel stain (optional)
❖ Flat oil-based varnish

1 Basecoat the project surface with the gray paint.

2 Apply a thin, even coat of the crackle medium with the paintbrush. Allow it to dry for at least one hour.

3 Use full-bodied white paint (straight from the can) to achieve the cracks pictured here. Apply the paint with an even stroke from top to bottom.

Note: If you reload the paintbrush, continue painting where you left off. Avoid over-brushing. Do not brush back and forth.

Tip: Instead of using a paintbrush to apply the crackle medium and the paint, you may use a skinny foam roller. Roll in a straight one-way direction, slightly overlapping adjacent sections.

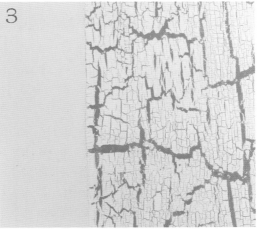

4 After you have applied the paint over the entire surface, you can force-dry the cracks with a hair dryer.

5 If desired, apply a coat of gel stain to further age your surface.

6 Topcoat with one or two coats of varnish. Apply *only* an oil-based varnish, as a water-based varnish will dissolve the crackle material.

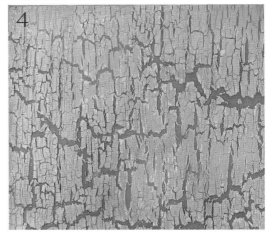

PUTTING TWO INCOMPATIBLE products together can cause a wonderful reaction. This stunning abstract finish was created with just one color over a basecoat.

If the richness of this deep blue intrigues you, use Japan Color paint. The Japan Color palette contains numerous, beautifully deep colors that match artist oil colors. They are sold in small 6-ounce (170 g) cans—no waste with quarts!

Most important, Japan Color dries flat. Standard paint-store paint only approaches this depth of color with paints that have a sheen (such as eggshell), and this technique requires a flat paint.

107 | Broken Paint

The blue used on this surface is Japan Color ultramarine blue. The basecoat is a very light gray. The gray basecoat offers a subtle contrast. To reduce the contrast even further, use a darker gray basecoat. For a higher contrast, use a white basecoat.

MATERIALS & TOOLS

- ❖ Eggshell latex paint, light gray
- ❖ Foam roller, 4" (10.2 cm)
- ❖ Mineral spirits
- ❖ Japan Color, ultramarine blue
- ❖ Two paint pails

- ❖ Flat oil paintbrush, 3" (7.6 cm)
- ❖ Hair dryer
- ❖ Oval sash paintbrush, 2" (5.1 cm)
- ❖ T-shirt rags
- ❖ Oil-based varnish

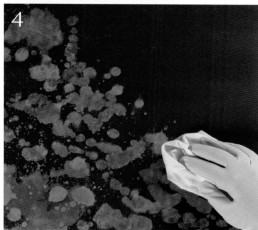

1 Basecoat the project surface with the light gray paint using the foam roller. Allow to dry overnight to cure (harden) the paint so the surface isn't absorbent.

2 Thin the ultramarine blue to a whole milk consistency with mineral spirits in a paint pail. Apply one coat using the flat paintbrush.

3 Dry the just applied blue paint with a hair dryer only until the shine disappears (the paint must be fresh to "bloom" properly. Do not over dry. Pour a small amount of mineral spirits into a pail. Dip the oval sash paintbrush about 1" (2.5 cm) into the mineral spirits. Hold the paintbrush close to, but not touching, the painted surface, letting the mineral spirits drip onto it. Continue the dipping and dripping until you've covered a small area, then blot the drips with a T-shirt rag. You may need to apply a little pressure or rub the surface slightly to remove the blue paint. Keep turning your rag to a clean spot to avoid depositing paint back onto the surface.

4 Continue step 3 until you are happy with the results. You can vary the depth by how much ultramarine blue you remove with the rag. If too much mineral spirits fall on the surface, or if you don't like the pattern of drips, don't touch the surface. Simply allow the mineral spirits to dry and then you may repeat the dripping process.

Tip: If the contrast is too high, overglaze after 24 hours using the ultramarine blue paint.

5 Topcoat with one or two coats of varnish.

108 | Intarsia

THE WORD *INTARSIA* comes from the Latin *interserere*, which means "to insert." Historically, intarsia meant an inlaid wood pattern. It is believed the technique developed in Italy in or around the 14th and 15th centuries.

Marble intarsia can be seen on the floors of buildings and churches throughout Europe. Marble and stone were inlaid in fanciful patterns or pictorial motifs such as lion heads and astrological symbols.

Intarsia creates pattern, color, form, and shape and is a wonderful way to include the look of semi-precious stone without the high cost or specialized knowledge necessary. With a combination of painting techniques, you can create a simple or highly involved design.

Malachite, lapis, and stone, each outlined in Fabulous Fakes, were used in this intarsia, but you can use any finish you like. Refer to the specific instructions to apply the finishes.

❖ Clear ruler, 24" (61 cm)

❖ Pencil

❖ Painter's masking tape, 1" (2.5 cm)

❖ Flat latex paint, white

❖ Latex paintbrush, 4" (10.2 cm)

❖ Eggshell latex paint, pale yellow/green

❖ Painter's masking paper, 3" (7.6 cm)

❖ Latex paint, gold

❖ Satin oil-based varnish

❖ All other materials and tools listed under Malachite (page 318), Provincial Lapis (page 338), and Faux Stone, (page 320).

1 Basecoat the project surface with the white paint using the paintbrush. Allow the paint to dry. Mark off the intarsia design area with the ruler and pencil, then tape along the outside of the design area on which you are working.

2 Draw your pattern with a thin pencil line using a clear ruler (which helps keep lines parallel or perpendicular to each other).

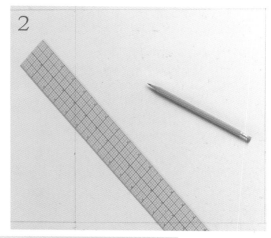

3 Tape along the outside of the pencil lines beginning in the interior of the design. Basecoat each section with the appropriate paint for the individual finishes, allowing the paint to dry between sections. In this case, the pale yellow/green paint was applied for the Malachite finish. Sand lightly after all the sections have dried. Follow the instructions under Malachite (page 318) to complete the center section. Allow to dry overnight; then remove the tape.

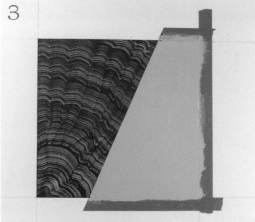

4 Tape the small squares along the outside of the pencil lines, inserting painter's paper along the outside edges. Basecoat the small squares with the gold paint. Allow to dry, and sand lightly. Follow the instructions under Provincial Lapis (page 338) to complete the squares. Allow to dry overnight, and then remove the tape.

5 Tape the rectangular sections outside of the white, securing the tape well by burnishing pressing (rubbing firmly) with your fingertips. Follow the instructions under Faux Stone (page 320) to complete the squares. Allow to dry, and then remove the tape.

6 Topcoat with one or two coats of varnish.

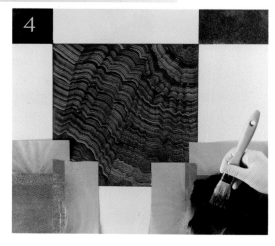

109 | Striping

PAINTING A STRIPE onto a piece of furniture may seem intimidating, but you'll quickly become good at it with a bit of practice.

Your stripe need not be perfect—remember, you're not a machine. Slight inconsistencies and unevenness merely reveal a bit of hand-painted personality.

It helps to have a good striping paintbrush. A striping paintbrush has long, soft, and flexible hairs that hold a good quantity of paint. Art materials stores sell high-quality striping brushes. The paintbrush size determines the width of the stripe, so consider purchasing both a #6 and a #3 sable striping paintbrush.

Location determines what style of stripe you will create. Thin accent stripes are done in indentations, wider bands on turned surfaces, and a variety of widths can be done along the edges of a surface.

Relax, practice, and look where you want the stripe to go—your hand will follow—and you will be making a steady and beautiful stripe in no time.

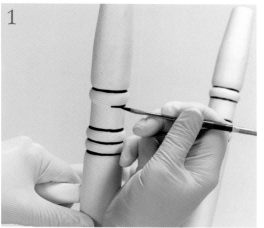

1 To create an incised stripe, thin the paint slightly with water or mineral spirits, as appropriate. Load the sable striping paintbrush with the thinned paint. Place the paintbrush tip into an indentation, and pull it toward yourself.

2 To create a broad, or band stripe, pick up slightly thinned paint on the ¼" (6 mm) paintbrush, hold it at a 45° angle to the surface, and pull it toward yourself.

3 Make a guide when you are striping a flat surface with no indentations. The guide can help create an even width for band striping or a line for a thin stripe. The guide is constructed the same way for both.

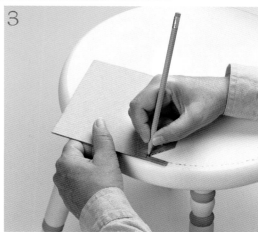

Determine the width of the band or the proximity of the stripe to the edge of your furniture piece. Mark the top edge of a square of cardboard that distance from the left side. Add a second mark 1" (2.5 cm) straight down from the first mark. Place another mark along the top edge of the cardboard 1" (2.5 cm) from the first mark. Draw a line from the first mark to the second, and from the second to the last mark. Create a notch by cutting along the lines with a craft knife.

Hold the guide with its left side resting along the edge of the project surface. Hold a pencil in your other hand, and place its point at the inside of the notch. Gently draw both the guide and the pencil long the edge to create a guideline. Load the paintbrush well with thinned paint and either draw it toward yourself along the pencil line (striping paintbrush) or between the edge and the pencil line (flat paintbrush).

110 | Soft Geometry

LOOK WHAT HAPPENS with a can of spray paint—a finish that creates itself!

Any color palette works, but using three colors to create Soft Geometry is easiest. The three colors should include a light, a medium, and a dark value.

Relax and enjoy the process as you create this soft look. If you think too much, your work will look labored. You will know how much to do and when to stop—when you like it!

Make sure you use a drop cloth and paint only in a well-ventilated area or outside if the day is not windy.

MATERIALS & TOOLS

- ❖ Flat latex paint, medium-dark gray
- ❖ Latex paintbrush, 4" (10.2 cm)
- ❖ Flat, rigid cardboard, large
- ❖ Spray paint, medium blue
- ❖ Spray paint, black
- ❖ Spray paint, white
- ❖ Gloves
- ❖ Drop cloth

1 Basecoat the project surface with the medium-dark gray paint.

2 Create the blue corners by resting the cardboard shield on the project surface at a 45° angle. The edges of the shield need to extend beyond the edges of the furniture piece. Point the spray can away from the shield, with the spray nozzle pointed toward the furniture piece. Mist the paint over the surface moving your arm and lightly covering the surface with paint. Do three corners of varying sizes in medium blue, allowing the paint to dry between corners.

3 Mist black (or the darkest color) over the fourth corner.

Note: Aim for see-through coverage; avoid opaque buildup. The darkest color will be applied very lightly.

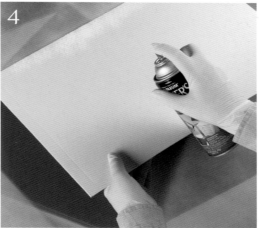

4 Position the shield; spray with white (or the lightest color). Repeat as many times, in different areas, as you like, allowing the paint to dry between areas. Some sections will become denser as the paint coats overlap creating a "soft" geometry.

5 Position the shield; mist using the medium blue (or your mid-tone color) paint. This step adds depth and interest.

6 Spray the final layer areas with white (or your lightest color).

7 Topcoat with one or two coats of varnish.

III | Torn Paper

THE TORN PAPER finish is amazingly simple, quick, and effective. It's best suited for modern or contemporary furniture, as it softens straight lines by adding a subtle tactile and visual texture.

There are two important concepts to keep in mind when using this finish. One: have enough paper. Two: keep the paper and the application area clean.

Using an artist sketchbook drawing pad allows you to flip to a clean, flat sheet each time you need to tear and glue. Too many sheets of floppy, loose paper can lead to frustration with glue and paper sticking to everything—you, the dog, the cat—you get the idea.

Choose smooth-surfaced furniture pieces with closed grain (open grain can cause air-pocket problems). The glued paper may be applied directly over any surface that does not resist water. If your surface is water-resistant, apply a primer coat before beginning.

- ❖ White glue, Elmer's® Glue-all
- ❖ Water
- ❖ Flat latex paintbrush, 4" (10.2 cm)

- ❖ Smooth artist acid-free sketchbook pad, 18" (45.7 cm) × 24" (61 cm), paper weight 50 lb
- ❖ Rubber roller, 4" (10.2 cm) to 6" (15.2 cm)

- ❖ Wallpaper cutting blade
- ❖ Satin oil-based paint, off-white
- ❖ Oil paintbrush, 4" (10.2 cm)

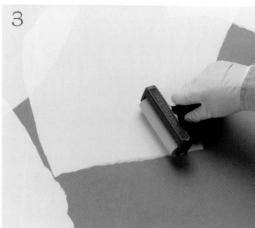

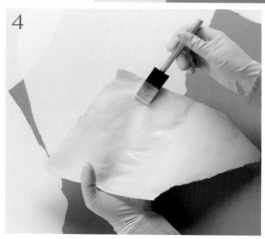

1 Thin the white glue with water to brushing consistency; apply it to the project surface using the latex paintbrush (this helps the paper adhere strongly to the surface). Allow it to dry completely, about one hour. The glue is completely transparent when dry.

2 Tear one or two edges of a sheet of paper into soft, irregularly curved lines (avoid straight lines). Brush glue over the entire back of the paper, covering it completely. Avoid getting glue on the face of the paper.

Tip: Add a few drops of food coloring to the glue to help you see it better against the white paper.

3 Lay the paper smoothly, glue-side-down on the project surface, extending it just beyond the surface. Firmly secure the paper and roll out air pockets with a rubber roller.

Tip: Use your fingertips to gently press out any small air bubbles. Don't worry about an occasional wrinkle, as it will lend itself to the look, but keep wrinkles to a minimum.

4 Continue tearing, gluing, and laying various shapes of paper, overlapping the other pieces as you work. Voids become part of the look when painted. To wrap edges, fold the paper over them and cut the paper at the corners to form a clean edge. Do not fold excess paper around the corners.

5 When the paper is completely dry, trim off any excess with the wallpaper knife. Apply the off-white paint using the oil paintbrush.

Note: If you prefer to use latex paint, you must seal the papered surface completely with shellac prior to applying the paint. There is no need to topcoat, as the satin oil-based paint is very durable.

MAKE A STATEMENT—the unex-pected is a delightful twist on an other-wise uninteresting surface. Have a bit of fun with words applied to furniture by using affirmations, names, a favorite saying, or your own poetic words.

112 | Words & Numbers

Stencil the kitchen chairs with family nicknames, ring the dining table with "bon appétit," or liven up the picnic table with the message "Ants Beware." Keep your pile of recipes clipped from newspapers and magazines right at hand, but cleverly hidden in a painted box stenciled with "Yum."

A stencil is the easiest way to apply lettering to furniture, but the stenciled effect may be eliminated by painting connections between the letters with an artist's paintbrush after the stenciled paint has dried.

- ❖ Pencil
- ❖ Painter's masking tape, 1" (2.5 cm)
- ❖ Ruler or tape measure
- ❖ Paper
- ❖ Alphabet stencil, 1" (2.5 cm)
- ❖ Stencil brush, ½" (1.3 cm)
- ❖ Satin oil-based paint
- ❖ Paper towels
- ❖ Angled artist brush, ⅛" (optional)

1 Determine (and mark, if necessary) the length of the path on which to stencil the letters. Place blue painter's tape along the bottom of the path. Find the middle of the path and mark the midpoint on the painter's masking tape.

Tip: Place a perpendicular piece of tape at the midpoint as a large visual aid.

2 Write out your saying in block letters on a piece of paper. Count the number of spaces between, and number of letters in, each word. Divide the total by two. To find the center, count, starting at the first letter, to that number. You will position the first half of your saying to left of the center mark.

Apply the letters from the center moving left (which means "writing" backward, so use care not to misspell). Keep your written saying in front of you and cross off the letters as you work. Continue until the first half is completed.

Tip: Use the spacing between the letters on the stencil to keep letters equal distances apart. Use the letter X to define the space between words. Stencils are usually clear or somewhat transparent, so you will be able to easily place the bottom of the letter along the tape line.

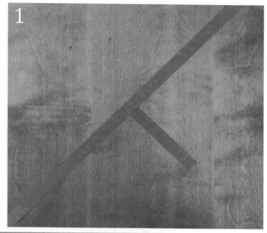

3 Tape the stencil in place, dip the stencil brush in the paint, and tap off the excess on a paper towel. Using a pouncing motion, stencil the first letter. Remove the stencil and clean off the paint around the letter. Allow the paint to dry or force-dry with a hair dryer, then proceed with the next letter to the left.

Tip: Using oil-based paint allows you to easily remove a misaligned or incorrect letter with mineral spirits.

4 Move back to the center and stencil the letters toward the right until all of your words have been stenciled.

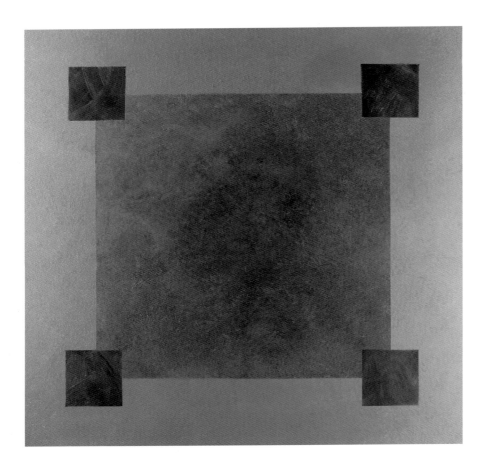

113 | From the Can

APPLY THIS METALLIC finish straight from the container. No mixing or adjustments needed!

Suitable for enhancing an entire large tabletop or as a decorative inset, the From the Can finish also adds a lovely accent to a wooden box lid. This versatile finish says contemporary, yet the formal colors allow it to speak in a traditional voice as well.

The design here is geometric, but organic or abstract shapes offer a striking modern statement. Snip into the "away" edge of the painter's masking tape to mark off curves.

When using painter's tape, be sure to remove it while the paint is still wet as the tape may pull dried paint away.

Refer to French Brush (page 140).

MATERIALS & TOOLS

- Flat latex primer
- Flat latex paintbrush, 3" (7.6 cm)
- Modern Masters® Champagne, ME 206 opaque
- Pencil
- Ruler
- Painter's masking tape, 1" (2.5 cm)
- Painter's taping paper
- Modern Masters® Sapphire, ME 655 semi-opaque
- Oval sash brush, 2" (5.1 cm)
- Cheesecloth, 90-weight
- Flat latex paintbrush, 1" (2.5 cm)

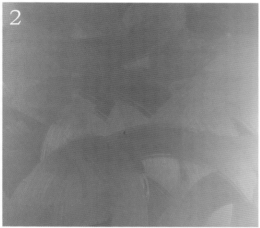

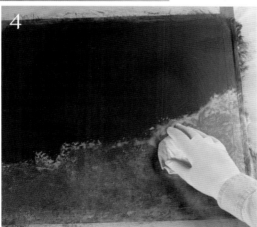

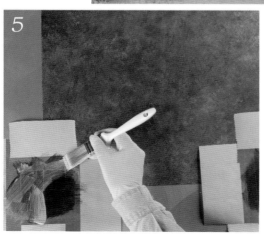

1 Basecoat the project surface with primer using the latex brush. Allow to dry one hour. Repeat with a second coat.

2 Apply a coat of champagne paint using the flat latex paintbrush and the French brush technique. Allow the paint to dry one hour. Repeat with a second coat.

3 Using a ruler and a pencil, mark off a 4" (10.2 cm) border. Apply the painter's tape along the outside of the pencil lines, securing painter's paper along the outside edges. Press and rub the tape with your fingers to avoid gaps.

Apply a coat of sapphire paint using the French brush technique. Remove the tape; allow the paint to dry, or force-dry with a hair dryer. Repeat with a second coat

4 Pounce the champagne paint over the surface working quickly with a slightly water-dampened cheesecloth, to soften the paint. Remove the tape and the paper. Allow the paint to dry about 30 minutes.

5 Mark off a small square that slightly overlaps one corner of the interior square. Apply painter's tape and paper along the marks. Paint the small square with two coats of the sapphire paint. Remove the tape. Allow the paint to dry. Repeat for each corner.

Apply one thin coat of champagne over the sapphire, either brushing the color on using curved brush strokes with the sash brush or pouncing it on with cheesecloth to create texture. Allow the paint to dry; then remove the tape and paper.

6 Topcoat with one or two coats of varnish.

114 | Stamping

STAMPING IS a wonderfully easy way to apply decorative motifs to a surface. The selection of rubber stamps is wide and varied; you will find unlimited motifs, themes, and designs. Go to any craft store and you will find a stamp or two that you will want to incorporate into a furniture piece, guaranteed!

If you plan to stamp with ink, ask your salesperson if the ink you've selected can be covered by a varnish. Most can, but checking is always best. Apply a varnish coat over the stamped surface to protect the ink.

To stamp small areas, add stamping medium to acrylic paint. You'll find both of those products in craft stores.

Whether you plan to stamp a border or a center motif, practice loading the proper amount of ink on the stamp and placing the stamp to properly line up the design. If the stamp's design is smaller than its wooden back, make yourself a guide: stamp the design on paper, cut it out, and tape or paste it to the top of the stamp. Aligning will be much easier.

❖ Ruler or tape measure   ❖ Inkpad

❖ Pencil   ❖ Paper (optional)

❖ Stamp

1 To create a perfect square or rectangular border, measure the length and width of the stamp design, then use multiples of the length plus one width-measurement to determine the length of a stamped line. Draw lines the appropriate length forming a square or rectangle on the project surface. Place the inked stamp at one corner, press lightly on the stamp, but do not rock it. Lift, re-ink, and continue stamping along the line. When you reach the end of the first line, a space the width of the stamp will remain. Place the stamp parallel to the second pencil line, and continue stamping. Repeat the procedure at each corner.

2 If the border you want to stamp isn't evenly divisible by length of the stamp, use this "no precision" option.

Draw all the guidelines. Begin stamping along a line, placing the inked stamp at one corner. Lift, re-ink, and continue stamping along the line. When you approach the end, tape a piece of paper along the adjacent line. Ink, then place the stamp, letting the overlap fall on the paper. Move the paper to the end of the next line, and continue stamping.

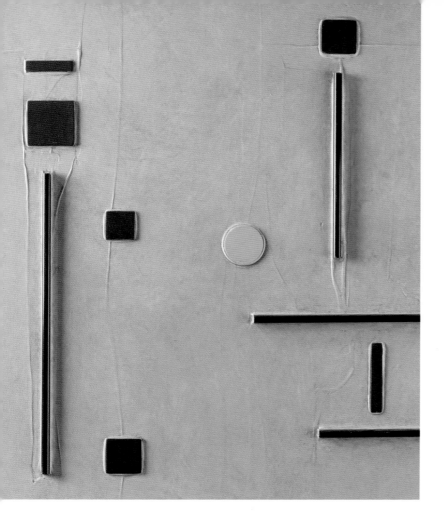

115 | Found Objects

WITH FOUND OBJECTS, anything goes, from elegance to whimsy. Explore, find treasures, and then have fun with this technique. The little geometric plastic pieces shown here came from a salvage store.

Make this finish sophisticated by inserting brass strips or other elegant objects. Go monochromatic for a modern appeal by painting over the objects. Keep in mind that lightweight objects work better. This finish creates interest on boring cabinet sides or intrigue on a tabletop.

Flat objects work best, but experiment. If you use high-dimension objects, incorporate glass bumpers into your design and then set a piece of tempered glass on top of the surface. Your glass supplier can help you choose the appropriate glass top.

To begin, arrange your found objects in a pleasing design. Draw a diagram or take digital photographs to serve as a guide as you refine your arrangement. You will not be able to re-create a drawn design exactly, so just let it happen.

- ❖ Found objects
- ❖ White glue, Elmer's® Glue-all
- ❖ Crazy Glue® or a two-part epoxy product (optional)
- ❖ Measuring container, four-cup
- ❖ All-purpose joint compound
- ❖ Flexible spreading blades, varied widths
- ❖ Paintable latex caulk (optional)
- ❖ Eggshell latex paint, white
- ❖ Flat latex paint, gray
- ❖ Latex glazing liquid
- ❖ Flat latex paintbrush, 4" (10.2 cm)
- ❖ Cheesecloth, 90-weight

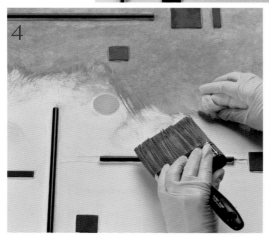

1 Glue objects no thicker than ¼" (6 mm) on the project surface with white glue. For objects that may not adhere with white glue, use Crazy Glue® or a two-part epoxy product.

2 Use the container to measure *exactly* one-part white glue to nine-parts joint compound (the glue adds durability). Mix well. Apply the compound smoothly (it's hard to sand), to a depth of ⅜" (9 cm) or less, over the entire surface. Trowel marks may also be part of the design.

Tip: Place your objects farther apart than your smallest size spreading blade.

3 While the joint compound is still wet, place the smaller objects into it using a slight twisting motion. Allow the compound to ooze up around the object to hold it in place. Allow the compound to dry completely. Lightly sand out any nibs or roughness.

Tip: Once the compound is dry, you may run a bead of caulk around the larger objects to ensure adhesion.

4 Basecoat the project surface with two coats of white paint; allow the paint to dry. Mix a glaze using one-part gray paint and one-part glazing liquid to one-part water. Apply the glaze using the 4" (10.2 cm) paintbrush. Immediately pounce with a wad of cheese-cloth to soften.

Tip: Apply glaze over the objects; then use a water-dampened cloth to wipe off the glaze before it dries. If the glaze dries and cannot be removed with water, try using denatured alcohol.

5 Topcoat with one or two coats of varnish.

THIS FUN PAINT turns any surface into a magnet. It's great for kids' rooms, even though it only comes in a dark charcoal gray color—simply paint over it using any finish technique you like. The Mottled finish (page 268) was used on the project shown. The magnets will still stick. Of course, if you are using a light colored paint, you may want to apply a primer over the magnetic paint.

Paint a small rectangle on a storage drawer and label it with magnetic letters. Amuse your child by painting his or her door and attaching magnetic

116 | Magnetic Paint

photo frames, objects, letters, or poetry. Paint a wall; then glue small magnets to each corner of school artwork, and create a gallery of "floating" art.

No more need to tape notes and whatnot to your door or wall! Hold notes with a decorative magnet. The magnetic charge is too weak to hold heavy objects, but strong enough to hold pictures, newspaper or magazine clippings, and photos.

You'll find magnetic paint in paint and home improvement stores.

Refer to French Brush (page 140).

MATERIALS & TOOLS

❖ Magnetic paint

❖ Angled latex paintbrush, 2" (5.1 cm)

❖ Sandpaper, 220-grit

❖ All other materials and tools listed under Mottled (page 268).

1 Apply the first coat of magnetic paint to a prepared project surface, using the French brush technique. Do not overwork the paint. Allow the paint to dry according to the paint manufacturer's instructions.

2 Apply the second coat using the same procedure as in step 1. The heavier the coating of magnetic paint applied, the stronger the magnetic attraction becomes. When dry, sand with 220-grit sandpaper.

Tip: This paint is very thick and grainy, so consider using an appealing texture over it. Follow the directions under Mottled (page 268), or use any preferred technique to cover the magnetic paint. Apply the magnetic paint with the same brushing technique as the chosen finish so the brushstrokes mimic each other.

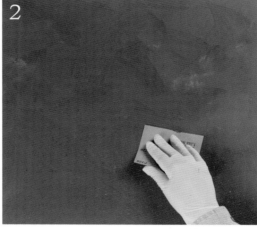

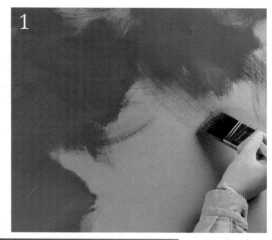

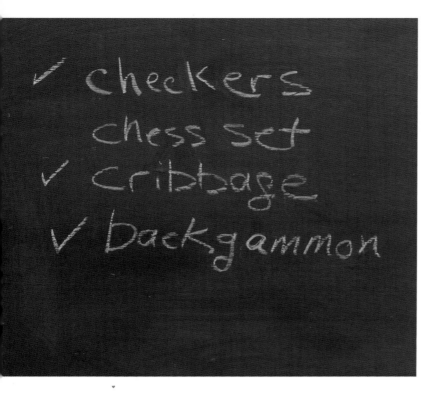

CHALKBOARD PAINT just lends itself to fun. Paint a square on a commonly used furniture piece and leave messages for family members. Paint on children's tables or other furniture pieces to inspire them to have fun decorating their own furniture. Paint the inside of an armoire and their artwork can be hidden away.

117 | Chalkboard Paint

Chalkboard paint is a smooth, almost flat, black paint that goes on beautifully with either a paintbrush or a roller.

Black and green are most commonly found, but a wide range of bright, cheery colors can be ordered from most paint stores or online.

- ❖ Chalkboard paint
- ❖ Angle-edged latex paintbrush, 3" (7.6 cm)

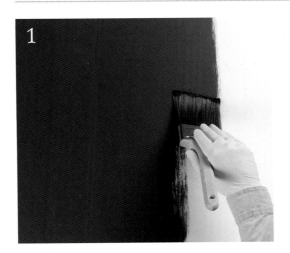

1 Apply the chalkboard paint over a properly primed surface. Hold the paintbrush at a 45° angle, and apply at least three coats, allowing the paint to dry between coats. Follow the manufacturer's instructions for drying times. The paint should cure 24 hours (harden) before using chalk on the surface.

If you apply painter's masking tape to an area, remove the tape immediately after painting (while the paint is still wet), as the dried paint on the tape may lift or chip the paint on the surface.

Tip: Chalkboard paint has a good shelf life, so store it in a heated environment and use it periodically to refresh your painted piece.

118 | Checkerboard Tabletop

A CHECKERBOARD PAINTED right on the tabletop is a wonderful addition to a children's room but also makes an adult game table attractive and doubly useful. The pattern used is the regulation layout for either chess or checkers.

While the instructions tell how to paint the checkerboard over a raw wood surface, you may also create it on a painted surface (and in any colors if the authenticity of the regulation board isn't a consideration).

The squares may be any size. You can easily alter the size of the checker-

board by dividing one of the edges by eight. Mark each edge using that measurement.

The number of squares must remain constant in order to use the board. The regulation chess/checkerboard consists of a field of 8 squares across and 8 squares down, totaling 64 squares. As a player faces the board, the square in the lower left-hand side is black and the lower right-hand square is red. This is the proper orientation, so lay out your board accordingly.

MATERIALS & TOOLS

- ❖ Ruler
- ❖ Pencil
- ❖ Painter's masking tape, 2" (5.1 cm)
- ❖ Flat latex paint, red
- ❖ Wallpaper cutting blade
- ❖ Flat latex paint, black
- ❖ Sponge paintbrushes, 1" (2.5 cm)
- ❖ Wet/dry sandpaper, 400-grit
- ❖ White eraser
- ❖ Tack cloth
- ❖ Soft rag
- ❖ Gel stain, Old Masters®, Golden Oak

1 Draw a 16" (40.6 cm) square in the center of your tabletop. Apply painter's masking tape along the outline. Paint the interior with one coat of red paint. Allow the paint to dry.

2 Mark the perimeter every 2" (5.1 cm). Draw a pencil line from every mark to the one directly opposite.

3 Run the tape along the inside of the left pencil line from top to bottom. Mark off the eight squares. Beginning with the lower left square, initial all the squares to be cut out with a "B." Cut out and remove them using the wallpaper blade and a ruler.

   Run another piece of tape along the edge of the row of squares and repeat the procedure, alternating the "B" squares. Continue until the checkerboard is complete. Press the edges of the tape firmly with your fingers.

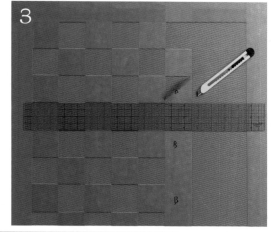

4 Apply one coat of black paint using the 1" (2.5 cm) paintbrush.

   Tip: Brush the black paint from the tape into the square to help avoid bleeding.

5 When the paint sheen dulls (about one hour), it is dry. Remove the tape.

6 Very lightly sand in the direction of the wood grain. If a bit of paint lifts, it will create a "worn" look, which is fine. Tack (wipe) to remove the sanding grit. Erase any pencil marks.

7 With a clean, soft rag, apply the gel stain to the entire surface and immediately wipe off to soften. Allow the stain to dry for 24 hours. Lightly sand again, as the staining might have raised the grain. Tack the surface.

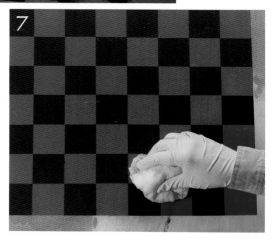

8 Topcoat with one or two coats of varnish.

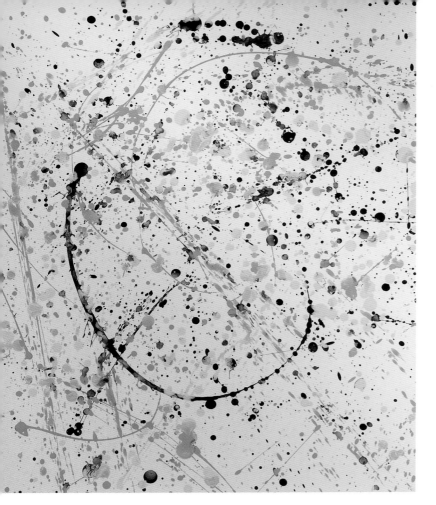

RELEASE YOUR JACKSON Pollock urges. Invite your children to assist. This whimsical and active finish looks spectacular done in the right colors on the right surface. It's perfect for the "retro" look, and fun on something unexpected.

The most difficult element to this finish is stopping—but do so when it makes you smile!

Experiment with a dark basecoat and light "drip and spill" paints. Amuse the children by using a "glow-in-the-dark" paint as one of the colors on a table for them.

119 | Drip & Spill

Even though this finish looks a bit chaotic, you can achieve a graceful and sophisticated movement of paint and color on a surface. This is a bold and confident finish because there is no turning back—you will not be able to wipe off a mistake.

You'll feel like a conductor while creating this finish as you paint "from the shoulder" using your whole arm to move and flick the paintbrush.

MATERIALS & TOOLS

- ❖ Eggshell latex paint, white
- ❖ Foam roller, 4" (10.2 cm)
- ❖ Eggshell latex paint, off-white
- ❖ Eggshell latex paint, tan
- ❖ Eggshell latex paint, black

- ❖ Water
- ❖ Three paint pails
- ❖ Three angle-edge latex brushes, 3" (7.6 cm)
- ❖ Drop cloth, large

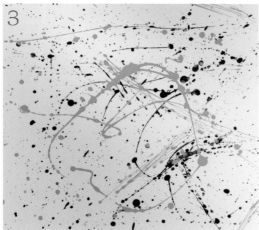

1 Basecoat the project surface with the white paint using the foam roller. Mix each of the other colors with water to a heavy cream consistency. Use a separate pail (and paintbrush) for each color.

2 Dip a paintbrush into the black paint. Hold it, point toward the project, about 3 ft. (91.4 cm) above the surface. Let the paint drip as you move the paintbrush around, or create splatters by using your arm to flick the paintbrush in a sideways movement (flicking from the wrist constrains the pattern).

Create fine lines by holding the paintbrush close to the surface and letting the paint drip off the tip for at least 2 ft. (61 cm) in a continuous string as you move the paintbrush. If the paint doesn't flow smoothly from the paintbrush, thin it with a bit more water, but do not thin it too much.

3 Vary the amount of each color used for a pleasing and harmonious composition. An equal amount of all three colors creates a dull look. Apply the tan paint using the procedures in step 2, but use 50 to 60 percent less "coverage" than that of the black paint.

4 Apply the off-white paint in the same manner, using 50 to 60 percent less "coverage" than that of the tan paint. Allow the surface to dry for two or three days.

Tip: If your proportions of any paint seem off, simply add more of the other colors until you have a pleasing balance. Just be careful that the paints don't get blended together.

5 Topcoat with one or two coats of varnish.

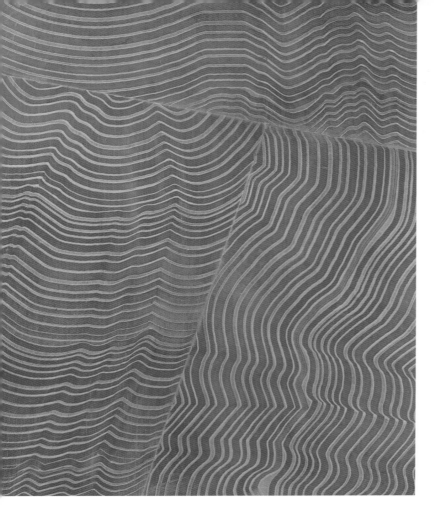

SQUEEGEE COMBING is an interesting, fun, and versatile finish that adds movement and interest to large flat surfaces.

Generally this finish is perceived as contemporary and modern. Render it with subtle tonal colorations such as ivory over white for an understated expression. Or use different paint sheen combinations; a red gloss over red flat for a sophisticated look. For high drama, try a high-contrast color scheme; white with black or deep burgundy.

120 | Squeegee Combing

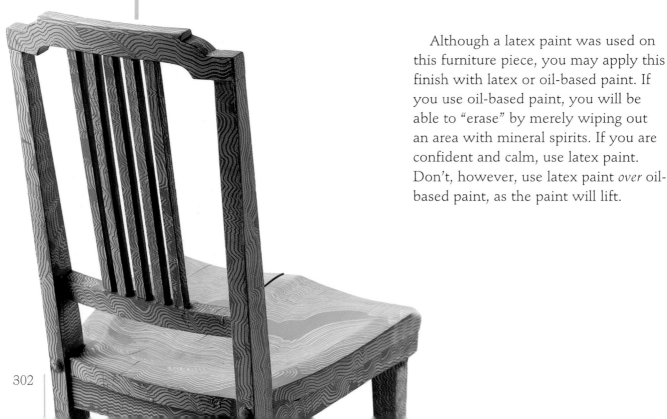

Although a latex paint was used on this furniture piece, you may apply this finish with latex or oil-based paint. If you use oil-based paint, you will be able to "erase" by merely wiping out an area with mineral spirits. If you are confident and calm, use latex paint. Don't, however, use latex paint *over* oil-based paint, as the paint will lift.

MATERIALS & TOOLS

- ❖ Rubber squeegee, 6" (15.2 cm)
- ❖ Craft knife
- ❖ Eggshell latex paint, medium greenish-gray
- ❖ Painter's masking tape, 1" (2.5 cm)

- ❖ Angled-edge latex paintbrush, 3" (7.6 cm)
- ❖ Eggshell latex paint, beige
- ❖ Gel stain, Old Masters®, Dark Walnut
- ❖ Rags

1 Cut inverted V-shaped notches along the edge of the squeegee with the craft knife. Vary the width of the notched areas and the distance between notches.

2 Basecoat the project surface with the greenish-gray paint. Allow the paint to dry.

Tip: A smooth basecoat helps the squeegee slide easily, yet if you have surface irregularities, they may lead to desirable "inconsistencies."

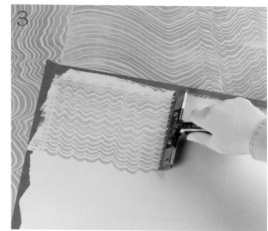

3 Divide your surface into sections, avoiding right angles (try for obtuse angles). Tape off one section. Brush slightly thinned beige paint over the section. Pull the notched squeegee through the wet paint, softly arcing and waving as you go. The type of pattern is up to you, soft or wild. Continue to follow your pattern over the entire section. You may add voids to your pattern by moving the squeegee farther over or slightly changing the angle of the pull. If you don't like how a section looks, wipe off the paint with a water-dampened cloth and start over. Allow the section to dry or force-dry with a hair dryer.

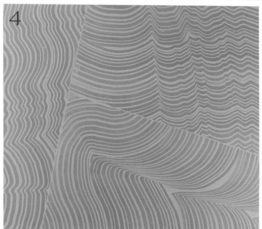

Tip: Thin the paint so it is only slightly "wetter." It should not run, but be loose enough to pull off with the squeegee.

4 Continue until all sections are completed, wiping the squeegee blade occasionally with a rag or paper towel to remove excess paint.

5 When all the sections are dry, apply the gel stain to soften and antique the finish. This will lower the contrast. Apply the gel stain with a rag and wipe off with a second rag until you create the desired look.

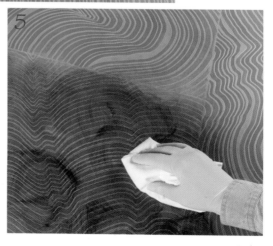

6 Topcoat with one or two coats of varnish.

Fabulous
FURNITURE
FAKES

121 | Faux Tiles

SPRUCE UP YOUR tired old kitchen table or add interest to outdoor furniture.

Furniture pieces painted with the Faux Tiles finish will be seen up close, so the technique must look refined. The quickest and most successful way to achieve this is by creating a narrow grout line. Since ⅛" (3 mm) masking tape is difficult to find, you will need to spend a little extra time cutting your tape to the appropriate size—but the effort is well worth it.

Many of the finishes in this book may be used to create the tile, particularly the Faux Stone, the Marble, the Provincial Lapis, and the Malachite.

Refer to French Brush (page 140), Parchment (page 90).

- Flat latex paint, white
- Flat latex paintbrush, 3" (7.6 cm)
- Ruler or tape measure
- Pencil
- Painter's masking tape, 1" (2.5 cm)
- Eraser
- Wallpaper cutting blade
- Flat latex paint, medium brown
- Flat latex paint, medium-dark brown
- Foam roller brush, 4" (10.2 cm)
- Latex glazing liquid
- Cheesecloth, 90-weight

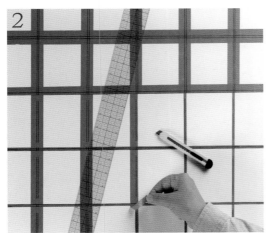

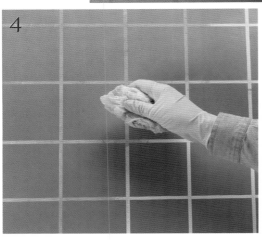

1 Basecoat the project surface with the white paint; allow the paint to dry overnight. Create a grid by dividing the length and width of the area to be "tiled" by the size of the tiles. For example, a tiled area 12" × 21" (30.5 × 53.3 cm) with 3" (7.6 cm) tiles creates a grid of four tiles down (12 divided by 3) and seven tiles across (21 divided by 3).

2 Pencil in all the grid lines on the project surface. Center the 1" (2.5 cm) painter's masking tape over each grid line. Create a 1/8" (3 mm) grout line by marking the center of the tape on both ends, then marking 1/16" (1.6 mm) to both sides of the center. Erase the center mark. Connect the marks on the opposite ends. Repeat on every tape line. Cut along all grout lines with the wallpaper blade, avoiding the areas where the grid lines cross, and remove the excess tape.

3 Work in a small area. Use the paintbrush to apply both brown paints using the French brush technique. Immediately soften the brushstrokes and blend the paint with the paint roller. Allow the paint to dry; remove the tape. Remove the penciled grid lines, if necessary.

4 Mix a glaze using one-part medium brown, one-part glazing liquid, and one-part water. Apply to the surface using the Parchment technique (page 90). While the glaze is wet, texture by pouncing the surface with a wad of cheesecloth. Allow the paint to dry completely.

5 Topcoat with one or two coats of varnish. If your project is to be used outdoors, use an exterior varnish.

122 | Parchment

THE PARCHMENT FINISH is one of the most foundational. This versatile finish radiates beauty on its own and as a base for stamped, stenciled, or painted decorative motifs. It can be used as an overglaze to age, reduce contrast, or lend depth to other finishes. Master this finish and have a myriad of possibilities open to you.

Whether you use oil-based or latex paint, the techniques used to create the finish are the same.

The Parchment finish should be soft, fairly even, and unobtrusive. Knowing when to stop manipulating the paint is key, as this finish will "get away" from you if you overwork it. Trust yourself, your hands, and your eyes, and a perfect result will quickly and effortlessly transpire. A subdued palette of earth-tones was used on the desk and shades of gray on the wood panel shown above, but the whole color spectrum is open to you.

MATERIALS & TOOLS

- ❖ Flat latex paint, white
- ❖ Flat latex paint, brownish-gray
- ❖ Latex glazing liquid
- ❖ Water
- ❖ Flat latex paintbrush, 4" (10.2 cm)
- ❖ Cheesecloth, 90-weight, 36" (91.4 cm)

1 Basecoat the project surface with the white paint. You may want to basecoat a sample board to practice steps 3 and 4 before beginning to work on your project surface.

2 Mix a glaze using one-part brownish-gray paint, one-part glazing liquid, and one-part water. Apply the glaze, covering the surface completely, using the 4" (10.2 cm) paintbrush. This step does not have to be neat. Immediately move to step 3.

3 Slightly water-dampen the cheesecloth. Distribute the glaze to remove the brushstrokes, using a light pressure and a circular motion.

4 Soften the texture with a combination pat-and-wipe using a clean, water-dampened 36" (91.4 cm) piece of cheesecloth scrunched into a soft ball. Place the cheesecloth on the surface, lift slightly, and replace with a slight forward push.

Tip: This is really easy, but the motion does take practice. Avoid creating thin or heavy spots. Relax, and don't overwork the surface.

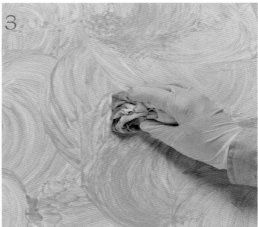

5 Topcoat with one or two coats of varnish.

Note: The wood insert at the top of page 326 was created with the paint colors listed in the materials list.

123 | Faux Marquetry

MARQUETRY IS THE craft of forming a decorative panel composed of shaped sections of wood veneer. It takes years to master that art, but you can easily simulate the look with stain on raw wood.

This simple yet elegant technique, appropriate for side panels and tabletops, makes an armoire's front doors stunning. Used in smaller scale on chests and boxes, the finish becomes a lovely, traditional detail (usually depicted in a half starburst or shell design).

This finish is usually done on wood, but you could certainly re-create the look of marquetry on other surfaces by combining it with Basic Wood Graining (page 328).

Refer to Gel Stains (page 255) and page 14 before beginning.

- Ruler or tape measure
- Pencil
- Painter's masking tape, 1" (2.5 cm)
- Gel stain, Old Masters®, Red Mahogany
- Flat oil paintbrush, 1" (2.5 cm)
- T-shirt rags
- Gel stain, Old Masters®, Dark Walnut
- Gel stain, Old Masters®, Golden Oak

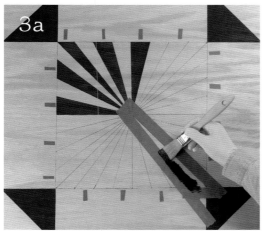

1 Mark off the design lightly with the pencil. The example shown is on a 16" (40.6 cm) square panel, but use any size surface, square or rectangular configuration, or any width border. Evenly mark off a 4" (10.2 cm) border on all sides to create four corner squares and a 14" (35.6 cm) inner square. Divide the small outer squares into two triangles.

Divide the center square into four triangles by drawing a line from corner to corner. Mark each side at 2" (5.1 cm) increments. Draw a line from each mark to the center point.

Tip: For more or fewer inner triangles, divide the length of one side of the square by the desired number and mark at the appropriate inch marks.

2 Tape the four border triangle edges. Stain with mahogany using the 1" (2.5 cm) paintbrush. Soften the stain by wiping toward the centers with a soft rag, taking care not to lift the tape. Allow the stain to dry slightly, and then remove the tape.

3 Place a small piece of tape *outside* every other inner triangle. Tape off a marked triangle, press the tape firmly to secure it, and apply the walnut stain using the 1" (2.5 cm) paintbrush, following the procedure in step 2. Repeat for each triangle. Allow the stain to dry slightly and then remove all of the tape.

4 Tape, then apply oak stain to the remaining inner triangles and then the border area, following steps 2 and 3. Allow the stain to cure for 24 hours.

5 Topcoat the surface with one or two coats of varnish or wax.

ELEGANT AND EASY, this finish works well as an inlay on large tables or desktops. Leather hides tend to be smaller than 19" × 30" (48.3 × 76.2 cm), so inlays with dimensions smaller than that most successfully mimic real leather.

You may apply the Faux Leather finish to contemporary furniture pieces; however, when used where one might traditionally find leather inlays, the finish is more believable.

124 | Faux Leather

Color variations in tanned leather range from reddish Cordova to a deep brown/black, so although the library table shown was painted in brown tones, your choice of colors is open. You may experiment using latex paints and mediums to create this finish, but the oil glaze gives a richness that the latex just cannot quite achieve.

❖ Painter's masking tape, ½" (1.3 cm)

❖ Painter's paper, 3" (7.6 cm) (optional)

❖ Flat oil-based paint, golden brown

❖ Flat oil-based paint, brown

❖ Alkyd glazing liquid

❖ Paint thinner

❖ Flat oil paintbrush, 3" (7.6 cm)

❖ Newspaper

❖ Cheesecloth, 90-weight, 24" (61 cm)

1 You may apply the Faux Leather finish to the entire project piece, allowing the tape lines to form panels, or use 3" (7.6 cm) painter's paper to protect the outer surface to create an inlaid look. Faux Leather complements both painted and stained surfaces.

Basecoat the project or inlay surface with the golden brown paint or a color that is about 50 percent lighter than your glaze color. Apply the painter's masking tape, creating the desired inlay size. Press the tape firmly in place with your fingertips.

Tip: Using a clear ruler and a T-square keeps the tape lines straight.

2 Mix a glaze using one-part brown paint, one-part glazing liquid, and one-part paint thinner. Apply the glaze to the entire project surface using the paintbrush.

3 While the glaze is still wet, smoothly lay the sheet of newspaper onto the glazed surface. Keep the newspaper flat. Lift the newspaper; then replace it on the project surface overlapping the first area slightly and avoiding right angles. Repeat this process over the entire project or inlay surface. Begin step 4 while the glaze is still wet.

4 Soften some of the edge lines by patting with the smooth side of a cheesecloth wad. You just want to soften the lines and fold the texture into the finish. Allow the paint to dry; then remove the tape.

5 Topcoat the surface with one or two coats of wax. For greater protection, apply a satin oil-based varnish before waxing.

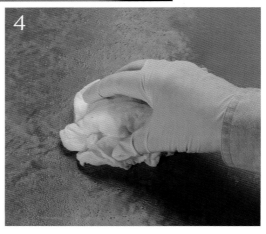

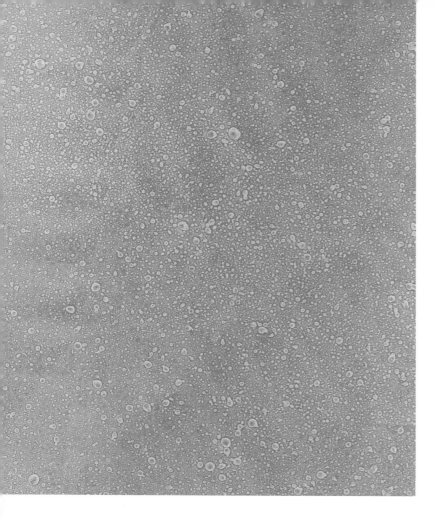

125 | Shagreen

SHAGREEN IS A high-end treated leather used on very special objects and furniture pieces. The roughened, untanned, and green-dyed leather once came from the hide on a horse's back. Shagreen is now commonly made of the skins from sharks and stingrays. You will create this lovely finish from paint, leaving all the sea life in peace.

Shagreen was traditionally prepared by embedding plant seeds in the soft, untreated hide. The hide was then covered with a cloth and trampled upon to push the seeds into the skin. When the skin dried, the seeds were shaken off leaving the leather peppered with small indentations.

Although used prior to it, the shagreen finish was very popular during the Art Nouveau era, so Art Deco styled furniture benefits from this finish. Still used today, shagreen is a beautiful finish on contemporary and traditional furniture.

- ❖ Flat latex paint, linen white
- ❖ Flat latex paintbrush, 3" (7.6 cm)
- ❖ Flat oil-based paint, pale green/ yellow
- ❖ Alkyd glazing liquid
- ❖ Mineral spirits
- ❖ Flat oil paintbrush, 3" (7.6 cm)
- ❖ Foam roller, 1" (2.5 cm)
- ❖ Spray bottle with settings
- ❖ Water

1 Basecoat the project surface with the linen white paint using the latex paintbrush. An optional basecoat color is a pale/light value steely/dirty gray.

Note: This technique is best created on a flat surface. Small projects must remain horizontal during the entire process. You may wish to basecoat a sample board and practice steps 2 to 4 before beginning to work on your project piece.

2 Mix a glaze using one-part green/yellow paint, one-part glazing liquid, and two-parts mineral spirits. Apply the glaze evenly to the entire surface using the oil paintbrush. If a gray basecoat was applied, use a medium dark steel-gray glaze.

3 Create a dimpled texture by rolling the foam roller in a random pattern over the wet glaze. Avoid over-rolling and work quickly so the glaze remains wet.

4 To create the distinctive spotted pattern, hold the water-filled spray bottle over the wet glaze, nozzle skyward, and spray straight up into the air. The falling water drops "break" the oil-based paint into circles. Spray over the entire project.

5 Adjust the nozzle to create larger circles and spray randomly. The completed surface will have mostly small circles with occasional larger circles. Allow the water to evaporate and the project surface to dry completely.

6 Topcoat the surface with one or two coats of oil varnish or wax.

126 | Faux Goatskin

THE SOFT LOOK of goatskin complements contemporary furniture and
works beautifully on traditional pieces
as an inlay. Typically goat hides are
small, so similar shapes and sizes are
pieced together to cover large areas.
Scale the size of your torn paper pieces
to fit your surface.

This finish is done with oil-based
paint and Japan Color for three partic-
ular reasons. The edges of the sections
get wiped out to create a "pieced-
goatskin mark," the Japan Color raw

sienna and raw umber earth tones are
the perfect shades for this finish, and
they come premixed in convenient
half-pints.

Plan to apply this finish to the entire
surface in one session; the paint must
not dry completely until you are finished.
You may force-dry between steps with
a hair dryer, but be careful not to over-
dry the area.

MATERIALS & TOOLS

- Flat latex paint, off-white
- Latex paintbrush, 3" (7.6 cm)
- Smooth, acid-free artist sketchbook pad, 18" × 24" (45.7 × 61 cm)
- Flat oil-based paint, white
- Flat oil paintbrush, 2" (5.1 cm)
- Japan Color, raw sienna
- Japan Color, raw umber
- Cheesecloth, 90-weight
- Oval sash paintbrush, 2" (5.1 cm)
- Painter's masking tape, 1" (2.5 cm)
- Paint thinner
- Flat oil-based varnish or wax

1 Basecoat the project surface with off-white paint using the latex paintbrush.

2 Tear several sheets of paper into graceful arcs or curves. Place the paper on the project surface, masking off a section. Hold down the edge you'll be painting off of with your hand.

Apply the white oil-based paint randomly using the oil paintbrush, painting off the paper's edge into the section. Wipe the paintbrush on a rag or paper towel, then repeat using raw sienna and covering a smaller area. Repeat using the raw umber.

Tip: Use the raw sienna and raw umber in different amounts within a section to simulate the unique coloration of each goatskin.

3 Continue to hold the paper in place and softly blend the colors with a cheesecloth wad.

4 Use the clean oval sash paintbrush to blend out the cheesecloth texture. Hold the paintbrush perpendicular to the surface and then pounce. Softly swipe the paintbrush into the center occasionally to simulate the fur. Don't overdo this. Remove the paper and allow the section to dry, or force dry with a hair dryer, until the sheen becomes matte.

5 Repeat steps 2 to 4 to complete all sections. When creating a section that touches another, arrange the paper to very slightly expose the edges of the previously painted sections.

The oil-based paint lifts the paint from the previously painted hide, creating an outline. If the paint doesn't lift off easily, wipe from the edge of the paper onto the painted area, just enough to leave a join-line, with a cheesecloth slightly dampened with paint thinner.

6 Topcoat with one or two coats of varnish or wax.

127 | Malachite

MALACHITE IS DELIGHTFUL on occasional tables and looks quite contemporary. Whether used alone or in combination with other faux stone techniques such as Intarsia (page 278) or with faux wood inlays, it presents a worldly richness and sophistication.

Use it on large surfaces for drama. The finish shown here simulates slab-cut malachite, which is often used on fine furniture. When you paint, you are re-creating the laying of the stone pieces, so draw obtuse angles and scale the size of the sections appropriately for the surface area.

You will also be re-creating with an eraser the multiple elongated oval curves that appear when malachite is sliced. You will want four patterns to avoid repetition and to avoid wear on the eraser.

Check the pattern by brushing paint on a piece of aluminum foil. Slice the eraser until you have a pattern you like.

In its raw form malachite is lumpily globular, a form called "botryoidal," (bah-tree-OYD-al) which means "grape cluster." It's a fun word to know and say.

The rippling ovals curve, forming a line that can be a tight or flattened arc. Just about anything goes (except forming round "bubbles"), so relax and have fun!

MATERIALS & TOOLS

- ❖ Eggshell latex paint, pale mint green
- ❖ Latex paintbrush, 3" (7.6 cm)
- ❖ Ruler
- ❖ Pencil
- ❖ Flat oil-based paint, deep rich green

- ❖ Alkyd glazing liquid
- ❖ Paint thinner
- ❖ White rubber eraser, notched
- ❖ Craft knife
- ❖ Aluminum foil
- ❖ Painter's masking tape, 1" (2.5 cm)

- ❖ Painter's paper, 3" (7.6 cm)
- ❖ Flat oil paintbrush, 2" (5.1 cm)
- ❖ Cheesecloth, 90-weight
- ❖ Hair dryer (optional)
- ❖ Gloss oil-based varnish

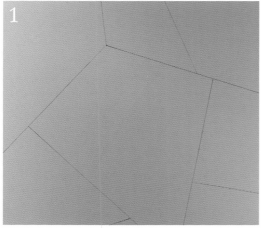

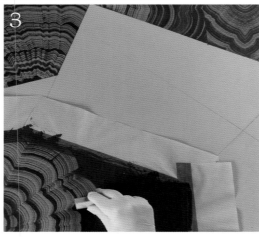

1 Basecoat the project surface with the latex paint using the latex paintbrush. Draw your inlay pattern using a pencil and the ruler. Avoid 90° angles.

2 Notch all four sides of a white rubber eraser with the craft knife.

3 Apply painter's masking tape along all the edges of a section, placing painter's paper along its outside edge. Mix a glaze using one-part oil-based paint, one-part glazing liquid, and one-part paint thinner. Brush the green glaze evenly over the section using the oil paintbrush. Gently pull your eraser over the "inside" of the section using a rippling motion to make curved and pointed parts of the first arc. Slightly twist the eraser occasionally to create an interesting pattern. Stop and restart without removing the eraser to emulate natural rock pressure lines.

Pull the next arc following the pattern, or leave voids, or change to another side of the eraser.

Allow the section to dry until the paint becomes matte, and then complete all of the sections. Vary the direction of the arcs from section to section. Allow the project to dry overnight.

4 Mix a stained overglaze with two-parts original glaze to one-part paint thinner. Brush over the entire surface, using the oil paintbrush, to create a more believable malachite texture and to reduce the contrast. Soften the glaze by patting with a wad of cheesecloth. Allow to dry overnight.

5 Topcoat with one or two coats of varnish.

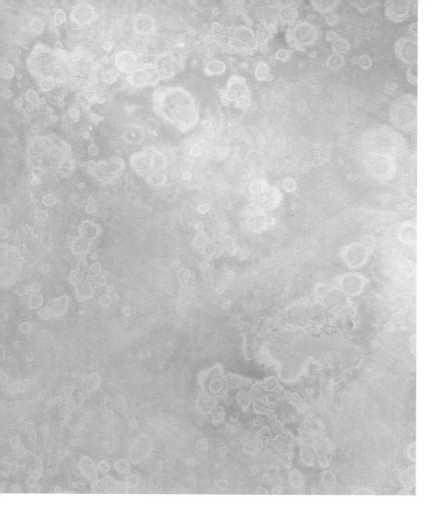

128 | Faux Stone

THE FAUX STONE finish offers a believable and quick way to create the look of stone without a lot of fuss and muss. The materials do the work for you.

There are many types of stone in the world—somewhere there is a natural stone that resembles the one in the finish described here! This finish offers you a basic approach to creating the appearance of stone. Select different colors or use multiple colors or even multiple applications of the techniques. As with wood graining, the use of natural earth colors makes this finish say "stone."

The only "trick" to this technique is to avoid letting your glaze dry before you are satisfied with your result.

MATERIALS & TOOLS

- ❖ Flat latex paint, white
- ❖ Flat latex paintbrush, 3" (7.6 cm)
- ❖ Latex paint, light tan
- ❖ Latex glazing liquid
- ❖ Water
- ❖ Two paint pails
- ❖ Cheesecloth, 90-weight, 24" (61 cm)
- ❖ Denatured alcohol
- ❖ Oval sash paintbrush, 2" (5.1 cm)

1 Basecoat the project surface or inlay area with the white paint using the flat latex brush.

2 Mix a glaze using one-part tan paint, one-part glazing liquid, and one-part water (you may use any earth tone color latex paint in place of the tan). Brush over the entire surface using the latex paintbrush. The amount of water added to the glaze will vary the look—experiment to find a look you like. Dampen the cheesecloth with water and wring it out well. Texture most, but not all, of the glaze with the cheesecloth by pressing and lifting while the paint is still wet.

3 Pour a bit of denatured alcohol into a bowl. Dip your fingers into the alcohol. Hold them above the surface, then flick the alcohol. Repeat as many times as needed to create a variety of splatters, but avoid flooding the surface.

Note: The untexturized areas develop a more graphic look when splattered.

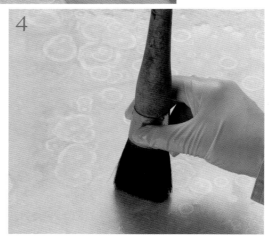

4 Hold the oval sash brush perpendicular to the surface, and pounce randomly to soften the contrast and to blend selected areas, while the paint and alcohol are still wet. Do not over-pounce.

Tip: If you do go too far and end up with a blur, allow the surface to dry, reapply the glaze and begin again.

5 Topcoat with one or two coats of varnish.

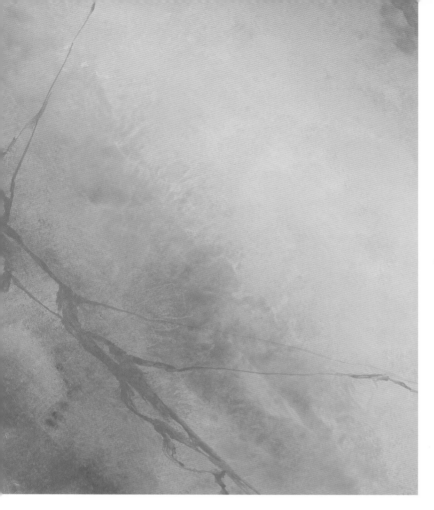

129 | Marble

THE SIMPLE TECHNIQUES used on this finish create a realistic marble, one that avoids looking overworked and clumsy, but appears effortless and elegant.

The following instructions detail how to achieve a basic and believable faux marble that you can apply to almost any surface.

Try combinations of colors: black with white, shades of gray, green with beige, or deep green with white. Keep your marble colors natural and you will create a finish that fools all who see your completed piece.

One of the tricks is to keep your paint movement following roughly a 45° angle (this is usually the pattern the earth produced when it formed certain marbles). Also, apply veining to less than 20 percent of the marble.

You will be applying three glazes, one after the other, and blending, so a quick touch will be helpful, as the paints must remain moist.

Tip: If you not feel confident enough to manipulate latex paint, use oil-based paints following the glazing recipe on page 254. Oil-based paint blends easily and offers a longer working time.

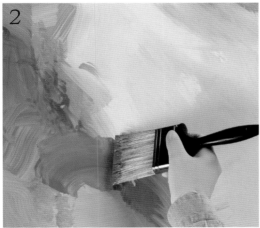

1 Basecoat the project surface with white paint.

2 Mix one-part paint, one-part glazing liquid, and one-part water to make the white, beige, and taupe glazes. Brush the white glaze in a 45° direction, covering about one-half of the surface. Wipe the paintbrush on a rag or paper towel; apply the beige glaze covering less than half of the surface. Blend the beige slightly into the white. Wipe the paintbrush; apply the taupe glaze covering one-fourth of the surface; blend some of the taupe into the other colors. Move to step 3 while the glazes are still wet.

3 Make a soft ball with a slightly water-dampened cheesecloth. Blend the three colors together leaving some of the cheesecloth texture in the paint. Allow the paint to dry.

4 The veining color is often slightly lighter than the darkest color; mix a bit of white glaze into the taupe.

Mix the veining paint to skim milk consistency with water. Dampen the feather with water, and then load it with the paint. Tickle the feather across the surface with a light pressure, pulling in a straight line. Form larger veins by laying the feather down and slightly rolling it. Keep the veins straight-sided, not scalloped or wiggly. Begin in the darkest area and pull through to other areas. Go off the edge or let the vein disappear. Avoid right angles and intersecting X-crossed veins. Blot the veins with cheesecloth as you work so they recede into the surface.

Tip: Practice veining on a sample board.

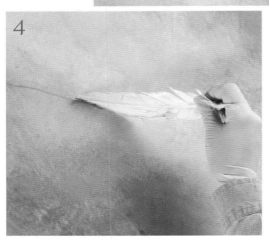

5 Topcoat with one or two coats of varnish.

THE UNIQUE ASPECT of this finish is in its liquid solution: milk. Also called *casein*, it's environmentally safe and non-toxic—an excellent and safe choice for painting children's furniture.

Milk paint dries to an extremely flat sheen, producing a lovely antique look to country style furniture. It's associated with the Colonial period and with the Shaker community whose members still use it on their furniture. Don't limit this versatile finish to the expected styles though; it's perfect for island style and shabby chic.

The paint comes in a powder form and is mixed with water to make either a full-bodied or a thin, glaze-like paint. Follow the mixing directions that accompany the product, as different

130 | Shaker Finish

companies have slightly different mixing recipes. The paint comes in both soft pastel and strong rich colors.

There is a slight milky odor when it is applied, but it dries completely odorless. This paint will spoil, so mix only what you need. The leftover paint may be stored in the refrigerator for a few days.

This translucent finish is done over raw wood. The most beautiful topcoat for this paint is hand-rubbed wax, but topcoat with one or two coats of flat oil-based varnish to keep watermarks away. Follow the manufacturer's instructions if you use an acrylic topcoat.

MATERIALS & TOOLS

- ❖ Measuring cup, 1 pint (500 ml)
- ❖ Water
- ❖ Milk paint, Old Fashioned Milk Paint®, Snow White
- ❖ Flat latex paintbrush, 3" (7.6 cm)
- ❖ Sandpaper, 220-grit
- ❖ Wax

1 Following the manufacturer's instructions, mix 6 oz. (170 g) powdered paint into 1 pint (500 ml) of warm water. Allow the paint to rest for 10 to 15 minutes before applying it to the raw wood surface.

2 Apply the milk paint in the direction of the wood grain. Allow the paint to dry for at least one hour.

3 Apply a second coat. The coverage should look somewhat grainy. Allow the paint to dry for at least one hour.

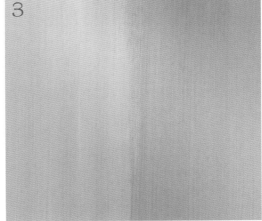

4 Apply a third coat. This gives a transparency without visible brushstrokes. If you prefer, you may continue until the coverage is opaque. Allow to dry overnight; then sand smooth.

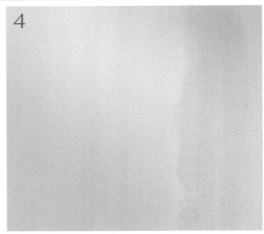

5 Topcoat with one or two coats of wax.

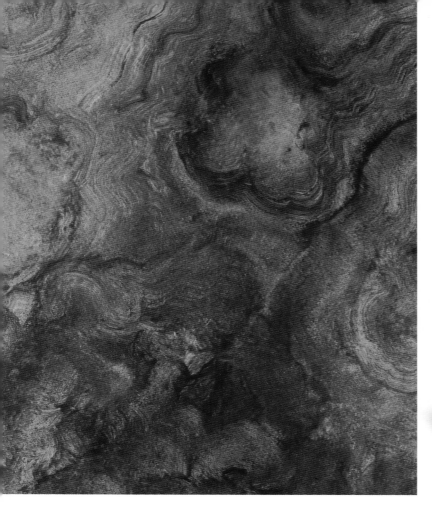

131 | Burled Wood

BURLS ARE THE gnarly and knotted warts found on trees. They are highly desired as veneers and for "highlight" panels on high-end furniture designed to showcase the uniqueness of the wood. They are often used to make boxes and clocks, as well as small turnings and bowls.

Burls are great fun because anything goes—grain crashes into itself and wild swirls meander across the surface. All this finish takes to be wonderful is a relaxed attitude! Enjoy the process and you will create a lovely burl. This is a great finish to try on a multiple caffé latte day, as squiggles and twitches make the best burl patterns.

As with any faux wood technique, the colors used say "wood" more than anything else.

MATERIALS & TOOLS

- Eggshell latex paint, light tan
- Flat latex paintbrush, 3" (7.6 cm)
- Satin oil-based varnish
- Flat oil paintbrush, 3" (7.6 cm)
- Paint tray
- UTC, burnt umber
- UTC, raw umber
- Gloves
- T-shirt rags
- Satin oil-based varnish
- Paint thinner (optional)

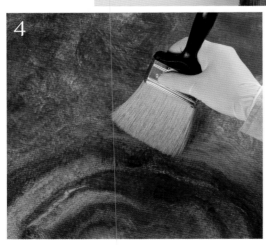

1 Basecoat the project surface with the light tan paint using the latex brush. This will be the lightest color in your burl. You may use another color if you prefer.

2 Brush a thick coat of varnish over a workable surface area with the oil paintbrush. (A workable area is indicated with tinted varnish in the example shown.) Pour a small puddle of burnt umber on the ridged, upper area of the paint tray. Pour a raw umber puddle next to, but not touching, the other UTC. Pour varnish in the trough portion. Wad the T-shirt rag into a small, loose ball.

Dip the rag into the burnt umber and then into the varnish. Smoosh the tip of the rag around on the varnished portion of the project surface, creating a ragged oval, an abstract shape, or a short, curved line. Use medium pressure, as if wiping up a spot of something. Squiggle the rag, pushing it with a nervous little twitch. If you miss a spot, pat color into the void.

3 Repeat the smooshing using a clean rag, varnish, and raw umber.

Develop a radial (sunburst) pattern as you work back and forth using both colors. Create more burls with burnt umber than with raw umber. If the varnish on the project surface begins to dry out, apply a bit more with a rag. If the drying is accelerated by hot, dry air, dip the rag into a small amount of paint thinner occasionally.

4 Dry-brush lightly, moving the oil paintbrush in a radial pattern, from the center of a "burl" outward to simulate a growth pattern. The varnish will be wet and tacky, so wipe the paintbrush on a dry cloth now and then.

5 Topcoat with one or two coats of varnish.

TWO THINGS CREATE realistic wood: color and grain. Using the basic techniques of combing, ragging, and flogging, you can create grain to simulate almost any type of wood. Beautiful on its own, this finish also works well as an accent border with the other finishes in this book.

Although not a furniture piece, doors (both steel and painted) are a wonderful surface for wood graining. If working on a door with inset panels, be sure to follow what would have been the natural direction of the wood grain.

You can find many specialty brushes

132 | Basic Wood Graining

and tools on the market to produce wood graining, and while they are wonderful tools, the only two you ever really need are a good flogger brush, and a set of steel combs.

To achieve the proper finish color, start with the proper basecoat color. If you are trying to match an existing wood, the basecoat paint must match the lightest color of the wood. Use an eggshell sheen for the basecoat, whether latex or oil-based.

Oil-based varnish is used for wood graining, as its longer drying time is forgiving and simple to erase with mineral spirits should a mistake happen.

MATERIALS & TOOLS

- ❖ Eggshell latex paint, Benjamin Moore Paints #1047 Aquavelvet
- ❖ Flat latex paintbrush, 3" (7.6 cm)
- ❖ Measuring cup, 1 pint (500 ml)
- ❖ Satin oil varnish, clear
- ❖ Paint pail
- ❖ UTC, burnt umber
- ❖ UTC, raw umber
- ❖ UTC, raw sienna
- ❖ Chip brush, 3" (7.6 cm)
- ❖ Steel wood graining combs (these usually are sold in a set)
- ❖ T-shirt rags
- ❖ Flogger brush

Note: A chip brush is an inexpensive, rough-bristled paintbrush

1 Basecoat the project surface with latex paint using the latex paintbrush.

Translucent, tinted varnish is the medium for Basic Wood Graining. Pour 1 pint (500 ml) of varnish into the paint pail. Drip small amounts of all three UTC colors into the varnish slowly until you create a color you like (start with about three-parts burnt umber, two-parts raw umber, and one-part raw sienna). You may need to add more colorant to make enough solution for large pieces, but continue slowly; if too much colorant is added, it will float and not mix, and the varnish will never dry.

Tip: The colorant never dries; wipe up spills immediately or it can spread everywhere.

2 Repetitive raking creates a realistic wood grain. Apply tinted varnish in the direction of the grain using a chip brush. Rake a comb back and forth quickly, multiple times, from top to bottom until a grain pattern emerges.

3 Pull a soft T-shirt rag from top to bottom, jittering the motion slightly, to create a vaguely rippled linear pattern. The wrinkly line creates a very believable wood grain.

4 Hold the flogger brush parallel to the surface, bristles downward. Slap the surface with quick snaps, working from the top down. Flog the entire surface a couple of times until you are satisfied with the look. Allow to dry for 24 hours.

Tip: Real wood grain never crashes into itself, so your grain lines need to run parallel to each another.

5 Topcoat with one or two coats of varnish.

133 | Mahogany

IN THIS TECHNIQUE color makes the finish believable. Mahogany serves as a beautiful finish for tabletops and inset side panels, and makes an inferior wood piece a superior one.

Mahogany is a quiet wood; the grain is fine, and what grain you see is fairly straight-lined without knots or whirls. It's also an elegant wood, and this finish should be selected for use on stylish furniture pieces.

Mahogany goes beyond Basic Wood Graining through its deeper basecoat color, the addition of Venetian red UTC to the graining varnish, and an additional paintbrush technique.

Refer to Basic Wood Graining (page 328).

- Eggshell latex paint, Benjamin Moore #1048 Aquavelvet
- Flat latex paintbrush, 3" (7.6 cm)
- Measuring cup, 1 pint (500 ml)
- Satin oil-based varnish, clear
- Paint pail

- UTC, burnt umber
- UTC, raw umber
- UTC, Venetian red
- Chip brush, 3" (7.6 cm)
- T-shirt rags
- Flogger brush

- Chip brush, 1½" (3.8 cm)
- Steel wood graining combs (usually sold in a set)

Note: A chip brush is an inexpensive, somewhat rough-bristled paintbrush.

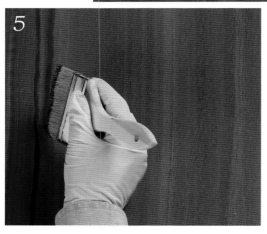

1 Basecoat the project surface with latex paint using the latex paintbrush.

Translucent, tinted varnish is the graining medium for Mahogany. Pour 1 pint (500 ml) of varnish into the paint pail. Drip small amounts of all three UTC colors into the varnish slowly until you create a color you like (start with about three-parts burnt umber, two-parts raw umber, and one-part Venetian red). You may need to add more colorant to make enough solution for large pieces, but continue slowly; if too much colorant is added, it will float and not mix, and the varnish will never dry.

Tip: The colorant never dries; wipe up spills immediately or it can spread everywhere.

2 Apply graining varnish with a large chip brush using a straight top-to-bottom stroke. Texture the varnish by lightly pulling a soft T-shirt rag over the surface from top to bottom. Jitter the motion slightly to create a vaguely rippled linear pattern. The wrinkly line creates a very believable mahogany grain. Repeat over the entire surface.

3 Hold the flogger brush parallel to the surface, bristles downward. Slap the surface with quick snaps, working from the top down. Flog the entire surface to soften the rag marks.

4 Dip the tip of the small chip brush into the graining varnish. Hold it at a 45° angle to the grain and lay in a dark accent by dragging the chisel-edge down the entire length of the grain. Use this accent sparingly, perhaps one per side. Allow to dry for 24 hours.

5 Topcoat with one or two coats of varnish.

134 | Rust

THIS FINISH MAY SHOW a heavy corrosion, or the beginning of rust formation. The example shown here signifies the earlier stage. Apply more of the yellowish and burnt orange paints to make a rustier looking surface.

This is a great look for patio furniture, interior occasional tables, and objects such as urns for both inside and outside.

MATERIALS & TOOLS

- ❖ Latex antique bronze paint, Modern Masters® Antique Bronze, ME 204 (opaque)
- ❖ Latex paintbrush, 3" (7.6 cm)
- ❖ Flat latex paint, black/brown

- ❖ Natural sea sponge
- ❖ T-shirt rags
- ❖ Latex glazing liquid
- ❖ Flat latex paint, brick red

- ❖ Flat latex paint, earthy yellow
- ❖ Water
- ❖ Water-based varnish, Modern Master® Dead Flat

1 Basecoat the project surface with the antique bronze paint using the latex paintbrush.

2 Apply the black/brown paint, covering the entire surface. Apply this paint so it is thicker in some areas and thinner in others (sloppily). Allow it to dry to the matte stage, but not to dry completely.

3 Dab a wet sea sponge over the barely dry paint with one hand, and remove the black paint with a T-shirt rag in the other hand. Work back and forth until the antique bronze shows through on most of the surface. You may have to scrub at the paint a bit, but if it hasn't dried completely, it will come off.

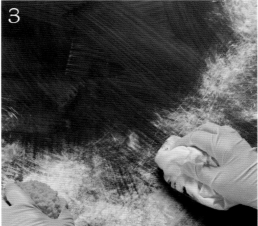

4 Mix four-parts glazing liquid, four-parts paint, and one-part water to make both the brick red and the yellow glazes.

Brush the yellow glaze over 75 percent of the surface using the dampened sea sponge. Rinse the sponge, press to remove the excess water, and apply the red glaze over 60 percent of the surface.

Blend and soften the glazes with a water-dampened T-shirt rag. In some places the two will meld into a warm orangey color. Some of the antique bronze color should show through here and there. Leave heavier glaze deposits over the black/brown paint areas. Allow to dry.

Note: Either glaze may be sparingly sponged over the surface to create a depth to the rust that you like.

5 Topcoat with one or two coats of varnish.

135 | Bronze

BRONZE IS A copper and tin alloy. The color may look similar to the verdigris copper, owing to the copper content in bronze. This finish emulates the color of bronze statuary. Bronze generally receives a chemical patina to maintain the deep luster of the newly made casting. If you study photos of bronzes, you will find a wide range of coloration.

This finish demonstrates what happens when "incompatible" paints work together. The application method is unique: latex paint applied over metallic paint, which makes it separate and crawl over the surface. Ordinarily this is bad, but on this finish, it is good.

MATERIALS & TOOLS

- ❖ Spray paint, Rust-oleum American Accents® Designer Metallic
- ❖ Two paint pails
- ❖ Water
- ❖ Semigloss latex paint, black
- ❖ Flat latex paintbrush, 3" (7.6 cm)
- ❖ Cheesecloth, 90-weight
- ❖ Hair dryer (optional)
- ❖ Dull or satin oil varnish

1 Basecoat the project surface solidly with the spray paint. Pour water into one pail, and black paint into the other as soon as the basecoat dries to the touch. Dip the paintbrush 1" (2.5 cm) into the black paint; then dip the loaded paintbrush into the water and thinly apply the paint to the surface using the French brush technique.

2 Fold in the black paint with a cheesecloth pad. Allow this layer to dry to the touch or force-dry with a hair dryer. The surface will look mostly bronze at this point.

3 Continue to build up semitransparent layers by repeating steps 1 and 2. You want to see the metallic bronze under the black, but have the finish softly obliterating it.

4 Topcoat with one or two coats of varnish.

WEATHERED AND AGED copper acquires a beautiful natural patina—one that is very easy to duplicate. There are many patina kits on the market that have pre-mixed colors. While they are good, there never seems to be enough to do a large furniture piece. This technique will allow you to work on entire patio sets, tabletops of any size, and even cabinetry.

There are also many good copper spray paints on the market. Use any you like for the copper basecoat, following the manufacturer's instructions.

136 | Verdigris Patina

You may also use one of the pre-mixed, water-based copper metallic paints.

A chemical reaction created by the atmosphere causes the copper to turn green. It "blooms" slowly (transparently), growing almost opaque. Areas of transparency and heavier blue/green glaze lend a realistic air to the finish.

MATERIALS & TOOLS

- ❖ Spray paint, Rust-oleum® Bright Copper
- ❖ Flat latex paint, warm black/brown
- ❖ Latex glazing liquid
- ❖ Water
- ❖ Three paint pails
- ❖ Two flat latex paint-brushes, 4" (10.2 cm)
- ❖ T-shirt rags
- ❖ Flat latex paint, blue/green
- ❖ Flat latex paint, white
- ❖ Water-based varnish, Modern Masters® Dead Flat

1 Basecoat the project surface with the spray paint.

2 Mix a glaze using four-parts black/brown paint, four-parts glazing liquid, and one-part water. Brush the glaze quickly over the entire surface using one of the latex paintbrushes. Wipe out the center with the T-shirt rag. Do not allow the paint to dry.

3 Dry-brush the wet paint using the clean latex paintbrush, to soften and blend. Wipe the paintbrush on a rag to clean for use in step 4. Allow to dry.

4 Mix one-part paint, one-part glazing liquid, and one-part water to make the blue and the white glazes. Brush the blue glaze over the entire surface. Immediately brush white glaze over 10 percent of the blue. Wipe out the center with a clean T-shirt rag. Dry-brush to soften. Allow to dry.

5 Topcoat with one or two coats of varnish.

LAPIS IS THE Latin word for stone; the Persian word Lazhward, means blue; apparently at some point these two words came together. Although lapis lazuli (gem lapis) is better known, provincial lapis is more common. Gem lapis is the lightest, most consistently colored portion of lapis. Provincial lapis is used for most furniture inlay because

137 | Provincial Lapis

of its availability, greater color movement, and interesting depth. It is the lapis form used in this finish.

A stunning way to introduce the rich, deep, mysterious color of blue into any environment, it's beautiful on small, modern and contemporary occasional tables.

- Flat latex or spray paint, gold
- Flat latex paintbrush, 3" (7.6 cm)
- Japan Color, cobalt blue
- Japan Color, Prussian blue
- Alkyd glazing liquid

- Paint thinner
- Flat oil paintbrush, 3" (7.6 cm)
- Oval sash brush, 2" (5.1 cm)
- Cheesecloth, 90-weight (optional)
- Particle/dust mask

- Metallic powder, rich gold
- Satin oil-based varnish

Note: If you cannot find the Japan Color cobalt or Prussian blues, you may substitute by using artist's tube paint.

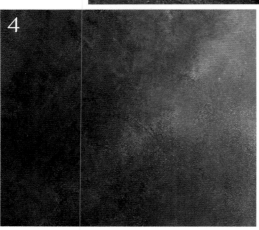

1 Basecoat the project surface with the gold paint and allow it to dry.

2 Mix one-part paint, one-part glazing liquid, and one-part paint thinner to make the two blue glazes. Slip-slap the cobalt glaze randomly over two or three areas of the project surface, using the flat oil paintbrush. Slip-slap the open areas with the Prussian blue glaze.

3 Firmly pounce with the sash brush, holding it perpendicularly to the surface, and moving at a 45° angle. This will blend the two colors together. If you would like more gold to show through, pat a few places with a cheesecloth, and then use the sash brush to remove the rag texture. Move to the next step while the paint is wet.

4 Do not inhale the powder; put the particle mask on before opening the powder.
   Place 1 tablespoon (15 ml) of gold powder into the center of a 6" (15.2 cm) square of cheesecloth, and fold. Hold your hand about 4 ft (1.2 m) above the surface and lightly tap the cheesecloth with your finger. The powder will float down onto surface. Fan your hand below the powder so it doesn't fall straight down onto the surface. Continue to apply the powder until you like the look.

5 This step is optional but adds a subtle variation. Pounce some of the powdered areas with the sash brush to produce a green accent. Do this sparingly, and follow the 45° movement.

6 Topcoat with one or two coats of varnish.

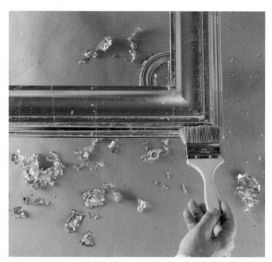

Antiquing & GILDING

138 | Stain Antiquing

ADD EXTRA PUNCH to simple staining with this easy to accomplish finish.
Apply Stain Antiquing over a freshly
stained surface, or enhance a previously
stained piece of wood or cabinetry.

When working on an older or already
stained piece, wash the surface well
and allow it to dry thoroughly before
you begin.

MATERIALS & TOOLS

- ❖ Gel stain, Old Masters®, Golden Oak
- ❖ Flat oil paintbrush, 1" (2.5 cm)
- ❖ T-shirt rags
- ❖ Gel stain, Old Masters®, Dark Walnut

1 Dip a rag into the oak stain and apply using a circular motion. Use the small paintbrush to reach into corners or crevices.

2 Wipe the excess stain off with a clean rag. Allow to dry.

3 Apply the walnut stain to the edges and corners of the project surface; leave a clear oval area in the center. Wipe the stain into the center with a clean rag until the entire surface is antiqued.

4 Topcoat with one or two coats of varnish.

139 | Staining & Distressing

OKAY, THIS IS the finish that allows you to vent all your pent-up frustrations! You get to beat, scrape, scratch, and otherwise destroy a surface. Everything you were ever taught about how not to hurt furniture is turned around and used when distressing a surface.

The beauty of age attracts us. Distressed furniture is like an old friend with signs of a life well lived; it shows years of service and use.

Natural wear happens in some places more than others, such as edges, around door handles, on legs and corners. With this in mind, decide where wear would likely occur on your surface, and attack it.

Common household items do the job, but go ahead and get inventive. Do enjoy creating beauty with imperfection.

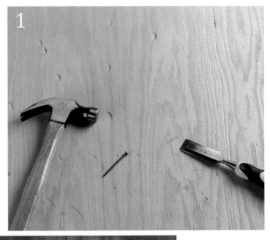

1 Clean old surfaces before beginning. Pound the project surface with both ends of the hammer to dent the wood, tap holes with the nail, or lay the nail on its side and pound for an interesting dent. Gouge large scrapes with the chisel by running it along one edge of the metal ruler. Distress corners with the hammer or chisel. Just have fun and mess it up.

2 Dip a rag into the oak stain and apply it to the center of the project surface using a circular motion. Apply the walnut stain along the edges, in recesses, cracks, and dents with a clean rag. Don't bother being neat. Use the small paintbrush to reach into corners or crevices.

3 Soften and blend the stains with a rag. Add more age by wiping the surface with a dirty rag to leave a deposit of heavier stain here and there. Your aim is to achieve a look of age, dirt, and a worn surface. Allow to dry.

4 Topcoat with one or two coats of varnish.

140 | Distressed Latex

WHAT A GREAT finish for raw wood furniture or those "must have" garage sale pieces. This finish may be applied over well-cleaned previously stained or varnished wood.

This is perfect for the country look and especially appropriate in children's rooms, as use and abuse enhances this finish. Furniture finished this way tends to have a New England seaside look.

Use your favorite colors to complement or contrast with other furniture or the room in which your surface will live.

MATERIALS & TOOLS

- ❖ Hammer
- ❖ Flat latex paint, blue
- ❖ Flat latex paintbrush, 4" (10.2 cm)
- ❖ Flat latex paint, linen white
- ❖ T-shirt rag
- ❖ Denatured alcohol
- ❖ Gel stain, Old Masters®, Dark Walnut

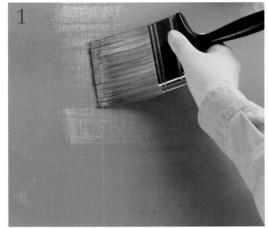

1 Clean old surfaces before beginning. If your furniture piece isn't already nicked and dinged, distress it with the hammer. Apply the blue paint, leaving some bare areas in the middle, the corners, and edges. Allow to dry.

2 Apply the white paint, covering the blue in the center of the surface, but leaving some blue paint and a few bare spots showing on the edges and corners. Allow the paint to dry to the matte stage, then dip a T-shirt rag into denatured alcohol and rub away some of the white paint, leaving a slightly patchy look. Also soften any brushstrokes. Allow to dry completely.

3 Dip a rag into the stain and apply it using a circular motion. Let the stain remain in dents and nicks, and leave a heavier deposit at the edges and corners. Soften the stain with a clean rag.

4 Topcoat with one or two coats of flat varnish or wax.

THIS IS ONE of the loveliest ways to antique a furniture piece. It's appropriate for just about any style and period. The graceful and soft finish can make a piece of furniture stand out or blend into an environment.

141 | Oil Paint Antiquing

Old, worn, or overly dark pieces of furniture with lovely lines or shape can be rescued with this finish. You will be amazed how that dresser or table you thought outdated and boring comes alive and looks like a whole new piece.

MATERIALS & TOOLS

- Flat latex paint, white
- Flat latex paintbrush, 4" (10.2 cm)
- Flat oil-based paint, beige
- Flat oil-based paint, green
- Alkyd glazing liquid
- Mineral spirits
- Flat oil paintbrush, 3" (7.6 cm)
- Cheesecloth, 90-weight
- UTC, burnt umber
- Oil-based varnish

1 Clean old surfaces before beginning. Remove any drawer pulls or other hardware. Base-coat the project surface with the latex paint using the latex paintbrush. Allow to dry.

2 Mix one-part oil-based paint, one-part glazing liquid, and one-part mineral spirits to make the beige and green glazes. Apply the beige glaze with the oil paintbrush and wipe out the center with a piece of cheesecloth. Do not allow the glaze to dry.

Note: Complete all the steps on one side before moving to another side.

3 Dry-brush using the oil paintbrush to soften the glaze, then pounce slightly using the same paintbrush, to soften the dry-brushed strokes.

4 Apply the green glaze with the oil paintbrush. Drag a cheesecloth rag through the glaze lightly from side to side to create some interest. Dry-brush gently with the latex brush to soften the pull strokes and blend the glaze. Allow to dry for 24 hours.

5 Mix the burnt umber into the varnish and brush over the entire piece using the oil paintbrush to further simulate age. The tinted varnish affects the colors, especially the green, turning it into a far more "mysterious" hue.

6 Topcoat with one or two coats of oil-based varnish.

142 | Aluminum Gilding

ALL SEMI-PRECIOUS metal leaf types—copper, aluminum, and composition (imitation gold)—are applied following the same procedure, so use the leaf you prefer following the instructions for this finish.

A gilded surface, the most elegant and sophisticated of all the finishes, is the look that all the metallic paints and powders attempt to emulate. It's the real McCoy.

Good preparation of your furniture piece is all-important, as your gilding will only be as beautiful as your prep. Leaf covers nothing—it reveals everything.

Leaf sticks to a material called "gold size," which comes to the proper tack (stickiness) after a certain amount of time. If you apply the leaf when the gold size is too wet, you will "flood" the leaf and it will look grainy and awful. If you apply the leaf when gold size is too dry, the leaf will have skips (areas where the leaf doesn't adhere). To tell when gold size has reached the proper tack, put a knuckle to the surface and pull it away. You should feel a tight pull.

The best gold sizes are oil-based, as they level out beautifully. A "quick" gold size, fine for small projects, comes

143 | Copper Gilding

to tack in about an hour and stays at tack for about an hour. For medium to large projects, use a 12-hour gold size; it comes to the proper tack after about 12 to 13 hours and stays at tack for 6 to 12 hours.

Copper, aluminum, and composition leaf come in packages of 500 sheets consisting of 20 books with 25 sheets each. The cost varies depending on the type of metal, but purchase from a gilding supply store to get the best price, or check online.

Caution: Once you learn how to apply leaf to a surface—because the process is so wonderful and the results are

so beautiful—you might develop "gilding fever," an overwhelming desire to gild everything in sight.

Keep gilded items away from excessive heat and humidity, which can damage the gilding.

Note: Apply the gold size in a very well-ventilated area, as it has strong fumes. However, everything sticks to gold size, so avoid dusty or wind-blown areas.

(Continued)

MATERIALS & TOOLS

- Low-sheen oil-based enamel or spray paint, taupe or brick red
- Flat oil paintbrush, 3" (7.6 cm)
- Wet/dry sandpaper, 400-grit
- 12-hour gold size, Mixton A Dorer LaFranc®
- Metal leaf, aluminum or copper
- Tamper brush, 2" (5.1 cm)
- Oil-based varnish

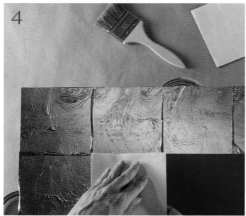

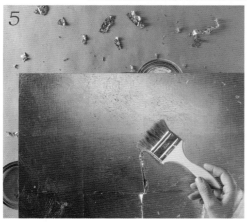

1 Apply three coats of enamel paint basecoat, allowing the paint to dry between coats. Allow the final coat to dry for 24 hours, then tufback. The surface must be smooth and nonporous. Apply the gold size very thinly for maximum coverage. Maintain a consistent and even application.

2 Leaf is thinner than tissue paper and very delicate. Do no touch it with your hands, as your body oils will tarnish it (unless it is aluminum). Work in a protected area free of drafts. If you have difficulty gilding on a horizontal surface, turn the piece vertical to allow gravity to help. Hold the book of leaf in your hand, roll back the lower covering paper (this ensures good placement), and place the leaf over the surface.

3 Move to the right and place the second sheet over the first by barely 1/4" (6 mm). Continue gilding, moving to the right. After completing one row move down a row and work left to right again. Once you have covered the entire surface, fill in any areas that you skipped.

4 Softly brush over, not against, the seams and entire surface with a tamper brush. Clean off all skewings (excess leaf) by dusting with the brush. Allow to dry overnight before tarnishing or varnishing.

5 Apply one or two coats of varnish.

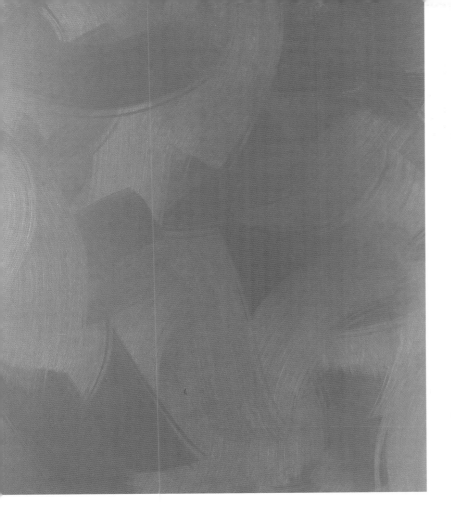

144 | Burnished Metal

BURNISHED METAL OFFERS a subtle, pretty finish reminiscent of swirl-burnished sheet metal. It's suitable for furniture with contemporary lines. The finish is strong, durable, and very easy to touch up—plus, all metallic paints work with it.

Metallic paints are notorious for having an uneven appearance, owing, in great part, to their reflectivity. Purposefully adding movement with brushwork, as this finish does, allows light to dance off the surface, producing interest and playfulness.

Refer to French Brush (page 140) before beginning.

MATERIALS & TOOLS

❖ Latex paint, Modern Masters® Champagne (opaque) ME 206

❖ Angle-edged latex paintbrush, 3" (7.6 cm)

1 Apply the metallic paint using the French brush technique. Allow the paint to dry, about one hour.

2 Repeat step 1.

3 Topcoat with one or two coats of varnish.

145 | Carved Surface Gilding

WRAP YOUR REFLECTION in the warm glow of gold on a mirror frame or watch the radiance of light against gold on candle or wall sconces. Always an elegant touch, gold also adds warmth and a feeling of well-being.

Gilding on a carved surface takes a bit more care than gilding on a flat project surface, but the compensation surpasses the effort.

You must take care to avoid size pooling in the recesses. Use the stiff-bristled artist's paintbrush to remove any excess size.

If you have difficulty gilding on a horizontal surface, turn the piece vertically, as gravity helps a bit.

Refer to Aluminum Gilding and Copper Gilding (pages 350 to 352).

- Low-sheen oil-based enamel or spray paint, brick red
- Flat oil paintbrush, 3" (7.6 cm)
- Steel wool, fine-grade
- Wet/dry sandpaper, 400-grit (optional)
- 12-hour gold size, Mixton A Dorer LaFranc®
- Short flat/bright artist's hog bristle paintbrush, 1" (2.5 cm)
- Composition leaf
- Very soft bristle* tamper or blending brush, 2" (5.1 cm)
- Satin oil-based varnish

*Note: A badger hair paintbrush is best.

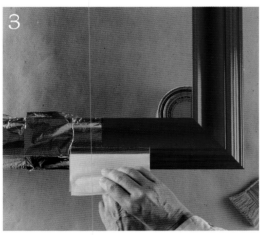

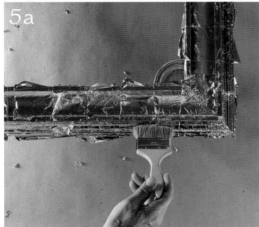

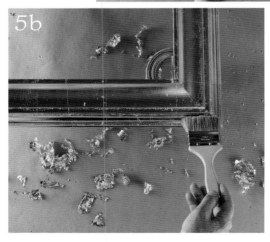

1 Apply three coats of enamel paint; allow the paint to dry between coats. After the third coat, allow the paint to dry for 24 hours. Lightly rub the entire surface with the steel wool (if your surface is flat enough to tuf-back, use that sanding method). Wipe lightly with a tack cloth to remove any grit. The surface must be smooth and nonporous.

2 Apply the gold size very thinly, stretching out the size with the brush. Keep the coverage consistent and even.

3 Leaf is thinner than tissue paper and very delicate. The biggest trick to gilding is getting the fragile sheets to lie down; even a bare puff of wind wreaks havoc, so work in a protected area. Do not worry about skips; just relax and cover the surface.

   Hold the book of composition leaf in your hand, and place the first leaf over the surface. Set the top and gently move the book away, allowing the leaf to settle into place. Never touch the leaf with your fingers, as this causes tarnishing.

4 Place the second leaf so it overlaps one-half of the first leaf. Place all subsequent leaves this way.

5 Tamp down the leaf by softly brushing over, not against, the seams and over the entire surface. This ensures that all of the leaf is attached to the surface. Clean off all skewings by gently "dusting" with the brush. Allow to dry overnight before tarnishing or varnishing.

6 Topcoat with one or two coats of varnish.

Note: Never apply tape of any sort to a gilded surface, even if varnished, as it will lift.

THIS FINISH BEGINS with a successfully gilded, but unvarnished, surface. The application method for composition leaf, the base for creating Tarnished Patina, is the same as that for aluminum leaf and copper leaf.

If you like the look of copper gilding, try the tarnishing process on the copper leaf. The results will be slightly different, but just as remarkable. Aluminum leaf will not tarnish.

Composition leaf tarnishes easily, so it requires careful handling until it is sealed. The plus side to its delicate nature means you can purposefully tarnish it to achieve some attention-grabbing results.

146 | Tarnished Patina

Traditionally, chemicals are used to create the tarnish. This finish employs a safer alternative—an everyday household product—white distilled vinegar.

Even though you will be applying a tarnish, the tarnish resulting from fingers is not desirable, so never touch the leaf with your hands until it is sealed.

Refer to Copper Gilding (page 351 to 352).

Tip: It is the nature of tarnishing that you will never achieve the exact same result twice, so if you are trying to match two or more pieces, tarnish them at the same time.

MATERIALS & TOOLS

- ❖ Spray paint, Rust-oleum® "American Accents" Colonial Red or any orangish brick red
- ❖ Wet/dry sandpaper, 400-grit
- ❖ Sandpaper, 400- and 600-grit wet/dry
- ❖ 12-hour gold size, Mixton A Dorer LaFranc®
- ❖ Composition leaf
- ❖ Tamper brush, 2" (5.1 cm)

- ❖ White distilled vinegar
- ❖ Glass measuring cup
- ❖ Glass bowl
- ❖ Badger or very soft natural bristle paintbrush, 3" (7.6 cm)
- ❖ T-shirt rags
- ❖ Spray bottle with "mist" setting
- ❖ Oil-based varnish

1 Basecoat the project surface with red paint, tufback and clean; gild the surface with composition leaf, tamp, and clean away all skewings.

2 Mix 1 cup (250 ml) of vinegar and ⅓ cup (75 ml) of water in a glass bowl. Dip the paintbrush in the vinegar mix, then pounce it on the leafed surface. Avoid brushing, which will leave marks. Move over the entire surface, but don't rework any area.

　The "tarnishing" appears after 45 minutes. Blot (do not rub) any remaining vinegar with a rag. Be very careful, as the leaf is "imperiled" at this point and you do not want to lift it.

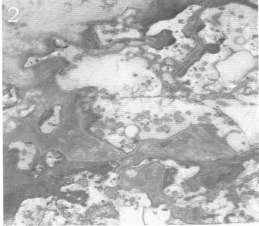

3 Apply undiluted vinegar following the same application procedure as in step 2. Check on the surface after about an hour. When you like the amount of red showing through, stop the tarnishing process by misting the entire surface with water and blotting carefully with a rag. Allow to dry overnight.

4 Topcoat with one or two coats of oil-based varnish in any sheen. Do not use water-based or spray varnishes; they contain agents that will tarnish the leaf in an unwanted manner.

Note: Never apply tape of any sort to a gilded surface, even if varnished, as the leaf will lift.

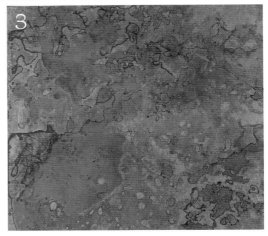

147 | Noton

NOTON IS A Japanese form of broken leaf gilding. The color play between the dark basecoat and the leaf create a visually intriguing composition. The organic nature of a broken application makes the contrast between the glimmer of gold and the inkiness of the black surface doubly interesting.

Balance is important to achieve the overall grace of Noton. Distribute the leaf so it covers at least 80 percent of the basecoat, or be understated and go for 20 percent leaf coverage.

Refer to Copper Gilding (pages 351 to 352).

1 Apply three coats of black paint, allowing the paint to dry between coats. After the third coat, allow the paint to dry for 24 hours, then tufback. The surface must be smooth and nonporous.

2 Apply the gold size very thinly, stretching out the size with the flat paintbrush. Keep the coverage consistent and even. Allow the size to come to tack.

3 Drag the leaf over the surface. Tear the leaf into interesting shapes and sizes, and if you have them, use the skewings (excess leaf) saved from other gilding projects. Avoid right angles as you work. Use wax paper to press the leaf down so you can check your composition, or simply let it happen. The examples show the application progression.

4 Carefully tamp all leaf into place. If you have very small areas, place wax paper over the surface before tamping, but lift it immediately.

5 Dampen the rag with mineral spirits and carefully clean off the exposed size. Allow the surface to dry overnight.

6 Topcoat the surface with varnish even if some remaining size is still slightly tacky. Apply to an area only once; do not over-brush. Allow to dry. Apply at least two more coats of varnish, allowing each to dry between coats. Tufback to smooth out any roughness from the leaf before applying the final varnish coat.

3a

3b

3c

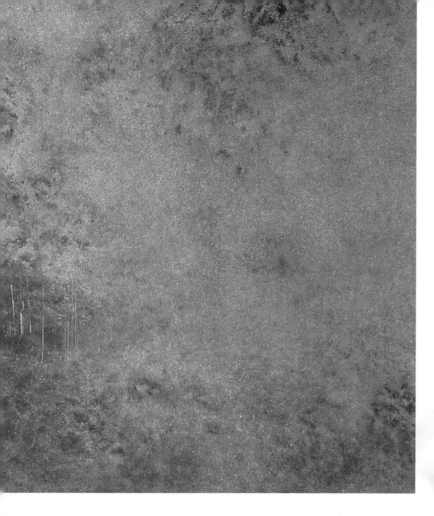

148 | Antiqued Gold

THIS VERSATILE AND easy-to-do finish creates beautiful results. It's appropriate for just about any piece of furniture or object, for the interior or exterior. You will move from step to step while the paint is wet, making this a quick and simple finish.

For finishing pieces to be used outside, select exterior paints, and follow the manufacturer's instructions.

There are many gold paints on the market: metallic or flat in spray or brush-on form, and in oil-based and latex formulas. Use the paint most convenient to you, but spray paint gives a smoother finish.

This finish must be done on a flat, horizontal surface. Vertical surfaces must be laid flat. If your surface has small legs, pounce the black paint on and rag off to coordinate with the flat areas.

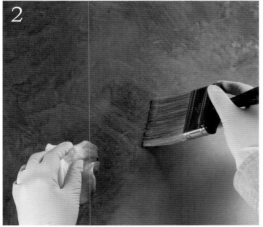

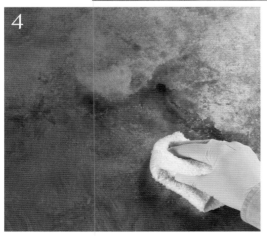

1 Basecoat the project surface with the gold paint.

2 Pour enough black paint into a paint pail to complete your surface. Add enough water to thin the paint to about whole milk consistency. Brush the black paint on and immediately pat with a cheesecloth wad.

3 While the black paint is still wet, dip the paintbrush 1" (2.5 cm) into the water; then selectively pounce areas on the piece. You are trying to puddle and pool the wet paint.

4 Soften the paint here and there by patting with a terry cloth rag. Take care to reveal areas of gold and deposits of black. If you remove too much paint, allow the surface to dry out and repeat the process.

5 Topcoat with one or two coats of varnish. The latex paint has been weakened by the addition of so much water and the topcoat will protect your beautiful work.

149 | Pickling

PICKLING IS ONE of a number of very old methods used to change the color of wood. The approach gives a very beautiful patina to any raw wood surface and is much less offensive than fuming, another color-altering technique.

Fuming is a process in which the vapors of a gas are used on woods that have natural tannin. Furniture makers have fumed wood for years. Charles Stickley of the Stickley furniture of the Arts and Craft period used the technique to achieve the beautiful colorations in his furniture. The wood was placed in large fuming sheds and a (usually very secret) chemical combination was infused into the shed. Rather like a smokehouse for furniture!

Pickling, on the other hand, uses vinegar and steel wool. Putting the two together creates a chemical reaction that results in the solution used for pickling. It's easy to do, but be careful not to drip or spill the solution on your surface, as that will show.

MATERIALS & TOOLS

❖ White distilled vinegar

❖ Two steel wool pads, coarse

❖ Paint pail

❖ Sandpaper, 220-grit

❖ Flat latex paintbrush, 3" (7.6 cm)

1 Soak the steel wool pads for 36 hours in ½ gallon (2 L) of white distilled vinegar.

2 Sand the raw wood smooth, lightly tack, then apply the vinegar mixture with the paintbrush and let nature take its course. The color develops fully after 24 hours. You may apply one or more coats to reach the depth of color you like.

Tip: Experiment in an inconspicuous place such as the inside of a drawer to see what color develops.

3 Topcoat with one or two coats of varnish or wax.

Note: The pine chair shown has had one pickling application and received a slight grayish discoloration. The top of the table and the drawer received a double application of the vinegar solution. Both of these pine pieces were new, raw wood, and are now softly altered. The insert shows pickling on an oak-veneered board. Veneer is thin and the solution stained the wood quickly and deeply into a dark gray.

3

TROMPE L'OEIL MEANS "the eye deceived" in French. Just as those who see this will be surprised it's not real, you will be surprised at how easily this technique allows you to render a believable raised panel.

This artistic technique employs manipulation of lights and darks to add dimension to two-dimensional surfaces.

The most important consideration is the direction from which your light source comes. This light source remains consistent and will be your "map" for placement of light and darks. For ease of rendering, keep it simple, select a two o'clock or ten o'clock direction. A two o'clock light source was used here.

150 | Trompe L'oeil Panel

Other factors for success concern the shading colors. If you apply a finish over the basecoat, you will need to complete the finish to judge the *overall* color before choosing shading colors. Use a version of the overall surface color that is about 60 percent darker for the dark shading. Use a lighter version about 50 percent lighter for the light shading.

You may use one or more of the techniques outlined in this book to finish your project piece. The desk front shown is Parchment (page 308), the top is Marble (page 322), and the center is Burled Wood (page 326). Choosing the finish to use is part of the fun.

1 Basecoat the project surface using your chosen colors and techniques.

2 Draw the outside edge of a rectangle for the coved border. Adhere tape along the inside of all lines, then also along the outside and inside edges of the first tape. Remove the first tape for a 1" (2.5 cm) border. Paint the border linen white using a latex brush.

3 Tape border corners at a 45° angle (for a bevel). Work one section at a time. Dry the paint with a hairdryer. Do not remove the panel border tape.

4 Double-load the latex paintbrush with dark and light paint. Stroke the paintbrush on the aluminum foil to slightly blend the colors in the center of the paintbrush. Pull the paintbrush along the center of the border. Place the dark shade toward the center at left and bottom sections. Place the dark shade toward the outside at the right and top sections. Allow paint to dry; then remove the corner bevel tape. Repeat for all border sections.

5 Place a section of tape at the upper left and lower right corners along the bevel right sides. Mix a lowlight color using three-parts black and one-part dark shading color; thin it with water to a whole-milk consistency. Load one edge of the artist's paintbrush with lowlight color; blend it on the aluminum foil. The paint should extend no farther than ¼" (6 mm) across the bristles. Place the color edge of the paintbrush on top of the dark shade color and pull across both sections. Allow the paint to dry; then remove the corner tapes.

6 Shift the corner tapes to the bevel left sides. Load one edge of the artist's paintbrush with white; blend it on the foil. The paint should extend no farther than ¼" (6 mm) across the bristles. Place the color edge of the brush on top of the lighter color and pull across both sections. Allow to dry; then remove corner tapes.

7 Topcoat with one or two coats of varnish. Remove the panel border tapes.

MATERIALS & TOOLS

- ❖ Flat latex paint for base, any color
- ❖ Ruler
- ❖ Pencil
- ❖ Painter's masking tape, 1" (2.5 cm)
- ❖ Flat latex paint, linen white
- ❖ Flat latex paintbrush, 1" (2.5 cm)
- ❖ Hairdryer
- ❖ Flat latex paint for dark shade
- ❖ Flat latex paint for light shade
- ❖ Aluminum foil
- ❖ Flat latex paint, black
- ❖ Flat artist's latex paintbrush, ½" (1.3 cm)

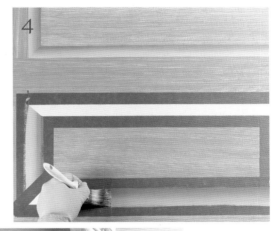

Index